The

Social Origins

of the

Modern
Middle East

Haim Gerber

The

Social Origins

of the

Modern
Middle East

Lynne Rienner Publishers
• Boulder, Colorado •

Paperback edition published in the United States of America in 1994 by
Lynne Rienner Publishers, Inc.
1800 30th Street, Boulder, Colorado 80301

and in the United Kingdom by
Lynne Rienner Publishers, Inc.
3 Henrietta Street, Covent Garden, London WC2E 8LU

First published in 1987 by Lynne Rienner Publishers, Inc.

Library of Congress Cataloging-in-Publication Data
Gerber, Haim.
   The social origins of the modern Middle East.
   Bibliography: p.
   Includes index
      1. Near East—Social conditions.   2. Agriculture and state—Turkey—History.
   3. Agriculture—Social aspects—Near east—History.   4. Land tenure—Near East—
History.
   5. Near East—History—1517- .   6. Near East—Politics and government.
   I. Title.
   HN656.G47   1987   306'.0956 86–21925
   ISBN 1-55587-509-2 (pb : alk. paper)

British Cataloguing in Publication Data
A Cataloguing in Publication record for this book
is available from the British Library.

Printed and bound in the United States of America

The paper used in this publication meets the requirements
of the American National Standard for Permanence of ∞
Paper for Printed Library Materials Z39.48.

Contents

Tables

Acknowledgment

I would like to thank the Publication Department of the Harry S. Truman Research Institute for the Advancement of Peace for their help in rendering my manuscript as readable as possible.

Note on Transliteration

In my efforts to make the text as unencumbered as possible, I have not used all the Turkish letters but have endeavored to spell the Turkish words according to the way they are pronounced. In quotes, in notes, and in the bibliography, I have, of course, preserved the original Turkish spelling.

CHAPTER ONE

Introduction

This book sets out to trace the effects of the Ottoman socioagrarian structure on the modern countries of the Middle East and, more specifically, on those countries with a straight line to an Ottoman past. Its basic assumption is that the socioagrarian structure of the past is a key to understanding the present political structure of Turkey and the Arab states. This is an assumption that is still subject to controversy. Yet, in a British context, where Parliament was the arena in which relations between monarch and aristocracy unfolded, few would contest the centrality of the topic. Few, yet again, would deny the intimate connection between Russia's bitter agrarian past and the Bolshevik Revolution. As the historian Sir Lewis Namier so eloquently put it:

> The relations of groups of men to plots of land, of organized communities to units of territory, form the basic content of political history. The conflict-ing territorial claims of communities constitute the greater part of con-scious international history; social stratifications and convulsions, primarily arising from the relationship of men to land, make the greater, not always fully conscious, part of the domestic history of nations—and even under urban and industrial conditions ownership of land counts for more than is usually supposed.[1]

If the centrality of a socioagrarian background seems less obvious in the Middle Eastern context, it is not because the issue is less significant there, but probably because events took a course that led to a somewhat exceptional outcome. The extreme paucity of good research into the social history of the Ottoman Empire is no doubt another contributory factor.

If one regards the history of the Middle East in its entirety, one cannot help but receive the impression that the significance of agrarian institutions has been greatly underestimated. There are two points in particular in the history of the region when the agrarian structure seems to have been of key importance. One was during the transformation of the Ottoman Empire into modern Turkey and the Arab states, which took place without great social upheaval. In the current literature on social revolutions, insufficient attention has been paid to their pertinent agrarian backgrounds;[2] only lately have historians begun to focus on the rural classes as important factors in the creation of the great social revolutions. Nevertheless, "though Marx summarily dismissed the peasantry as so many 'potatoes in a sack,' and despite the generality of working class *social movements,* the major *revolutions* of our time have been made largely by country people."[3] If we place the Ottoman Empire in a single category with states such as historic China and Russia, we see that (outwardly, at least) amazingly similar starting points led to entirely different modes of evolution into the modern world. One explanation for this may be found in the character of agrarian development in each society. This is not to belittle the validity of other explanations, but is merely an attempt to add to them.

The impression that the significance of agrarian institutions has been given short shrift is strengthened when one takes stock of another period in the history of the region—that of the modern army revolutions. I have always suspected that these revolutions had some connection with agrarian class structure. In this I am following the late G. Baer's view that army revolutions in the modern Middle East were something of a substitute for total peasant revolution. Following his analysis of the various political reasons for the 1952 Egyptian Revolution, Baer added:

> Political factors, however, had not been the only cause of the Military Revolution; Egyptian society, too, had undergone important changes which found their expression in the early fifties. Up to 1950 social tensions following the Second World War found their release in the villages in outbursts of individual violence; in 1951, for the first time in modern Egyptian history, there occurred some rebellions of fallahin making common cause against their landlords. . . . This unrest in the Egyptian village revealed that the equilibrium of Egyptian society had been unsettled. Yet the old regime reacted only by announcing its intention to introduce some minor reforms (which were never carried out); the landlords, and the social system in general, were not affected. . . . Thus, the Military Revolution was the result not only of political difficulties, but also of social ferment; and the agrarian reform was conceived not only as a means to prevent the restoration of the old political system but also as a response to social unrest. In order to reestablish social equilibrium in the Egyptian countryside and to forestall Communist revolution, landed property would have to be redistributed.[4]

My main source of inspiration in writing this study has been Barrington Moore's *Social Origins of Dictatorship and Democracy,* which deals with the process of modernization as it occurred in several major civilizations.[5] The main body of Moore's book is devoted to an ideographic description of six societies (England, France, the United States, China, India, and Japan), prefaced by a theory that is in essence an attempt to trace some meaningful thread through the mass of detail.

Although most modernization studies address themselves to the question of the Industrial Revolution and economic progress in general, Moore went further and tackled the thorny problem of the evolution of special forms of political regimes. Moreover, he tried to identify under what conditions these evolutions are peaceful, and when they involve great social upheaval and revolution. The major focuses of his analysis were social groups and social classes: the peasantry, the aristocracy (or, at least, the landed upper class), and the urban bourgeoisie. He was particularly interested in the landed upper class and its relationships with other classes: With whom did it contract to create a strong power base for itself? What was the exact nature of these alliances? Moore assumed that an aristocratic government is not compatible with parliamentary democracy, because tight control of the peasantry necessitates a strong repressive apparatus. On the other hand, some form of parliamentary democracy is likely to appear in situations where a capitalist economy reigns and where the great bulk of society is composed of the middle class, given that such an economy requires freedom and opportunity to influence potential consumers, and such a society does not need a strong internal repressive apparatus.

In the case of England, we observe an isolated island kingdom relatively immune to foreign invasion. Ever since the Middle Ages the monarch had maintained a subtle balance of power with the aristocracy. The crown neither urgently needed nor could actually establish a standing army. This balance of power provided a solid base on which to build a parliamentary democracy. A second base was the early capitalization of agriculture by English landlords, a process that began as early as the twelfth century with the discovery of the unique quality of English wool and the onset of the Continental demand for it. Landlords began to evict traditional peasants and to erect sheep pens in place of deserted villages. This process gathered momentum in subsequent centuries, when new developments accelerated the pace of eviction. By the eighteenth century, little remained of the old English peasantry. So it was that the issue of massive peasant revolution was removed from the agenda of English public life.

Western scholars, and particularly those studying Third World societies, are likely to view British democracy as a work of great genius, not emulated by the Third World because of certain inherent defects in the latter. However, an examination of the growth of British democracy before the Glorious Revolution suggests that its development was purely accidental, the result of a sequence of events neither preconceived nor planned. It also suggests that the fortunate outcome was based, paradoxically, on a series of factors that would be considered undesirable and, indeed, unacceptable in every modern polity. (Lawrence Stone's analysis, which is offered in the next few paragraphs, may serve as an example.[6])

The basic factor was the pervasive weakness of the English monarchy vis-à-vis other classes. Little as this was to the liking of most of the English kings, they could not do much about it. The sixteenth-century Tudor sovereigns, especially, attempted to emulate the French monarchy, but with limited success, chiefly because the survival of strong feudal institutions in England provided the people with extremely powerful levers against the monarch.

In order to become an absolute ruler, an English king would have to vastly augment his sources of revenue. Here he would encounter the opposition of both Parliament and the Common Law. The main potential untapped sources of revenue were the grandees of the realm, but they enjoyed the ancient privilege of tax exemption; by using Parliament and by insisting on the "sacredness" of the Common Law, the nobility managed to thwart assault by the crown. This failure of the crown meant that the government continued to function without standing armies and without a state bureaucracy worthy of the name. In times of emergency, reigning monarchs could rely only on the support of their own servants, or on the goodwill of the landed magnates. Thus, the failure of the monarchy was the success of parliamentary democracy in England. Historical accident prevailed, rather than conscious political planning.

In France, according to Moore, the impulse toward capitalization of agriculture was weaker than in England, but was nevertheless strong. From the late Middle Ages onward the French peasantry had been in effect in complete control of the land, but still owed rent to the aristocracy, which for the most part was domiciled in the big cities. The cleavage inherent in this situation bred discontent and bitterness, and the French peasantry grew ever more rebellious with the passage of time. The revolution in France was to lead to a bourgeois democracy because, first and foremost, the special privileges and political position of the aristocracy were eliminated, thereby overcoming the main hurdle to democracy; and because, second, in the course of the revolution the peasantry entered into an alliance with the urban Third Estate. The institutional reflection of that alliance was bourgeois democracy.

In Japan (and Germany), the impulse toward modernization was weaker than in either England or France. There the revolution came from above, by way of an alliance between the landed upper class and a feeble urban bourgeoisie. Such alliances, according to Moore, usually result in fascist regimes.

Although Moore did not deal specifically with Russia, what he wrote about China applied to Russia as well:

> The great agrarian bureaucracies of these countries served to inhibit the commercial and later industrial impulses even more than in the preceding instances of Japan and Germany. The results were twofold. In the first place these urban classes were too weak to constitute even a junior partner in the form of modernization taken by Germany and Japan. . . . And in the absence of more than the most feeble steps toward modernization a huge

peasantry remained. This stratum, subject to new strains and stresses as the modern world encroached upon it, provided the main destructive revolutionary force that overthrew the old order and propelled these countries into the modern era under communist leadership.[7]

In India, where the impulse toward modernization was the weakest, the country nevertheless evolved to become, at least partially, a Western-style parliamentary democracy. According to Moore, democracy in India was made possible because the British prevented an alliance between the landed elite (the *zamindars*) and the nascent bourgeoisie, headed by members of the free professions. In the course of the struggle for independence this bourgeoisie was led by Mohandas Gandhi, who preferred an alliance with the peasantry, needing its mass support for his policy of passive resistance. Thus, when independence came, the bourgeoisie remained in the saddle, and a parliamentary democracy was inevitable. The price of democracy in this case was the virtual perpetuation of abject poverty for hundreds of millions of people.

China, Russia, and India were alike in that in all three the impulse toward modernization was weak, while traditional agriculture was irreparably undermined. However, in the first two cases the outcome was a peasant revolution leading to a communist regime, while in India no such revolution took place. Moore believed that the explanation for this difference could be found in the specific structure of the village in each society. In India, the caste system helped to absorb feelings of resentment. In China, no such mechanism existed; on the contrary, landless peasants were not considered full members of the community and were the subject of ridicule. Thus, the social structure in China encouraged rebelliousness, a tendency greatly inhibited by the Indian village structure.

It is only natural that such an ambitious book as Moore's would be subject to serious criticism. The most complete and thorough critique was written by Theda Skocpol. Dismissing the case of India as superfluous (without explanation), Skocpol proceeded to present a short model of Moore's explanatory paradigm.[8] Moore posited three routes to the modern world— "bourgeois revolution" (England, France, the United States); "revolution from above" (Japan, Germany); and "peasant revolution" (China, Russia)— the major differentiating factor being the strength of the impulse toward modernization. This impulse was said by Moore to be the strongest in those countries that took the first route, weaker in the second, and weakest in the third. Skocpol, correctly, criticized Moore for treating this factor in a mysterious way (Whence the impulse toward modernization?). Indeed, this is probably the weakest point in an otherwise splendid book.

An important part of Skocpol's critique involves the exposure of empirical errors in Moore's analysis. A case in point is the emergence of English democracy. According to Skocpol, the idea of an alliance between the aristocracy and other classes is not a valid explanation for the emergence of parliamentary democracy. Rather, the crucial factor was that the landed upper class of the nineteenth century (as much as it was antidemocratic at heart) was unable to contain the political demands of the lower classes because, as we have seen above, it lacked tangible means of coercion.

Skocpol's own theory, which is also extremely pertinent to our topic, follows largely in the footsteps of Moore's methodology.[9] In it she investigated the causes behind three major social-agrarian revolutions—the French, the Russian, and the Chinese—all of which took place in polities designated as agrarian bureaucracies (a category to which she explicitly assigned the Ottoman Empire). As she defined such a state:

> An agrarian bureaucracy is an agricultural society in which social control rests on a division of labor and a coordination of effort between a semibureaucratic state and a landed upper class. The landed upper class typically retains, as an adjunct to its landed property, considerable . . . undifferentiated local and regional authority over the peasant majority of the population. The partially bureaucratic central state extracts taxes and labor from peasants either indirectly through landlord intermediaries or else directly, but with (at least minimal) reliance upon cooperation from individuals of the landed upper class. In turn, the landed upper class relies upon the backing of a coercive state to extract rents and/or dues from the peasantry. At the political center, autocrat, bureaucracy, and army monopolize decisions, yet . . . accommodate the regional and local power of the landed upper class and . . . recruit individual members of this class into leading positions in the state system.[10]

I later show that the Ottoman Empire in fact differed from this model in important ways, with no less important consequences. Nevertheless, the model provides an excellent starting point for our discussion.

According to Skocpol, the social structure in agrarian states universally encourages peasant unrest and rebelliousness because the peasantry feels extremely reluctant to relinquish part of its produce.[11] For peasants to revolt, however, they must be in possession of "tactical space"—that is, they must be independent of their overlord in their daily lives, living in independent, autonomous communities that merely owe rent and dues to the overlord. In a situation of close, day-to-day dependence, peasants are unable to organize themselves for a rebellion.

For social revolutions to take place in agrarian states, a number of factors should coincide. In the three cases studied by Skocpol there were, first, a large-scale weakening of the power of the state and a loosening of its control of the peasantry; and second, intensive activity on the part of intellectual elites, who had been marginal in the old order and were thus entirely alienated from it. In France, China, and Russia the great revolutions took place because the agrarian bureaucracy was unable to cope with the challenges raised by the modern world. For example, one such challenge was the need for a tax reform that would increase the burden on the aristocracy. However, this was well nigh impossible, because those regimes were politically dependent on the support of the aristocracy. Consequently, in all three cases there occurred a series of political crises that the ancien régime was unable to resolve. Central authority was weakened or undermined, and the ever present tendency of the peasantry to revolt surfaced again. Only this time, the large-scale destructive force was channeled by the new intellectual elite toward the total destruction of the old order.

Apt though Skocpol's criticism of Moore may be, Moore's great methodological breakthrough remains unshaken. Alliances between classes may be useful for some historical situations and not for others. The modern socio-political formation of a country is forged in the process of mutual sociopolitical formation of a country is forged in the process of mutual interactions among all the social groups active in that society. This last point is especially pertinent for the Middle East, where, as we shall see, societies evolved in substantially different ways from all the cases analyzed by Moore. Moore described societies that underwent an industrial revolution and became parliamentary democracies. He also discussed societies that were traditionally great agrarian empires and that became communist states. The Middle East presents an entirely different picture. As with China and Russia, the Ottoman Empire was basically agrarian, and the impulse toward modernization was rather weak. But in contrast to China and Russia, no peasant revolution took place. Instead, in the course of the twentieth century, army juntas rose to power and established military regimes, and in two of these societies, Lebanon and Turkey, some sort of parliamentary democracy took root. This is in stark contradiction to Moore's analysis, and we are confronted with a rather perplexing puzzle. I am nevertheless of the opinion that one can construct a theory that explains the modern Middle East in the terms of Moore's paradigm.

To achieve this, in the first five chapters of this book I present a detailed analysis of the socioagrarian structure of the Middle East before the modern era (i.e., the post-World War I period), at the time the region was ruled by the Ottoman Empire. This time frame lends itself to tripartite periodization: the sixteenth century, the seventeenth and eighteenth centuries, and the nineteenth century. The stage was set in the sixteenth century for subsequent socioagrarian development. The institutional format of the Ottoman Empire—including agrarian institutions and class structure—had its origins here. In the next two centuries, the so-called period of Ottoman decline, these structures came under a great deal of stress. The nineteenth century saw the emergence of efforts to rejuvenate the state through legal reform—usually referred to as Tanzimat—as well as the major economic and political impacts of the Industrial Revolution.

In Chapter 6, these developments are tied to the present through an analysis of socioagrarian developments in the twentieth century. The sixth chapter demonstrates that the internal logic of these developments during all four centuries is vitally important to understanding the sociopolitical trends that are taking place before our eyes.

One peculiarity in the structure of my argument calls for special comment. Although on the whole each chapter is based both substantively and chronologically on the one that precedes it, Chapter 3 is an exception. It deals with one particular region—the Bursa region in west Anatolia—in the seventeenth century, while Chapter 4 covers the same period throughout the empire. the empire. I was influenced in this structural choice by the state of social research on the Ottoman Empire, a field that is so underdeveloped that any serious scholarly work must build its own empirical data base. As I had access to the Bursa archive, one of the best provincial Ottoman archives and one of the few accessible ones, my concentration on Bursa is a result of the unusually solid data furnished by this excellent source.

One may conclude that, pending further research, the agrarian structure that comes to light through the study of the Bursa archive was more or less typical of the agrarian regime throughout Anatolia during the period in question. I derive this conclusion not only from the similarity between my Bursa findings and the more general findings analyzed in Chapter 4, but also from the striking similarity between the findings regarding seventeenth-century Bursa and twentieth-century Anatolia (Bursa included), as detailed in Chapter 6.

CHAPTER TWO

The Classical Ottoman Land Regime

The Ottoman Empire was a strongly centralized polity. At its core sat the omnicompetent, central government, or sultanate, which dominated the periphery (that is, the society at large).[1] The chief expression of this centralization was the predominant position of the sultan, who was the spiritual-religious and temporal leader.

The Ottoman state was heir to both the orthodox Muslim tradition of the caliphate and of various Iranian states in central Asia. Its political structure derived from a synthesis of ancient Iranian and Muslim principles and was in fact a combination of autocratic rule and Muslim tradition, which decreed that the rightful ruler was the caliph, who was the religious leader of the "community of believers"—the *umma*—and successor to the Prophet Muhammad.

The house of Osman, which was the ruling dynasty of the Ottoman Empire from the year 1290 (or even earlier), weathered in the course of its history a great many crises; nonetheless, it persisted for more than six centuries and remained the reigning dynasty until 1922, when it was finally dismantled by Mustafa Kemal. This stability was surely a record in Islamic terms and undoubtedly a rare achievement for any civilization and is all the more remarkable insofar as the known record of Ottoman history contained very few upheavals. The Janissaries or crowds who brought about the downfall of several sultans, never, as far as is known, demanded or contemplated the replacement of a sultan by anyone but his perfectly legitimate heir.

One method used to achieve this stability was the frequent transfer of high-ranking officials from place to place and from post to post, and the habitual removal from office of the grand vezir, the chief minister of state. The vezir captured center stage at the beginning of the seventeenth century, when the sultan delegated day-to-day state business to his officials. He ceased attending to everyday affairs of state and thus, symbolically, distanced himself even farther from the common people. The brunt of responsibility for failure in war or government was borne by the grand vezir, who on occasion was made the scapegoat for state failures and was forced to pay with his life in order to safeguard and shield the reputation of the sultan. This sultanic policy, intended as it was to prevent the creation of feudalistic enclaves at the top of the Ottoman hierarchy, was surely one major reason for the extremely mobile bureaucratic structure that seems to have characterized the Ottoman government.

The emergence of any feudal enclaves was further prevented by the *musadara,* the custom of confiscating properties of high-ranking officials after their deaths. Scholars at one time thought that this custom was applied to all Ottoman state officials, but recent studies have proved otherwise. Barkan, for example, has published documents from the court archives of Edirne that indicated that men of state left properties to their heirs as a matter of routine;[2] similar findings emerged from a study of the *kadi* records (the protocol kept by the *kadi*) of seventeenth-century Bursa.[3] Hence, the institution of *musadara* seemed to have been applied to state officials who fell from grace in the eyes of the sultan, and to men of state of the first rank (who had done nothing to enrage the sultan, but whose wealth and power may have threatened him).

An institutional arrangement that greatly helped curb the emergence of opposition to the sultan's rule was the cardinal position of the *kadi,* or "judge," in Islamic civilization in general and in the Ottoman Empire in particular. In another study I have described the central role played by the *kadi* in all aspects of provincial administration.[4] Most of the sultanic orders were sent to *kadi*s, who often were enjoined thereby to personally attend to state affairs. Documents revealed that the *kadi*'s role in the Ottoman provincial administration was superior to that played by the governor of the province. Politically, this exceedingly important officeholder was, by dint of his education, devoid of political ambitions and, as far as we know, totally loyal to the central authority.

Possibly the most important way in which the Ottoman sultans strove to ensure complete control of the periphery—whether by conscious design or not—was by striving to prevent the emergence in the provinces of any landed upper class. At this juncture we need not dwell on this point in detail, for it constitutes the main topic of analysis in the following chapters.

The Ottoman center maintained its considerable strength, even during the seventeenth and eighteenth centuries when several provinces lay outside its tight control. Although a weakening of state authority in fact did take place on a geographic basis—places nearer Istanbul and the central government remained under firm control—there were no serious challenges to the legitimacy of the ruling dynasty during this period. Furthermore, even in some of the provinces where effectual control was greatly reduced, much of the external facade and its structural underpinnings remained unchanged (see Chapter 3).

Strong centralism, however, was only one aspect of the Ottoman political system. Another, which has been entirely disregarded by historians, was the liberal character of the Ottoman political system. By this I mean the extremely lenient policy adopted by the central government toward the periphery. The sultanate displayed great interest only in those areas within its immediate political vicinity and tended to neglect the institutions of the lower classes. For the periphery the consequences of this neglect were both beneficial and harmful. Although the periphery enjoyed a large measure of freedom and autonomy, it also was plagued by a total lack of governmental expenditure on public services.

Such autonomy had many expressions. There was no integrated, uniform legal system. The government observed with equanimity the differing legal systems in Mount Lebanon, Palestine, and the Hijaz, for example. Furthermore, it is my contention that under the Ottomans the city and village populations were ruled in a very loose manner, which allowed for a large measure of autonomy. Another expression of autonomy was found in the structure of the guilds; it was not by chance that the institutional leniency enjoyed by the lower classes was embodied in the agrarian privileges of the small landholders. The center, in its attempts to obstruct the formation of a landed upper class, strove to preserve the rights of the small peasants. This policy came into being along with the classical Ottoman land regime.

The classical land regime of the Ottoman Empire originated with the *timar,* or "fief," system that developed in the fifteenth and sixteenth centuries.[5] This was the period of the formation of the Ottoman institutional structure in general, and the agrarian regime evolved as part of that complex. However, this regime was not created ex nihilo; in fact, it is doubtful whether it was a matter of deliberate Ottoman creation. At least some of the major elements of this agrarian regime were inherited from the past, sometimes the distant past. Happily for the present study, the end result of the sixteenth-century Ottoman bureaucratic process constituted such a tremendous break with the past that only brief attention to the institutions that preceded this result is necessary.

The two main pillars of the Ottoman agrarian regime were the *miri* regime and the *timar* system. All agricultural or, more specifically, grain-producing land in the state was declared *miri,* that is, "belonging formally to the state"; only vineyards and orchards in or on the outskirts of settled areas were considered *mulk,* or "privately owned." There is no question that this division was influenced by ancient Islamic traditions; however, the connection between the basic Ottoman land law and the land law of classical Islam was complicated. Classical Islamic law distinguished between many different types of land, on the basis of a peasant's religion and according to whether the area had been conquered forcibly or acquired peaceably. Part of the agricultural land was considered entirely private and part belonged to the ruler.[6] Thus, the concept of the state/ruler as the nominal owner of agricultural lands was already well known to classical Islam. But the basic Ottoman separation of land into *mulk* or *miri* was not extant in the classical period. Nor was the relation between the religion of the peasant and the status of the land to be found in the Ottoman Empire. The concept of *kharaj* (the land tax) in effect disappeared.

Agricultural land, then, was state land (*miri*), whether occupied by Muslims or Christians, who were taxed identically. Any differences in this respect were a function of variations in the customary law inherited by the Ottomans in different regions. Agricultural land was encumbered by two types of taxes. One constituted a share of the produce and amounted to approximately one-tenth in Anatolia and some other areas, where it was called *ushr*. In Syria and Palestine the tax varied between one-quarter and one-third and was called *qasm*.[7] The second tax took the form of a certain sum of money levied against the land held by the peasant and was called *chift resmi* in the Ottoman jargon.[8] Because of their similarity to certain Islamic taxes, these two Ottoman taxes were sometimes given the old names: *kharaj muqasama,* a classical tax that was a proportion of the produce, and *kharaj muwazzafa,* levied as a sum of money per area of land.[9] But in reality these taxes were not analogous; in classical Islamic law these two types of taxes served to define two mutually exclusive types of land, while in the Ottoman Empire every piece of land was liable to both taxes.[10]

The question of the separation between *miri* and *mulk* land was an extremely complex one. In practice it was sometimes difficult to determine whether a certain plot was *mulk* or *miri*. After all, there were no cadastral maps in the sixteenth century, and in their absence it stood to reason that gardens were considered *mulk* land and cornfields *miri*. But this left room for abuse. Cornfields could be transformed into gardens, with a consequent change in the status of the land. But this did not occur on a substantial scale, chiefly because the Ottoman agrarian economy was a subsistence one; the main concern of the peasants was to prepare the stock of needed grain to sustain their families throughout the year. This concern probably eclipsed any other consideration, such as the legal status of the land. But it also showed that formal title to the land was probably not a priority for the peasant, at least until the mid-nineteenth century.

The *timar* system was the second main pillar of the classical Ottoman agrarian system. Every province acquired by the state—with a few exceptions—was divided into fiefs of one of three sizes—*timar, ziamet,* and *has* (*timar* was the smallest, *has* the largest). The fiefs were allotted to cavalrymen (*sipahis*), who were entitled by their rank to collect the taxes the peasants owed the state. In return, the *sipahis* guaranteed their military service to the state in time of war. This institution was at least a partially inherited one. In recent years a number of scholars have discovered that the beginnings of the *timar* system in fact lie in pre-Ottoman Anatolian states. But, again, there is no doubt that the institution attained its final form with the Ottomans.

The *sipahi* (fiefholder) had a right to collect and keep the land tax, but this did not confer on him any political or juridical power beyond that. Every Ottoman province had a governor and a *kadi,* who were charged with running the province, including the fiefs within it. It may be presumed, given human nature, that *sipahis* in the fifteenth and sixteenth centuries probably tried to overstep these limitations but, as far as we know, with little success. Fiefholders were administrators without roots in their localities. Deserving *sipahis* were promoted to larger fiefs, which may well have been on the other side of the empire, a fact that probably diminished their interest in the general affairs of their localities. In addition, there were extremely powerful opponents to *sipahi* hegemony on the scene, notably the *kadi.*

An interesting and important question about the *timar* system is why it should have come into existence in the first place. Why, for instance, did the Ottoman government levy taxes indirectly and fail to establish an army of its own choice? Those who express wonder at the fact that the Ottomans maintained such a cumbersome mechanism should remember that such a legal institution was exceptional in the fifteenth century; the politically undisputed right of the state to collect agricultural taxes from its citizens did not exist at the time in Western Europe.

It seems that the Ottoman state was technically unable to cope with the task, which must have been huge, for the tax, of course, could only be levied in kind. Somehow the state had to handle the large quantities of grain in an indirect fashion. The *timar* system was the solution. The *sipahi* collected the grain and dispensed it, and repaid the state by way of military service. Despite the gradual abolition of the *timar* system after the sixteenth century, the tax nevertheless continued to be levied in an indirect fashion, this time through the *iltizam,* or "tax farming." Both the *timar* and *iltizam* existed because of the magnitude of the main tax involved and both were collected in kind, although concurrent taxes were being levied in cash.[11]

The *timar* system was not a feudal system in any meaningful sense of the term; it was a bureaucratic institution intended to help the state solve various collection problems. Therefore, the *timar* system was established in places where the power of the state was strongest. In areas such as Mount Lebanon and east of the Jordan River, where the power of the state was only nominal, no trace of the *timar* system existed. Thus, in contrast to a truly feudal regime, the *timar* system was a direct derivative of the state's power.

There is another important aspect of the *timar* system to which we must now turn: the position of the peasants within its framework. They were legally tenants of the state; if peasants fulfilled their obligation to pay taxes, their right of usufruct was hereditary and secure. But they were restricted in the ways they could use the land. It had to be tilled. Failure to till land for three consecutive years was considered cause for lapse of the right to the land. Peasants could sell the land, provided that they had procured the prior consent of the fiefholder. Insofar as the land was *miri*, it was legally forbidden to turn it into a religious endowment (*waqf*).

The preservation of the integrity of the family farm and its security of tenure seemed to have been one of the main functions of the system. The *chift*—the land area ploughed by a pair of oxen in a ploughing season—was considered sufficient to sustain a family. In different parts of the empire the *chift* varied between 60 and 150 donums (the donum was approximately 1,000 square meters). One aim of the government's policy was to prevent fragmentation of this "lot viable" among an owner's heirs. The government was probably not very persistent in this policy. Michael Cook found that in the sixteenth century undivided *chifts* among peasant tenures were already, in fact, not very common and that an average peasant family possessed about one-third of a *chift*.[12] But apparently the state was much more persistent in enforcing another of its policies: preventing the loss of peasant land to members of the village community and the passing of the land to outsiders. This was achieved mainly through the laws of succession. Kin and members of the village community had priority rights in inheriting agricultural land left vacant by a former holder.

Cook's studies of the land and population surveys of various areas in Anatolia confirmed that this policy was successfully implemented. Village land as a rule was owned only by village members, not by urban engrossers. It would thus seem that the sixteenth-century Ottoman Empire had a very egalitarian land regime, the cornerstone of which was the village community and the small independent peasant. This picture is corroborated by an additional aspect of that land regime, much neglected in research until now —pasturage, the area lying beyond the arable fields or in uncultivable patches nearer to the village, was the common property of all members of the village community, who had exclusive right to it, at least in theory. This was a crucial aspect of the classical Ottoman agrarian regime, and one that revealed a great deal about its later evolution.

Theoretically, then, all arable land in the Ottoman Empire was state owned, but to ascribe great historical importance to this fact would be rather formalistic. The question of whether in reality the land belonged to anybody should be approached in practical terms, largely within the frame of reference suggested by Kenneth Cuno for Egypt. In other words, we should raise questions such as who, in practice, had access to the land. Who had the right to hold, sell, or pass it on by way of succession, and who, if anybody, could endow the land as a *waqf*? Whoever could fulfill these functions should in all probability be considered the practical owner of the land. If there were no person who fit the bill, then we should conclude that the land truly belonged to the state alone. If we apply these general considerations to the classical land regime of the Ottoman Empire, then for all practical purposes the peasants were in complete possession of the soil. I find it difficult to ascribe any importance to the fact that the ruler was the titular owner of the land and therefore deem it of little value to analyze Ottoman society in terms of the Asiatic Mode of Production.[13]

The traditional agrarian structure typical of the sixteenth-century Ottoman Empire underwent a period of severe crisis at the end of that century. In fact, Barkan considered it the beginning of the epoch of large estates in Turkish history.[14] A series of popular revolts, coupled with the large-scale breakdown of discipline in various state institutions (especially the army), brought about a period of near anarchy in the late sixteenth and early seventeenth centuries commonly referred to as the Jelali revolts.[15] This period was characterized by the unleashing of army units and gangs of undisciplined religious school students on the peasant population. Rebels exerted pressure on villages, which resulted in the large-scale flight of peasants from their homes. Some of the lands so vacated were said to have been captured by members of the Ottoman elite (*askeris*), who converted peasant farms into large estates, which were called *chiftliks*, the term designating a large estate in Ottoman (mainly Turkish) history. The whole phenomenon was apparently connected with the great demographic boom the Middle East experienced in the sixteenth century as did all of Europe. Fernand Braudel assembled an impressive array of data indicating a 100 percent growth in population early in the sixteenth century.[16] The main period of growth occurred between 1450 and 1550, followed by a Malthusian crisis that reversed the process. In Braudel's words: "By 1550 the turning-point had been reached. There were too many people for comfort. Towards 1600 this overload halted expansion in new directions."[17]

Braudel was the first to inspire historians to investigate the Ottoman records for possible parallels with European developments. The Turkish historian Ömer Lutfi Barkan amassed figures from sixteenth-century land and population surveys and concluded that developments in the Middle East were very similar to those in other Mediterranean countries.[18] Other provinces of the Ottoman Empire shared in this general trend, although they differed in some details.[19]

In view of the wide gap that at that time separated Islam from the Christian West, the similarity between East and West in population explosion surely indicated that there was a common cause. Today there is no doubt that the major cause in Europe was climate. The sixteenth century witnessed what is commonly referred to as the "small ice age," that is, the drifting southward of the North Pole's icebergs. This brought about a significant increase in rainfall and hence more abundant harvests and more food.[20]

To what extent can this climatological theory be applied to the Middle

East? The literary sources were not particularly encouraging. There was no mention of climate in the Ottoman chronicles; nor was any information on this problem found in the Ottoman archives. In the absence of literary sources, future research on this topic will have to rely on techniques such as the analysis of tree rings. A study by Zipora Klein, a geographer, may be a first step in this direction; she examined changes in the level of the Dead Sea during the last eight hundred years or so. She assumed that the level reflected the quantities of rainfall west and east of the Jordan River.[21]

Klein's methodology was quite complicated, and relied, among other things, on travelers' accounts and observable traces of the sea level left on walls touching the water. She was finally able to draw up a chart that indicated the historic changes in the Dead Sea level. The first half of the sixteenth century was clearly unique in terms of the quantity of rainfall, and this peak was exactly paralleled by the population increase in the East. The rainfall level declined drastically in the last decades of the sixteenth century, exactly when the population curve turns downward. Can this be a mere coincidence? Probably not. The long-term drop in rainfall following the sixteenth century probably had much to do with the so-called decline of the Ottoman Empire. This downward trend was again reversed only in the second half of the nineteenth century, a period also noted for economic development according to independent, literary sources

Was there a causal relation between the Jelali revolts and the agrarian changes? Cook doubted any such connection; he contended that there was no adequate evidence to support such a theory. However, this period did witness serious population pressure; it is hardly likely that there would have been no agrarian consequences. The Jelali revolts were largely the work of a tremendously inflated student population. These students were thrown onto society at large by an overburdened rural economy and rural society.

Nevertheless, the Jelali revolts took place a considerable number of years after the population decline. This hiatus is a true enigma; yet it is possible that the climatic factor may shed some light on the subject. If rainfall declined throughout the latter decades of the sixteenth century, then it was quite possible that pressure on the land mounted, notwithstanding the fact that the population growth already had passed its peak. A connection among population pressure, the Jelali revolts, and agrarian problems was therefore feasible. Sudden pressure on the land could have resulted in large-scale dislocation in traditional institutions and, among other things, acute competition for the land between various classes of society. There is no question that something of this kind did take place in the Middle East at the end of the sixteenth century. So far, empirical information is available only on Anatolia proper, but in all likelihood the process was not limited to Anatolia.

As noted previously, Barkan saw this crisis period as the beginning of the era of large estates. However, neither he nor any other historian pursued this issue in an empirical fashion into the later period. Such an investigation would show, I believe, that the process of large-estate formation did not continue on any massive scale. Charles Issawi seemed to be the only scholar who collected and assessed the information available on the demographic evolution of the Ottoman Empire after the sixteenth century.[22] He attempted to make some sense of the available data and eventually came up with two conflicting population figures for Anatolia in 1831: either 8.4 million or 4.8 million people. Although he found it impossible to reconcile these figures, he said that the latter was more plausible and added that this would represent a "small decline" in population from 1535 to 1831. In other words, population growth was probably stationary or slightly on the decline. A slight decline also was found in western Anatolia in the seventeenth century, and an overall picture of stagnation was detected for Ottoman Palestine.[23]

The major reason for the formation of large estates was competition for the land, which was caused by pressure and growing fragmentation, as well as an increasing appetite for land among various types of city entrepreneurs due to the growing demand for foodstuffs in the cities. Concomitantly, if the population declined after the sixteenth century and remained static for the next two hundred years or so (apart from short-term oscillations), then there was just that much less impetus to create large estates until the middle of the nineteenth century.

CHAPTER THREE

Agriculture and the Land Regime in Seventeenth-Century Anatolia

This chapter deals with agricultural life in a small region in the northwestern corner of Anatolia in the seventeenth century.[1] In this region, peasants were so involved in urban life that the city and the village were almost inseparable. Villagers came to the city to sell a variety of agricultural produce, to buy and sell property, to sue other villagers or urban dwellers, or to defend themselves in a profusion of court cases. The inhabitants of a village often came to town en masse to take part in court hearings. Quite frequently they abandoned their villages and migrated to Bursa (the central city of the region) to settle there permanently.[2]

Bursa court records tell us a great deal about the relation of village to city. Although in other parts of the rural Middle East at this time peasants did not recognize the orthodox Sharia (Islamic law) and apparently tried to avoid resorting to the Sharia courts,[3] in the Bursa region the peasants made quite frequent use of the institution. (They even went to court for the purpose of dividing up their post-mortem estates among their legal heirs.) Thus, we have access to detailed lists of estates of more than four hundred villagers who lived in the Bursa region in the seventeenth century—a superb source of quantitative information, albeit not devoid of severe methodological problems.

The Land Regime

Agricultural land in the Ottoman Empire generally could not be formally owned by individuals but only held in possession.[4] After the great agrarian regime established in the fifteenth and sixteenth centuries, only the state (or the sultan as its personification) actually owned the land. The state en-

---

Dates in this chapter are listed as Islamic year/Christian year.

trusted the land to individuals or institutions and did not concern itself with the daily management of the land. In practice, there developed a complicated two-fold system of those who legally and practically controlled the land on behalf of the state (the *timar* system and the *waqf,* especially the so-called sultanic *waqfs*) and those who actually held and worked it, that is, the peasants.

The Waqf

The institution of the sultanic *waqf* controlled the lion's share of the lands in the Bursa region.[5] These *waqfs* were huge charitable institutions founded by the sultans; in the case of Bursa the *waqfs* were founded in the fourteenth century, when the city was the capital of the state. A sultanic *waqf* consisted, on the one hand, of revenue-consuming institutions, such as large mosques, *medrese*s (religious schools), soup kitchens for the poor, and the like, and on the other, of revenue-creating institutions, such as a market, and the villages in the immediate vicinity of the city. The ruler awarded these villages to the *waqf* because they were the property of the monarch. In this way most of the villages in the Bursa region belonged to sultanic *waqfs*. In practice, this meant that the village paid all its taxes to the *waqf,* and *waqf* administrators kept a watchful eye on land transfers in the village (as we see later).

The Timar

We possess very little data on the *timar* system in the Bursa region. This is undoubtedly due to the fact that the *waqf,* not the *timar,* was the foremost agrarian institution in the region. Most of the extant references to *timar*s or *zeamet*s are to fiefs lying not in the immediate vicinity of Bursa but farther afield. Nevertheless, these scattered references made clear that the *timar* system still functioned as it did in the sixteenth century. Thus, a register dealing with the whereabouts of fiefs in the province of Bursa in the late seventeenth century indicated that most fiefs passed smoothly from father to son in the traditional fashion.[6] Similarly, fiefs were awarded for exceptional service in time of war, and holders of such fiefs lost them for subsequent failure to take part in the sultan's wars.[7] In fact, most references in this material to the *timar* system consisted of sultanic orders of nomination or confiscation of fiefs. Thus, in one document two sons of a *zeamet*holder who died in 1031/1621– 2* inherited the fief in equal proportions as *timar*s.[8] In another document a deceased, heirless *zeamet*holder whose fiefs consisted of villages in the regions of Bolu and Bursa was assigned a successor.[9] However, the available evidence did not mention the transfer of the villages from the *timar* system to the tax-farming system, a process that was supposed to have been very widespread during this period.[10]

The *zeamet*s mentioned in these two documents were not unified, coherent estates. They were a rather more or less haphazard list of sources of revenue, sometimes purely rural, sometimes urban, scattered across large areas of western Anatolia. This haphazardness was characteristic of practically all the *zeamet* documents under investigation and suggested sheer bureaucratic incompetence and thus explained the decline of the whole system. A *timar-* or *zeamet*holder could not possibly have lived on a regular basis in his fief when it was composed of plots of land so widely dispersed. Inevitably, he took up residence in a big city and contented himself with the collection of revenue.

The evidence suggested that the *timar* system was declining, albeit at a pace apparently much slower than was formerly thought. Although historians have supposed that by the seventeenth century the *iltizam* had largely replaced the *timar* as the chief means for the collection of land revenue, references to the *timar* by far exceeded in number those to the *iltizam*.

The Iltizam

Tax collection through farming of taxes, or *iltizam,* was in fact rare in the Bursa region. As we have seen, where the *timar* system existed, it continued to function quite smoothly in this period, and the primary materials held no record of a case in which a *timar* was transformed into a tax farm. At the same time, the great *waqf*s collected their village taxes through a salaried official, or *cabi,* and made only rare recourse to tax farming. In fact, I have found only three cases in which *waqf*s collected their taxes in this manner. Yildrim Beyazid *waqf* in Bursa farmed out all its villages to a certain villager for one year.[11] In another case, a smaller *waqf* farmed out its lands, again for just one year.[12] In the third case, a *multezim* (assignee) of some *waqf* villages in the Bursa region who had fulfilled all his obligations to the Treasury was thereupon notified that his contract was to be renewed for another year, along with those of other *multezim*s who had likewise fulfilled their obligations.[13]

Thus, the *iltizam* made but little headway in the Bursa region in the seventeenth century. I did, however, find some clearer signs of its use in some areas farther afield (but still in Bursa's orbit). Thus, in one document a person identified as the *multezim* of the *mukataas*[14] (the tax-farming regions) of Yenishehir, Ine-Göl, Iznik, and Kite sued someone for having broken into the warehouse where he stored the grain collected as taxes.[15] In a document from the end of the period there were traces of the *malikane* system (the *iltizam* granted for life).[16] In this document a *malikane*holder from the region of Iznik claimed that villagers from outside the *mukataa* had seized a piece of land inside it and refused to pay taxes.[17] There is, as yet, no information on the circumstances in which these tax-farming rights were granted or why the *iltizam* in the Bursa region itself was so undeveloped.

Could it be that the *iltizam* did not develop as rapidly as was formerly supposed? (see Chapter 4.)

Land Ownership

Information derived from the court records of Bursa indicated quite unequivocally that in that region collective ownership of land (*musha*) did not exist; no mention of it was made in literally hundreds of documents under scrutiny. At the same time, records of agricultural land transactions did indicate that private and permanent possession of land existed. If these lands had been of the *musha* type, the selling party would merely have been able to sell its share in the total. But in no instance was this the case; without exception, an exact description of the borders of the land in question and the names of the bordering neighbors were recorded. The sold lands often were specified by individual names; thus, there is no doubt that people did own permanent plots of land.[18] Moreover, one rare document, which gave details of the sown lands in the possession of all the inhabitants of a particular village, showed that there was hardly a peasant who held his or her land in one piece; most owned several separate tracts.[19] All this evidence served to indicate quite clearly that collective ownership did not exist in the Bursa region in the seventeenth century.

The peasant, the actual occupier of the land, also had certain rights to it. These rights were mainly defined by the land laws of the fifteenth and sixteenth centuries, which in turn were probably continuations of older customary laws.[20] The basis of the system was the *chift*, a land area that varied between 60 and 150 donums (about 1,000 square meters) and that was defined as the area that can be sown by a pair of oxen in one ploughing season. The Ottoman government of the classical period made efforts to ensure that such an area, considered a "lot viable," would be in the possession of each peasant family and would remain in its hands.[21] By law, a peasant's holding could not be usurped or confiscated if he fulfilled the basic obligation of tilling the land at least one year in three.[22] The peasant enjoyed the right to bequeath the land in his possession to his heirs, but in order to prevent too rapid parceling of the land the law specified that only sons could inherit. This was called "simple succession" (*intikal-i adi*) and did not involve the payment of a tax. In the event that the peasant only had daughters (or more remote relatives), they still possessed the right of priority to inherit the land, but they had to pay a tax, called *tapu* (entry fine), which supposedly reflected the land's value in relation to neighboring lands.[23]

On the basis of the research material presented here, it seems quite evident that the right to security of land tenure was not jeopardized in seventeenth-century Bursa. I have come across hundreds of documents in which peasants sold lands to others or conducted other transactions with citizens, *waqf* managers or *sipahi*s. In fact, villagers quite often sued when their lands were usurped. The object of these suits was almost always pasture land; rarely was a complaint lodged for illegal usurpation of sown land. I would venture to draw the conclusion, therefore, that such cases were indeed infrequent and tenure of land was fairly secure.

The peasant's right to bequeath his land to his heirs was not mere theory in the Bursa region in the seventeenth century. My sources contained a number of cases in which the *sipahi* or the *waqf* manager tried to disinherit legal heirs, but none pertained to adult sons. Thus, in one document two women from the village of Hamidler sued a Bursa citizen. They claimed that their father had died leaving no son but only two daughters and that the *waqf* manager had ignored their rights and transferred the land to the defendant, for a *tapu* tax of 15,000 akche. The sisters produced in court a *responsa* (legal opinion) of the *sheyhulislam* to the effect that they had the right to pay the same *tapu* and receive the land.[24]

As indicated, heirs other than sons were entitled to the land if they were willing to pay the required *tapu*. If such an heir refused to pay the *tapu* and someone else were willing to pay for it, the former lost his or her right to the land. Such a case was also grounds for recourse to the *sheyhulislam* of the day, who upheld this ruling.[25] Documents such as these proved that the classical *kanun* (sixteenth-century Ottoman state law) in matters of land law was considered perfectly valid in the eyes of the *kadi*s and the grand muftis of the empire. It may be asked why security of land was to a large degree preserved. After all, it was in the interest of the *sipahi* and the *waqf* manager to usurp lands and to transfer them to others; this would mean more money in *tapu*. It seems to me that the explanation was rooted in the political power of the village community in the Bursa region. This community must have had a customary code of behavior of its own, which included, among other things, precise information on landownership. True, there was no hint of the existence of such a legal mechanism in my sources. But Paul Stirling has demonstrated how such a mechanism worked harmoniously in a twentieth-century Anatolian village community.[26] Given that the village community in the Bursa region was quite powerful, it is not farfetched to assume that that community also would have a say as to what was right and wrong in the area of landownership.

Another basic, important right that peasants in the Bursa region possessed was the free sale of their agricultural land on the market. *Kadi* records of seventeenth-century Bursa contained a large number of documents that recorded the free sale of agricultural land. In each of these cases, what was in fact sold was the right of possession of the land, and this was transferred with the prior consent of the *sahib-i arz* (landowner), the usual mode of reference to the *waqf* manager or the fiefholder. In no case was a request to sell land turned down by the "landowner," although in one case a peasant was sued by such a "landowner" on the charge of having sold his land without express permission. In this case, the sale was nullified.[27] There were no recorded restrictions on land sales, notwithstanding the policy of preventing the land from slipping out of the hands of the peasants. On the other hand, selling was clearly in the interest of the *sipahi* and the *waqf* manager, for, as I have said, selling meant the payment of *tapu*.

All manner of sales was recorded in these documents. In some cases, villagers sold to other villagers;[28] in others, urbanites sold to other urbanites.[29] But the common type of sale was villagers selling to urbanites, that is, to inhabitants of Bursa, a remarkable phenomenon that amounted to a serious urban penetration of the countryside.[30]

All kinds of land changed hands as well—large estates[31] as well as extremely small plots of land (only one or two donums).[32] Such small tracts probably constituted part of the "lot viable" of the village family, and probably they were sold in order to meet financial obligations. The large number of such sales recorded in the *kadi* records was a clear indication that villagers considered their agricultural land a commodity. In this context, it may not be superfluous to mention that almost all these transactions were paid for in cash. Hence, this is one proof that in the Bursa region the village economy was almost entirely integrated into the urban economy.

To conclude my analysis of the peasants' rights in relation to their lands, a brief discussion of their ability to turn their agricultural land into a *waqf* is in order. This type of transaction was strictly forbidden by law, for only purely private property could be made a *waqf*—which the agricultural lands were not. The actual power of landholders to make a piece of land a *waqf* is therefore an excellent criterion by which to judge the relative power of landholders vis-à-vis the central Ottoman government. Documentary evidence from the Bursa region in the seventeenth century indicated that there were no cases in which agricultural land was made a *waqf*. This fact is noteworthy, because we know that the *waqf* institution in the Bursa region was extremely popular, as it was in all other regions of the empire, and people tended to donate any kind of property they owned. The complete lack of a *waqf* made up of agricultural land cannot therefore be considered fortuitous. The only explanation for this situation is that, at least in the Bursa region, the state had enough political authority to enforce its law. To what extent this situation prevailed in other parts of the empire remains to be seen.[33]

The Peasant Economy: Land Distribution

Post-mortem estates in the *kadi* registers of Bursa contained no evidence of the agricultural land that the region's peasants possessed. Although this makes the task of tracing the distribution of land among the peasants difficult, there is an indirect method that may enable us to overcome this obstacle, albeit without precision. Peasant estates, and occasionally urban estates, sometimes included a peculiar itemization of the quantity of grain sown. This information supplied a lead as to the relevant land area. Peasants in the Bursa region at any given time worked about one-half their land,[34] leaving fallow the other half. We also know that there were very firm customary rules about the quantity of seed to be sown per unit of land; in hundreds of documents in the Bursa records areas of land are described by the amount of seed that they could "absorb."[35] In other words, the quantity of seed was meaningful to members of the society in question. Michael Cook found that the quantity of seed that could be "absorbed" was ten *mudd* (1 *mudd* = ½ ton) per *chift* of land.[36] In my own investigation I found confirmation in a single document in which a plot of land was described in two ways—as a plot of 2 *chiftlik* and as a plot that could "absorb" 20 *mudd* of seed.[37] Therefore, it is safe to assume that these were more or less constant relations. With these two basic assumptions in mind, conversion of this information about the quantity of seed sown into a calculation of land areas was a simple arithmetic exercise.

Unfortunately, however, such information was rarely found in the estate records (it was available in only forty cases). It was therefore necessary to find another device; I based subsequent calculations on the premise that one could expect to find a close statistical relationship between the size of land plots and the number of plowing stock on the same estate.[38] Here I made the somewhat bold assumption that peasants whose estates did not include such oxen had no land. The logic behind this assumption was that oxen were quite inexpensive in the Bursa region, and therefore there was no compelling reason why a farmer who had land would not own plowing stock.

My next step was to check the forty estates with sown seed (for which I had by now the exact land areas) and discover whether there really existed a relationship between the land area and the number of plowing stock. In fact, a very high correlation coefficient was found ($R = 0.81$), thereby confirming my assumption. I then went one step farther and calculated the average land area per head of oxen for these estates. The outcome was 0.4 *chift* per head. With this piece of information in hand I could finally calculate the actual land areas of most of the villagers' estates (see Table 3.1).

Before we analyze the findings, we must examine an important document that bore upon the same question. It consisted of a survey of the real estate owned by inhabitants of Sirme and its neighboring villages.[39] The survey was conducted as the outcome of a conflict about distribution of tax on real estate. Oddly enough (and in fact uniquely), the survey included houses, vineyards, and orchards as well as "agricultural land" (*tarla*). The

Table 3.1
Land Distribution Among Peasants in the Bursa Region
in the Seventeenth Century

Area	Period A		Period B		Period C	
(*chift*)	No.	%	No.	%	No.	%
0.	54	35	30	33	69	38
0.4	15	10	9	10	12	7
0.8	49	31	24	26	48	27
1.2	7	4	7	8	9	5
1.6	22	14	8	9	22	12
2	1	1	5	5	8	4
2.4	3	2	–		3	2
3–5	4	3	9	10	9	5
10	1	1	–		–	
Total	156	101	92	101	180	100

survey gave the monetary value of these types of property for each villager.
The following entries from the survey will serve as an illustration.

Name of Villager	Monetary Value of Property (in akche)

1. Mehmed Chelebi b. Mustafa
   - House and orchard (2) — 12,000
   - Vineyard (2) — 3,500
   - Orchard (11) — 21,500
   - Arable land (23) — 14,120
   - Total 51,120

2. Mustafa Chelebi b. Osman
   - House — 3,000
   - Orchard (6) — 10,300
   - Arable land (27) — 16,250
   - Total 29,550

3. Ibrahim b. Musli
   - House — 6,000
   - Orchard (1) — 2,000
   - Arable land (2) — 600
   - Total 8,600

In order to convert these money values into land areas, I tried to compile information on land values by way of sale transactions recorded at random in the *kadi* records of Bursa. Only in a few dozen cases was it possible to extract sufficient data from the document, and most of the cases were from the middle decades of the seventeenth century. After making the necessary adjustment to the inflation rate, I concluded that the average value of one donum of arable land in the Bursa region at the end of the seventeenth century was about 70 akche. With this finding in hand I constructed a table of land distribution in the said village (see Table 3.2)

I would be the first to advise caution in interpreting this table, especially in view of the rough procedure employed in my efforts to reach an approximation of the value of a land unit. Nonetheless, I think that the figures do have some value; even if land areas in the village were in reality double the findings in the table, this would not materially weaken the conclusion I have drawn from them.

Methodologically, one point is especially important in this document, that is, the information about those with no agricultural land at all. Here, of

Table 3.2
Land Distribution in the Village of Sirme, 1681

Dunam	No. of Owners	%
0	40	53
1–5	8	11
6–10	5	7
11–15	1	1
16–20	2	3
21–30	6	8
51–60	3	4
61–70	2	3
71–80	1	1
91–100	1	1
101–150	3	4
201–250	4	5
Total	76	101

Source: B 107/321, 42a ff, 20 Rejeb 1092.

course, no methodological "device" was used; these peasants simply had no land. So at least in this respect the document is entirely reliable. The proportion of this group within the total, about 50 percent, is higher than the proportion of landless found in the estate records, but the sources are alike in that in both of them this category is not only the biggest—it is substantially bigger than any other. The differences in the size of this group from one source to the other can be attributed to special conditions in the village of Sirme. So, to a certain degree, the two sources seem mutually corroborative.

Indeed, this first category of landless peasants was obviously one of great importance. After all, the number of landless peasants and their general position is one of the most important criteria by which to evaluate any rural society. At first glance, the size of this group in the rural society of the Bursa region seemed astonishing. But a more penetrating look at the details revealed that not all of the group really constituted a severe agrarian or economic problem; many had other ways of earning a livelihood. It can be inferred from their estates that some voluntarily relinquished the pursuit of sown agriculture to specialize in other branches, particularly gardening or sheeprearing. Thus, Sayyid Ali Chelebi, who died in 1105/1693, had no arable land but did have a sumptuous village house and a large number of orchards. On the whole he was quite well to do, and so it was quite clear that he chose to specialize in gardening.[40] Similar conclusions appeared to have validity for other estates as well.[41]

Another branch of agriculture that appeared to have been an alternative to field cultivation was sheepbreeding. Although most villager estates were without sheep, a certain number nevertheless had large flocks of sheep. Thus, in the estate of a villager from Bilad Yunus, there was no trace of sown agriculture, but there were 54 sheep.[42] In another estate in the same village, whose owner died twenty years later, there was mention of 140 sheep, again with no indication of sown agriculture.[43] Yet another villager, who died at the end of the century and had no agricultural land, left a flock of 300 sheep.[44] Still others who also apparently had no land were agriculturists.[45] Sometimes there were border cases in which the villager had no land, and it is doubtful whether the other property on his estate was sufficient to sustain him and his family. In such instances, we have to decide somewhat arbitrarily whether the case was one of real landlessness.

Some of the landless villagers, in fact, did engage in nonagricultural occupations; some were village prayer leaders (imams),[46] some were shopkeepers,[47] and some were even artisans.[48] After I examined all the estates of landless villagers for other occupations, I reduced the number of those in this category, as is shown in Table 3.3.

Thus, even after we have explained some instances of landlessness among peasants, it is still evident that the landless constituted almost one-quarter of the peasants in the village. However, a certain proportion of this

Table 3.3
Landless Peasants with No Other Occupation

	No.	%
Period A	43	27
Period B	20	22
Period C	42	23

group consisted of youths who had not yet inherited land because their fathers were still alive. We know that when such youths married and established families, they founded farmsteads of their own and thus were liable to taxation.[49] It may be asked, however, why they could not reclaim new land from the wilderness or at least usurp parts of the village pasture. After all, important as grazing land was to the village economy, grain production was far more so. Although pasture existed alongside minute plots of land, the obvious lack of reclamation efforts indicated that pasture was most likely confined to mountain slopes and similar barren land (land reclamation was generally discussed in the documents with reference to difficult mountainous soil).[50] In addition, most of the recorded cases concerned events at the end of the sixteenth and the beginning of the seventeenth centuries, but none referred to usurpation of village pasture land. Thus, little in the way of land reserves existed, and the youth had to wait for their inheritances to obtain land. We do not know the size of this group, but it certainly accounted for some percentage of the landless. If it constituted only 10 percent of the villagers (a mere guess), then 10–15 percent of the villagers had either no land at all or had only minute plots. This was quite in line with twentieth-century figures, and it did not indicate that a major problem of landlessness was in the making.[51]

One sign, or even proof, of this was the fact that we have found in the Bursa *kadi* records only two cases of tenancy contracts between landowners and peasants. In one document a *muderris* (religious teacher), an inhabitant of Bursa, owned lands in the village of Dekincik that he leased to a villager. He described the matter as follows:

> When I worked the said fields with the permission of the *kadi* of the day, the said Ahmed came, too, together with my other employees and worked with the oxen. Afterwards the said Ahmed asked to lease from me the said fields and I, too, leased to him the said fields and thus we made a *muzaraa* [sharecropping contract] by the terms of which the land and the seed are mine, whilst the rest of the work is his. I handed over the said fields to the

said Ahmed, for the duration of three years . . . by way of *muzaraa*. And he, too, received them in the said manner and tilled them. After the harvest, and after paying tithe and other taxes from the produce to the *waqf,* we have divided up between us the rest and each side took his share.[52]

This document showed that the classical Islamic legal contract of *muzaraa* was in use in the Bursa region in the seventeenth century.[53] On the other hand, I have not come across any other type of contract by which agricultural land was leased in a sharecropping arrangement (or, for that matter, in any other arrangement). Clearly, then, sharecropping and tenancy were not particularly widespread in the Bursa region in the seventeenth century; no records for Bursa or Edirne mentioned the terms *murabaa* or *ortakchilik*, which were used to denote sharecropping in a later period in Anatolia and the Fertile Crescent. I believe these terms were not extant in the seventeenth century because large estates were rare in this region.

According to the available data, the villager estates were small in size. The average land plot was 66 donums in Period A (1600–1630), 79 donums in Period B (1631–1670), and 68 donums in Period C (1671–1700). These are much larger areas than the average 30 donum plot at the height of the population boom in the sixteenth century.[54] My findings do corroborate to a certain extent Cook's conclusion that the late sixteenth century was a period of increasing pressure on the land.[55] In the seventeenth century this pressure eased, and hence we find larger average plots per villager. However, the largest group of villagers were found in the category with the least land—about one-half *chift,* which was barely sufficient to sustain a small family. At the same time, there were practically no large landowners within the village. A villager who owned 10 *chift* (800–1,000 donums) was rare, and this in itself cannot be considered an exceptionally large estate.

All in all, the Bursa region was a regime of smallholders. In most villages farms were small, even minute, and often barely sufficient to maintain a family. A certain proportion of the village population was landless. However, this landlessness, as far as we know, was not caused by any process of land agglomeration by the wealthy. Even the richest stratum of villagers rarely owned large tracts of land. Landlessness and the small size of landholdings must therefore have been chiefly the result of the division of plots through inheritance. The landless peasants were, however, too few to constitute anything like a rural proletarian army, and the larger estates were not big enough to necessitate the formation of such a proletariat. This basic truth endured even when the somewhat larger estates of the urbanite agriculturalists or the *chiftliks* appeared on the scene.

Pasture

Pasture was already a vital part of the village economy in the classical agrarian regime of the fifteenth and sixteenth centuries. Many of the agrarian codes in Barkan's great collection contained an article to the effect that no one was to lay hands on the ancient pasture area of the village and divert it to another use.[56] In the Bursa region of the seventeenth century, every village devoted a part of its land to pasturage. Many, if not all, the villages had as one of their communal employees a cowherd (called in the sources *sighirtmac*) whose daily duty was to graze and guard the village livestock. The holder of this position could be and was sued by villagers for alleged negligence when, for instance, livestock was seized by wolves.[57] Apparently, these cowherds were the only employees that many villages had, and thus they personified the essence of the village community.

In fact, because the pasturage area was common land and belonged equally to all, it constituted the main basis for the existence of the village community in the Bursa region. This was especially true given the complete absence of communal ownership of agricultural lands (*musha*). Whatever the cadences of status and economic well-being in the village, as far as the pasture was concerned no differentiation existed, and all livestock owners considered themselves equal.

Historical records suggested that the pasture was always a burning issue in the villages of the Bursa region, a fact made evident by a large number of legal conflicts in which entire villages took part. Thus, in one document the villagers of Alishar sued the inhabitants of the neighboring village of Timurtash, claiming that the latter had usurped part of the pasture area that traditionally belonged to the former village.[58]

Examples such as these are not rare.[59] Not the least interesting aspect of all these cases was the fact that a large number of villagers, possibly the entire adult village population, appeared en masse in court with no legal representative of any sort to speak for them. This probably indicated a considerable degree of solidarity and strength on the part of the village community and served as excellent proof of a wide measure of legal and political autonomy.

Peasants of the Bursa region waged war for their pastures not only against other villages; city entrepreneurs, often bearing military titles, were often sued, too. Thus, according to one typical document, the villagers of Ishiklar Kebir sued several entrepreneurs and managers and claimed that "Some of the places around the said village belong to the *waqf* of Hazret Emir and some to the *waqf* of Sultan Yildrim Beyazid II and as of old we sow and plow them. And some of these places have been pasture for our cattle, and they have never been pasture for sheep and goats. But, nevertheless, the forenamed, as well as some *sipahis* and *Janissaries* raised sheep and placed them there forcefully, causing us great harm."[60]

Not surprisingly, conflicts about pastures sometimes took place between villages and nomadic or seminomadic Turcoman tribes, or Yuruk, the famous nomadic and tribal remnant of the old Turkish population of Anatolia. Apparently, no corner of Anatolia was without them, and the Bursa region was no exception. Side by side with urbanites and villagers, they constituted the third element of the human geography of Anatolia. Their main occupation was, of course, sheepbreeding. Most of them still preserved the ancient tradition of transhumance—they roamed between winter pasture in the low-lying plains and summer pasture at the top of the mountains. An adequate description of this type of human activity in Ottoman times is still lacking, although Planhol, who has written the classic account of its decline in recent decades, tried to investigate its early roots.[61] In 1804, Hammer cited a long list of such summer pastures (*yayla*) throughout the peninsula.[62]

Not surprisingly, the mountain dominating Bursa, the Ulu Dagh, the highest mountain in western Anatolia, constituted one such major pasturage. The exact relationship between transhumance and pastoralism in the seventeenth century is unfortunately not at all clear because we possess very few references to these nomads. However, there is no doubt that they did exert a certain measure of influence on domestic farming. Thus, in one document there was a rare reference to the Yuruks. The inhabitants of the village of Akche sued a group of them, claiming that "the aforementioned come to the vicinity of the village in winter time and they pass the winter there, while in the summer they go away. While this has been the situation as of old, it is now summer but, nevertheless, they do not go, but rather pasture their cattle in the pasture area belonging to us by *tapu.*"[63]

In this context it may be of some interest to mention the fact that one sultanic *waqf* in Bursa (the *waqf* of Yildrim Beyazid) even had as one of its basic revenue-producing assets a vast flock of 32,000 sheep, for which a pasture area of some 20 *chift* (about 500 acres) was allotted. Why and under what circumstances such an unusual endowment was granted was not made clear, but the very existence of a flock of this size was evidence of a specialized pastoral economy.[64]

Within the context of pastoralism it is important to bear in mind the difference between village pastoralism (cattle) and Turcoman pastoralism (sheep). Sown agriculture and sheepbreeding were often mutually exclusive activities. Cattle were necessary in the pursuit of sown agriculture (especially for plowing), while sheepbreeding was not and was therefore to a certain extent an alternative to sown agriculture. Indeed, we have seen that in the Bursa region this was exactly the situation; only a few peasants possessed sheep. The documents concerning conflicts about pasture supported this conclusion. The pastures were mostly cattle pastures. In none of the lawsuits brought against village herdsmen was there reference to sheep; most references were to cattle, and there was occasional mention of horses. Description of pasture sometimes indicated quite explicitly that the area in question consisted of village lands unsuitable for agriculture.[65]

Urban Involvement in Agriculture

Agriculture in the Bursa region was not conducted solely by peasants. In fact, one of the most interesting aspects of the body of documents under study was the large-scale involvement of urbanites in agricultural affairs. Bursavites were intensely concerned with all aspects of agricultural life. Of course, they were especially interested in orchards, and estate descriptions referred to vast sums of money invested in them. But this activity can hardly be described as agriculture in the full sense of the word. The more meaningful side of the phenomenon was the intense involvement of urban citizens in sown agriculture, which was carried out in the villages around the city. The exact extent of this involvement is unknown, but the large number of documents concerning it indicated that it was quite extensive. Thus, in our previously mentioned survey of land sales by villagers in the Bursa region, it was noteworthy that the overwhelming number of people who bought these lands were urbanites. This fact was certainly not commensurate with sixteenth-century land law. But whether there was a legal revolution is not yet wholly clear. It is still possible that the sixteenth-century land policy of the Ottoman government has been idealized, but only further research will verify this point. However, the peasants' right to sell was grounded in legal opinions of the highest authority, as evidenced in the attempt made by a brother of a peasant to prevent him from selling his land. The peasant sold the land freely on the market; his brother claimed that he had priority right to buy the land for the price offered. However, the *sheyhulislam* who was approached thought otherwise. Here is the text of this important *fetva* (Islamic legal opinion):

> Zeid sold and transferred to Amr, with the permission of the "landlord," his land, which was in his possession. Then came Bekir, Zeid's brother, and said to Amr: "Being Zeid's brother I have priority over you in the matter of buying the said land." Can he pay whatever Amr had given and take the said land? Answer: He cannot. If, in this way, a former *kadi* gave verdict to transfer the land from Amr to Bekir, is his verdict valid? Answer: No.[66]

One way to convey an idea of the extent of urban involvement in agriculture is to analyze the estates of those Bursavites whose major occupation was agriculture.[67] (See table 3.4.)

Two points are noteworthy in this regard. The first is what we may call

Table 3.4
Estates of City-Based Farmers in Seventeenth-Century Bursa (akche)

	Period A: N = 55			Period B: N = 76		Period C: N = 150		
	Nominal	Adjusted	Average per Estate	Nominal	Average per Estate	Nominal	Adjusted	Average per Estate
Houses	1,302,746	1,691,878	30,761	1,259,750	16,562	2,272,508	1,761,634	11,744
Estates	(16) 1,100,430	1,429,129	25,984	(20) 887,550	11,678	(25) 1,059,200	821,085	5,474
Gardens	1,120,010	1,454,558	26,446	896,930	11,801	2,982,136	2,311,733	15,411
Cattle	(339) 278,820	362,104	6,583	(427) 352,173	4,634	(510) 369,730	286,612	1,910
Sheep	(425) 14,350	18,636	330	(4521) 648,660	8,535	(1201) 194,562	150,823	1,005
Debts	432,879	562,180	10,221	1,271,789	16,734	3,906,024	3,027,925	20,186
Sums owed	631,004	819,485	14,899	868,320	11,425	1,398,132	1,083,823	7,225
Total	(net) 6,695,835	8,695,889	158,107	8,886,850	116,932	13,958,439	10,820,495	72,136

Source: Kadi Records of seventeenth-century Bursa.

the structural aspect, that is, the general problem of urban involvement in agriculture; the second is the more limited problem of the apparent changes in these estates during the course of time. The former is really a remarkable phenomenon. It shows that city and village in the Bursa region were not separated from each other by anything like an iron curtain. Just as villagers enmeshed themselves in the affairs of the city, so urbanites involved themselves with equal passion in rural matters. Urban entrepreneurship in Bursa encompassed a wide range of activities; it was in no way restricted to commerce and artisanship. Moreover, the urban involvement in rural affairs was not passive possession by absentee landlords. Only a few of the urbanites involved in agriculture had *chiftliks*, (in general the farm not defined as a *chiftlik* was much smaller). In all probability farms were worked by the estate owner himself, perhaps with some family help in peak periods. If the owner used hired help at all, it was only to a very limited extent. The number of slaves he possessed was also very small. Even the *chiftliks* that the members of this category possessed were generally not large enough to allow the development of large-scale capitalistic agriculture.

As against this generally intense involvement of the urban group in village agriculture, Table 3.4 indicates that the wealth of the urban agriculturalists decreased sharply and constantly throughout the seventeenth century. In fact, it decreased more persistently and more sharply than the wealth of any other group. The figures in Table 3.4 consistently show an acute drop throughout the period under consideration. How can we account for this apparently drastic decline in the wealth of the city-based agriculturists? There was probably a decrease in the attractiveness of the countryside in relation to urban investment. This region, like others in the Ottoman Empire, experienced a demographic peak in the second half of the sixteenth century, which resulted in a greater demand for foodstuffs as well as an increased need for more investment in the rural area. Only a study of this area in the sixteenth century, which has not been undertaken so far, could verify this theory. Another plausible explanation, also at present no more than a hypothesis, is that agriculture attracted less investments because extensive trade, and especially trade in Persian silk, was more attractive, a fact also reflected in the phenomenal rise in the average wealth of the merchants of Bursa.[68]

The general trend in diminished income also was apparent in estate lists of particular assets. The wealth at the disposal of urban agriculturalists decreased in houses, *chiftliks*, orchards, and cattle. At the same time, there was increasing indebtedness. Altogether, the practitioners of this occupation were steadily pauperized with the passage of time. Noteworthy were the differences between the estates of urbanite farmers and peasants. The latter showed a rising trend in size of estates in the middle third of the seventeenth century and a decrease in the last third. Therefore, it seems that peasants were affected by different forces than were urban agriculturalists, the main difference being that unlike the urban entrepreneurs the peasants did not work for the city market.

Chiftliks

The most interesting aspect of urban involvement in agriculture in the Bursa region was the association of urbanites with large estates or *chiftliks*.[69] Documentary materials seemed to indicate that the *chiftlik* in the Bursa region was the primary form of urban involvement in sown agriculture. *Chiftlik* was not always the term used to designate a large estate. Its origin is the *chift*, or pair, that is, the pair of oxen needed to pull one plow.[70] In the fifteenth and sixteenth centuries the term signified the amount of land a pair of oxen could plow in a plowing season (which probably lasted for one month). This area differed according to location, and on the whole varied between 60 and 150 donums (the donum being about 1,000 square meters).[71] However, as early as the sixteenth century the term *chiftlik* began to change in meaning, and by the seventeenth century it definitely was used to designate an estate—that is, a large house adjacent to arable land of varying size, which could consist of less or much more than one *chift*.

There are those who claim the *chiftliks* were mainly created in the great period of anarchy at the end of the sixteenth and the beginning of the seventeenth centuries during the time associated with the Jelali revolts.[72] This large-scale popular uprising upset the entire social fabric in Anatolia and caused widespread flight from the land. The vacated lands were then occupied by members of the Ottoman military-political elite, who converted them into large estates called *chiftliks*. There were some documentary indications that such events did indeed take place. Thus, a sultanic order of 1017/1608 stated explicitly that all categories of the military elite had usurped vacant lands and had refused to restore them to the peasants on the latter's return, claiming they had received the said lands from *sipahi*s or *waqf* managers.[73] This does not prove that *chiftliks* were created solely in this way or that this was the major avenue to their creation. In fact, the documents did not distinguish clearly between a *chiftlik* and a regular peasant farm that was not called a *chiftlik*; after all, *chiftlik* was not a formal designation, but rather a popular term. Regular documentary mention was made of tenures that were more extensive than land areas of *chiftliks*. I can only speculate why some farms were singled out for this designation, which was somewhat arbitrary. Perhaps the houses of the *chiftliks*, which were generally sumptuous and expensive in contrast to the peasants' dwellings, give rise to this differential term.

The main motivation for creating *chiftliks* appeared to have been commercial—the wish to turn a small peasant farm producing a meager surplus into one producing for the city market. This end could have been accomplished during the Jelali revolts through usurpation of lands as well as through regular, legitimate business methods. It seemed that in the Bursa region the latter was the more usual process. The fact that commerce was mainly at the root of the phenomenon of the *chiftliks* was apparent from the large quantities of grain mentioned, in the inventories of these farms, and from the sizable number of cows listed; the latter were part of the large-scale dairy farms that operated in some of the *chiftliks* and produced dairy products for the city.

Another common theory as to the origin of the *chiftliks*, one not supported by the material from Bursa, was advanced by Stoianovitch. He speculated that the *chiftlik* was the *hasa* of the *timar,* the domain of the fiefholder, who became ever stronger at the expense of the small peasants until eventually the latter were reduced to the inferior status of tenants or sharecroppers, subservient to the landlord in every respect.[74] Were this the case, we should find at the most one *chiftlik* per village. But the phenomenon actually encountered was the concentration of a number of farms in one village (mostly near the town) as well as villages farther afield with no *chiftlik* at all. Moreover, most if not all *chiftliks* in the Bursa region sprang up on *waqf* soil and had nothing to do with the *timar* system. Therefore, there were some differences between the *chiftliks* in the Balkans and those in Anatolia, and one should be wary of applying conclusions drawn from either one of these cases to the other.

Ownership was an extremely revealing aspect of the *chiftliks*. One of the most important social groups possessing *chiftliks* in the Bursa region was the elite, which included some persons who were at the very top of the Ottoman political pyramid. The most notable case in the documents was the estate of one Dervish Pasha. At the beginning of the seventeenth century he purchased jewelry for the enormous sum of 3.5 million akche and mortgaged a *chiftlik* in the village of Balikli, called Muhi ed-Din Bey Chiftlighi, which contained 297 head of cattle, 25 male slaves, and 12 female slaves.[75] This was the largest estate recorded in these documents and could well have served as a basis for large-scale capitalistic agriculture. A *chiftlik* in the same village was owned by a top Ottoman official (a *bashdefterdar,* or head treasurer) a half century later.[76] According to another document relating to the same estate, it included sown land of at least 10 *chift,* that is, 800–1,000 donums.[77] A certain Ishak Pasha had a *chiftlik* in the area of Gemlik, which in 1085/1674 was confiscated by the Treasury.[78] Other *chiftlik* owners in the Bursa region included Vezir Omer Pasha[79] and Mevlana Mehmed Efendi, an Anadolu Kazaskeri.[80] These were the most conspicuous examples of members of the top Ottoman elite who owned *chiftliks* in the Bursa region; the number of low-echelon members of the elite who had such estates was much larger.[81]

Men of religion, no less than members of the military establishment and no less surprisingly, were distinct among those who possessed *chiftliks* in the Bursa region. Thus, Molla Dervish Mehmed Efendi, a famous personality in the annals of the city,[82] and Mehmed Efendi b. Habil each owned a *chiftlik*.[83] In a third document a *chiftlik* changed hands between two important religious personalities—the seller was Mevlana Ibrahim Efendi (hence a *kadi*), and the buyer was a *sheyh* (head) of a Sufi covenant in Bursa.[84] All in all, I have come across no less than thirty examples of important religious personalities who owned *chiftliks* in the Bursa region.[85] The *ulema* (men, or doctors, of religion) did have a special interest in *chiftliks*.

There was no information on the day-to-day involvement of the *ulema* in the affairs of the *chiftliks*, and it is not likely that they were so engaged. They probably had stewards for this task, yet it did seem quite clear that at least as far as buying, selling, and the like were concerned, the *ulema* took care of their own interests, pleaded their cases in court in person, and were in possession of full information about their *chiftliks*. There were indications, however, that some owners were definitely not in the vicinity of their properties, and therefore they appeared to have been absentee landlords. Thus, one Bursa citizen died a *kadi* of Salonika and left a *chiftlik* in a Bursa village.[86] Similarly, a *muderris* from Istanbul had a *chiftlik* in a Mudanya village.[87]

These cases suggested that for these men of religion, the *chiftliks* were a sort of retirement place, a source from which to draw their pensions. However, even if this were true, the *ulema* did not (at least exclusively) hoard wealth by way of expensive apparel, jewelry, and other uneconomic forms; rather they invested it quite cleverly in a fashion not unworthy of the term *capitalistic.*

I have claimed that the creation of *chiftliks* sprang from a capitalistic impulse. However, there were indications that the phenomenon was limited. A rare document from the end of the seventeenth century helped draw a general picture of the institution—a 1696 survey of the *kaza* of Bursa indicated those villages in which *chiftliks* existed; the survey also listed their land areas. There were sixty-nine farms in the *kaza* (see Table 3.5), and most were modest. Only in rare cases were the *chiftliks* as large as 1,000 donum (200 acres). By modern standards of landownership in the Middle East or Europe, this was a rather modest size; in fact, there were no great estates in the Bursa region. Although we have no comparable information for areas farther afield, it is probably safe to assume that there must have been a direct correlation between farm size and proximity to a great city—there can be no other reason for urban involvement with the *chiftliks* than their commercial potential. This potential decreased with the distance from the city. The farm size for the *kaza* of Bursa appeared to have been a sort of "ceiling" for the whole area. Moreover, many of the documents that indicated the extent

Table 3.5
Chiftliks in the Kaza of Bursa, 1696

Area (chift)	No. of Farms in category
0.5	6
1	11
1.5	5
2	13
4	21
5	4
6	4
10	2
11	1
15	1
24	1

Source: Kepeji 2776.

of the sown land of the chiftliks obscured a vitally important characteristic of this land—it was never in one integral piece. Scores of sales agreements for chiftliks made it abundantly clear that in exactly the same fashion as for peasant farms, the agricultural land was minutely divided into plots, probably of no more than a few donums each. Even in those cases where the overall land area of the chiftlik might justify the introduction of more capitalistic agricultural techniques, the minute parceling of the land precluded such a move, and there was no sign that anything like land integration was taking place.[88]

The chiftlik was thus a noteworthy and an impressive manifestation of urban initiative and a businesslike turn of mind, but its existence did not alter the basic land regime in the Bursa region in the seventeenth century, which was a regime of smallholders and independent, autonomous village communities. Why was the phenomenon so limited? The answer is simple—the produce of the chiftliks was intended exclusively for the Bursa market. Given the poor communications system of the time, it must have been impractical to export grain from the Bursa region, and Bursa itself in the seventeenth century was an agglomeration of no more than thirty thousand inhabitants, far too few to make conceivable the development of large-scale agricultural estates.

Moreover, during the course of time the chiftlik did not appear to have developed (see Table 3.6). On the contrary, judging from available statistics, the number of chiftliks did not increase significantly, and the value of the average chiftlik declined. If this finding is correct, then it would indicate that

Table 3.6
Chiftliks in the Estates of Urban Farmers

	No.	Value (nominal)	Value (adjusted)	Value Per *Chiftlik*
Period A	16	1,000,430	1,429,130	89,320
Period B	20	887,550	887,550	44,377
Period C	25	1,059,200	821,085	32,843

insufficient investment was being put into the institution to maintain its value and that the institution's attraction for the city elite was certainly not increasing. It would also mean that there was no tendency toward growing urban dominance of the countryside.

Urban society in the Bursa region exerted a major influence on the hinterland. The relationship constituted nothing less than an invasion of the countryside by the city. What was the nature of this influence? If we take as an example a village with four *chiftliks*, all owned by urbanites, of what relevance was this to the functioning of the village community? Was the political autonomy of that community preserved, weakened, or shattered? Did the *chiftlik* owners come to dominate the village in part or in full? These are crucial questions to which the next section may provide some tentative answers.

The Village Community

We now come to the last subject on which information can be derived from the sources under investigation: the village community in the Bursa region. The existence of substantive involvement by city businessmen in village agriculture might result in the loosening of ties between peasants. On the whole, however, the village community was quite strong. It may be useful to compare this situation to that of nineteenth-century Egypt. Gabriel Baer observed in that rural society three variables of cohesiveness: (1) *corvée* (forced labor), to maintain the irrigation canals; (2) *musha*, or communal tenure of land; and (3) a collective tax responsibility.[89] In seventeenth-century Anatolia these variables were irrelevant. The *corvée* did not exist at all, nor did *musha*. In fact, the common pasture probably constituted a stronger bond than did the institution of *musha,* wherever it existed. The pasture always served as ground for strife and conflict, and thus provided a permanent motive for common activity on the part of the entire village community.

Common tax responsibility also constituted a basis for communality of interest among villagers. This was especially true when inhabitants of one village possessed taxable property in another. In many such cases village inhabitants sued these strangers and demanded that they pay a portion of their tax liability.[90] These same taxes served as an important basis for village cohesiveness in another way as well. Their distribution among the villagers was not decided by any administration, but rather by the members of the village community and in cases of serious conflict, by a committee nominated by the *kadi* at the request of the villagers. Thus, tax distribution was the outcome of simple community dynamics, which were quite democratic in nature—at least insofar as the sources made discernible such a conclusion.

This wide measure of communal independence and autonomy was not reinforced by any single, strong, formal or informal leader.[91] Such officeholders were still in the misty future. The existence of such a democratic community, operating without any external control or internal leadership was a manifestation of a far-reaching primitive democracy that I consider characteristic of many aspects of social life in the Ottoman Empire.

CHAPTER FOUR

Agrarian Development in the Seventeenth, Eighteenth, and Nineteenth Centuries

Many scholars believe that in the late sixteenth century the pristine agrarian structure fell into rapid decline and gave rise to a regime of large estates. Previous studies show that the state abstained from assigning fiefs to *sipahis* and began to collect taxes by means of tax farming (*iltizam*). Before long these tax farmers (*multezims*) took possession of large tracts of land, which they converted into private property, as did state officials and provincial strongmen or notables (*ayan*). A landed elite thereby came into being, which increasingly turned the semibureaucratic Ottoman state into a semifeudal state.

This picture was by and large true of the Balkan areas of the Ottoman Empire, but less so of its Asian section. The situation as depicted for Bursa was also valid for the Asian region. Because there is a dearth of available primary sources that could shed light on the subject, the preparation of this chapter drew on an in-depth study of a new and formerly untapped source—the *fetva* collections, or Muslim *responsa*.

Wallerstein's "Modern World System" and the Middle East

A relatively new theory—namely, Immanuel Wallerstein's theory of the modern world system—has exerted a strong influence on comparative social history and may help place the present discussion into a meaningful, conceptualized framework.[1] This theory has powerfully influenced a large number of Ottomanists, who have all sought to utilize it to explain how and why large estates emerged in the Middle East from the sixteenth century onward. We shall therefore examine this theory in some detail in order to determine the extent to which it is applicable to the Middle East under the Ottomans.

Wallerstein claimed that a world capitalist system emerged in the sixteenth century.[2] He divided the world analytically into three different parts:

core, semiperiphery, and periphery. In the core countries (England and some of its neighbors in northwestern Europe) a capitalist economy started to emerge in the sixteenth century, and the trend gained momentum, culminating in the Industrial Revolution in the eighteenth century. The semiperiphery and to a larger extent the periphery were intimately connected with these developments. These areas underwent significant socioeconomic changes that generated a dependence on the economy of the core countries. This development caused an increased demand for foodstuffs and raw materials. As a result, raw materials were supplied by the peripheral areas, and these countries became linked to the world market. Within these areas a landed upper class took advantage of the newfound opportunities and exerted intensive pressure on the peasantry, thus creating what Fernand Braudel called "the second serfdom," that is, the emergence of feudal class relations in the countryside. This landed upper class was able to augment its political power at the expense of a weakened central government and a forcefully paralyzed indigenous bourgeoisie. In such countries (as exemplified by Poland) the landed elite enlisted the services of nonindigenous, middle-class groups (especially Jews) that fulfilled economic functions without presenting serious political demands. These developments touched off the decline of traditional indigenous handicrafts. "Without a strong State and a strong indigenous bourgeoisie, there was no effective pressure to establish protective devices for local handicrafts. As the efficiency of western European products grew, they undersold Polish products, and a once significant local handicraft industry all but disappeared."[3] In this way the countries of the periphery underwent a process of deindustrialization. Labor and other resources from crafts and industry were shifted to agriculture, and agriculturalists were increasingly subjugated to the highhanded authority of the landed elite. Through this process the countries in question become peripheralized.

According to Wallerstein's theory, the main economic division is between core and periphery; semiperipheral countries such as Russia are located in between because (largely for political reasons) they manage to resist being drawn into the world market. This theory provides a paradigm that makes the emergence of a regime with large estates in the Middle East not only intelligible but also inevitable. Its relevance is enhanced by the fact that Wallerstein himself and a number of other scholars have extensively applied it to the Ottoman context.[4] They all have unhesitatingly concluded that the Ottoman Empire was a typical case of a peripheral country.

How applicable is this theory to the Ottoman Empire? To what extent did the Ottoman Empire pass from a state of prosperous handicrafts in the sixteenth century to one of defunct or declining handicrafts in the course of the next two hundred years? How correct is the assertion that the main urban economic functions once fulfilled by a predominant, indigenous bourgeoisie passed into the hands of minority groups that were devoid of power or prospects? Although there may not be sufficient data to answer these questions in a definitive manner, there are enough available for a preliminary discussion.

Wallerstein's theory in its particulars seems only marginally applicable to the Ottoman scene. Attempts so far to apply it to this part of the world have unfortunately been largely unconvincing because they have disregarded relevant empirical facts. Although this theory may be true for the Balkan peninsula, it does not hold for the Asian parts of the empire. Many sources have shown that a clear trend toward large-estate formation was underway in the Balkans throughout the seventeenth and eighteenth centuries.[5] Recently this was admirably demonstrated by the meticulous study of Bruce McGowan, who found evidence of widespread usurpation of peasant farms by members of the administrative and military elite in the Balkans in the seventeenth century. The state opposed this trend only feebly or ignored it altogether. McGowan even observed that the *kadi* could not do much about it and formally sanctioned this usurpation of the state's rights to its lands.[7]

One point of major importance concerning developments in the Balkans is that the *chiftliks* were considered private property. As one scholar stated, they were "privately owned commercial states devoid of any obligations to the state. The *chiftlik* holder owned the land outright, and often the tools, animals, and seeds his tenants used. Here, the process of usurpation of state control was complete, and the terms of peasant tenure had also been altered."[8]

Far from posing a serious challenge to the thesis presented herein, McGowan's study corroborated it and deepened my understanding of the historicogeographical trends at work in the Ottoman Empire. It appears initially that the key issue here is the international demand for agricultural products. This is only partially correct.

McGowan made it absolutely clear that the *chiftliks* in the sub-Danubian region during the Ottoman period were intimately connected with international trade. Not only was there a European demand for the agricultural produce grown here, but river and sea transportation made it possible to meet this demand. As McGowan put it, "Consolidated monoculture was in those centuries almost always a response to foreign demand pressing on the Ottoman shores."[9] In the sub-Danubian region, as in Anatolia, there were social elements with the motivation and ability to establish large farms. However, did the European demand exert the same influence in these two regions? McGowan did not deal explicitly with the difference between *chiftlik* formation in the Balkans and in Anatolia, although he did refer to a possible difference when he said that: "A study recently published by Gilles Veinstein suggests, on the basis of the experience of the Izmir zone, that *it was the fiscal domination of the peasantry and not the organization of estates to serve the export trade* which was the primary rural source of power and fortune."[10] Even in the Balkans the phenomenon of large estates could easily be exaggerated. Most of the *chiftliks* were small, between 25 and 50 hectares (250–500 donums).[11] Moreover, McGowan noted with considerable surprise that the phenomenon did not become more extensive in the eighteenth century.[12]

It is tempting to suggest that the difference between the Balkans and the Middle East in matters of peripheralization could be reduced to differences in geographical accessibility. However, this reduction is problematic, particularly in the case of Egypt. No area in the Middle East was more accessible to foreign trade than was Egypt. For the peripheralization theory to be valid, it must be proven in the Egyptian context, specifically in relation to Egypt's foreign trade structure. According to Wallerstein's theory, important changes suffered by the economic structure of the periphery should be reflected in the structure of foreign trade. There should be a growing trend toward the export of raw materials to the core countries in exchange for the import of finished products, chiefly textiles. I have investigated this point in relation to Bursa, but without access to global figures.[13] More than two thousand estates proved to be excellent sources, for they included a complete listing of all clothes, usually with a hint as to their provenance. According to this source most textiles in seventeenth-century Bursa were not of foreign origin but rather were produced within the Ottoman Empire. This confutes the notion that local handicrafts were undermined by foreign products. I found no information whatsoever regarding international trade in foodstuffs, and I suspect that no grains or other agricultural products were exported from the Bursa region in the seventeenth century. I tend to agree with Cook that regions only slightly removed from the coast were debarred from international commerce by prohibitive transportation costs.[14]

However, as has been suggested, in order to investigate Wallerstein's theory within the context of international trade, the best starting point would unquestionably be Ottoman Egypt. Egypt is the only area for which we possess reasonably quantitative information on global trade. Whereas some scholars might claim that physical inaccessibility inhibited connections between provinces of the empire and the world capitalist market, this argument does not apply to Egypt, which because of the Nile, was most suited to international trade. If there were an area where Wallerstein's theory should be applicable, it would be Egypt. Unfortunately, however, it does not.

For all intents and purposes the internal structure of Egyptian international trade at the end of the eighteenth century appeared to corroborate Wallerstein's theory. Egypt exported rice as well as certain minerals and a small quantity of textiles to Europe. In exchange it imported mostly finished products, chiefly textiles.[15] But this is only one side of the story, and a very misleading one. Egypt's entire European trade constituted a very small proportion (about 15 percent) of the nation's global foreign trade.[16] Therefore, Egypt's foreign trade could hardly have exerted much of an influence on the country's resulting economic structure.

Egypt's trade with Europe was too small to cause deindustrialization. Europe simply did not sell large quantities of textiles to Egypt, perhaps because there was no price gap to offset transportation costs (this was before the Industrial Revolution). With regard to Egyptian export of foodstuffs, the European demand was too small to exert significant pressure on Egypt's economic structure and to push the country in the direction of large-estate formation.[17] This situation was to change entirely in the next century with the introduction of cotton. Here as elsewhere (see Chapter 3) the world market exerted a massive influence on a traditional economy only when there were unusually large profits to be made.

In Wallerstein's theory large-estate formation in the periphery was dependent upon peripheralization of the socioeconomic structure, that is, the weakening of the urban bourgeoisie. To what extent was such a process really underway in the Ottoman Empire? It used to be possible to maintain that Muslims in Ottoman society shunned capitalistic or quasi-capitalistic economic activities. Such a view is clearly no longer tenable. Halil Inalcik, Ronald Jennings, and others have shown that Muslims were involved in brisk and ambitious economic activity.[18] In other research I have illustrated in some detail the economic structure of a seventeenth-century Turkish city where Muslims were far more prominent in high-risk commerce than were Jews or Christians. The city, Bursa, was renowned as an important center of the silk trade and production. Large quantities of high-value Persian silk were imported to Bursa every year; the value of these consignments far surpassed that of other economic ventures. Yet the records show unequivocally that most merchants were Muslims. Silk production also flourished in seventeenth-century Bursa and was largely in the hands of Muslims.

One might argue that these were the last convulsions of a dying handicraft system. However, this was not the case. One early nineteenth-century source described a blossoming silk industry in Bursa. It was estimated that annual silk production in the city was 254 tons, a figure vastly greater than that of Bursa's estimated silk production in the seventeenth century. Moreover, a sizable proportion of that silk was utilized in the city itself. Thus, from the seventeenth to the nineteenth century there was no noticeable decline in silk production in Bursa.[19] In the 1830s, Bursa's silk industry, far from dying out, was given new lease on life by industrialization.[20] Although the source of entrepreneurship here was initially European, local businessmen, among them many Muslim Turks, soon followed suit. The rapidity of the industry's development and its early date are a blow to the theory that nineteenth-century Ottoman reform efforts were solely directed at the military sphere. In fact, the industrialization of the Bursa silk industry started a mere decade after that of Lyons.[21] The silk industry in Bursa grew phenomenally in Middle Eastern terms, and its growth undercuts the theory of peripheralization of the Middle Eastern economic structure.

Had Wallerstein been correct about the marginality of the indigenous bourgeoisie in Ottoman society, this would have been reflected chiefly in the sphere of credit relations because here the traditional Islamic aversion is all too well known. As a starting point we can investigate the role of the Jews, who in many peripheral countries played an important role in credit operations. In a previous study I analyzed the place of Ottoman Jewry within the context of the Ottoman (quasi-) banking system.[22] My starting point was a detailed case study of Bursa in the seventeenth century. Surprisingly, the records revealed that far from monopolizing the moneylending profession in that city, Jews were hardly involved in it. Thousands of estates of deceased from Bursa contained extensive details (including names) of sums owed by the deceased as well as sums owed to him. Jews rarely appeared in these lists as creditors. They were more often listed as debtors. Indeed, in seventeenth-century Bursa there was a group of professional moneylenders, most of whom were Muslim; none was Jewish.

This information was further confirmed by the case of seventeenth-century Edirne, one of the major Ottoman urban centers.[23] Documents published by Ö. L. Barkan showed that Jews were more often debtors than creditors. In one estate published by Barkan we find a Muslim, obviously a professional moneylender, in whose estate were listed more than one hundred names of Jews who owed him sums of money at the time of his death.[24] It can be concluded from this document that this person specialized in lending money at interest to the Jewish community of that city; the fact that Jews had access to a non-Jewish moneylender can be interpreted to mean that there was a paucity of Jewish moneylenders. I came to the conclusion that the evidence from Bursa and Edirne held as well for the Ottoman Empire in general.

In what way is the peripheralization thesis correct? Wallerstein's findings for the sixteenth and seventeenth centuries may hold for the period of the Industrial Revolution and then possibly not for the first years of that epoch. Dominique Chevallier demonstrated clearly that the real inundation of the Middle East by Industrial Revolution products started only in the 1820s when the steamship was introduced into regular service, thereby bringing about a dramatic reduction in transportation costs.[25] In former times textiles were hand produced, which effectively prevented the disappearance or even decline of traditional Middle Eastern handicrafts. But even in the context of the nineteenth century Wallerstein's theory must be substantially modified. Considerable empirical data showed that local indigenous handicrafts did not disappear quickly, even after the inundation of Middle Eastern markets by cheap European textiles.

Reports throughout the nineteenth century reiterated the persistence of the traditional textile crafts in the face of impossible competition.[26] It is sufficient in the present context to mention the opinion of one British observer writing in 1910.

> As it is, notwithstanding many obstacles which have mitigated against proper development, the earning capacity of the country is still very considerable; agriculture, and the local industries of silk, oil and soap manufactures, weaving and dyeing, are valuable sources of income, to which are added the value of the exports of wool, cattle, sheep, fruit etc., and the amount of the large cash remittances which Syrians abroad are constantly sending to their homes. The wealth of the people has increased, and their purchasing power has also become correspondingly greater; conditions of living have changed, and with the gradual disappearance of old customs and habits the wants of the people have also an increasing tendency.[27]

The gradual elimination of the textile industry was mirrored in other handicraft industries that were less closely involved with the Industrial Revolution. Moreover, the largest sections of the local craft industry probably remained entirely beyond the reach of foreign competition, particularly in the case of the building industry, carpentry, food production, and the like.[28]

On balance, therefore, one cannot postulate the total disappearance of craft industries in nineteenth-century Syria and Palestine. Studies concerning Anatolia confirmed this general finding.[29] First, the craft guilds were still strong and vigorous. Although Bursa's guilds reportedly declined (possibly due to particularly intensive capitalist development), the guilds in many other cities, including Istanbul, did not. Moreover, guild structure and function remained what they had been for centuries. Guilds were still able to curtail activity (including that of the modern capitalist sector) when it constituted a violation of customary law concerning economic and legal privileges. There was a striking continuity between this kind of practice and that found in seventeenth-century Bursa. The guilds of eastern Anatolia that historians considered extinct probably never really existed, for the appearance of an organized guild system required a certain sophistication of the craft industry.[30]

On this basis, Orhan Kurmuş reached the conclusion that the traditional assumption concerning the decline of handicrafts was entirely unfounded. Nor was there a real basis for the assumption that the indigenous, Turkish bourgeoisie had been waning. Certainly, foreign capital made major inroads into the fabric of the Anatolian economy, but local mercantile activity was by no means eradicated. As late as 1870, there was a thriving weaving industry in outlying cities such as Erzurum, which was run and financed by indigenous entrepreneurs: "Weaving was dominated by merchant capital. Town weavers were employed by 'capitalists' on piecework. Cotton yarn supplied by merchants was transformed into cloth on payment of a fixed price per piece. There was a high demand for these relatively finer clothes and weavers could find work up to 290 days a year."[31] Far from disappearing, as the traditional theory would have us believe, one British consul in eastern Anatolia claimed that "in forming an estimate of the real conditions of the weaving population in my district as compared with England . . . their condition, if not one of absolute content, is far superior to that of the same class in England."[32] Thus, there is no factual basis for the assumption (explicit or implicit) that there was a catastrophic decline in craft and commerce in Anatolia and the Fertile Crescent in the nineteenth century. Strategically, the area lost much of its independence (including economic independence) and was tied to the world economy, but vigorous activity remained and was destined to remain to the end. Far from being overwhelmingly crushed by Western activity, the region's economy was not infrequently encouraged by it.

Wallerstein was nevertheless partially correct in the context of the nineteenth century. With the European Industrial Revolution, the Middle East was truly relegated to the dependent position of providing a market for finished products in exchange for foodstuffs and raw material. Regarding the problem of industry in the Middle East, the difference may not be especially important. The point is, however, that in accepting Wallerstein's explanatory paradigm we are misled when we try to unravel the social and political developments of the modern Middle East. Were Wallerstein right, we should have expected the predominance of large landlordism in the Middle East in the seventeenth and eighteenth centuries, with far-reaching repercussions on the political regime in the twentieth. The fact that this predominance started only in the latter half of the nineteenth century was vitally important. A discussion of the role of various potential contenders to the role of landed elite as well as various factors that inhibited the appearance of such an elite follows.

The Gradual Decline of the *Timar* System

The *timar* system was not really a feudal institution, and *timar*holders were rarely, if every, transformed into true landlords. Consequently, much of the discussion on the possible appearance of a genuine landed upper class must address the process of the disappearance of the *timar* system. There was, however, abundant evidence indicating that the institution was quite resilient.

One of the most important sources that demonstrated the vitality and longevity of the *timar* system was the large number of documents relating to the institution in the *fetva* (*responsa*) collections dating from the seventeenth century onward.[33] Although the institution of tax farming (*iltizam*) was mentioned in only a handful of documents, the *timar* appeared in several hundred cases. It would be hazardous to view the number of occurrences of any subject in the *fetva* collections as a direct indicator of its prevalence in "real" life, although it would be equally unwise to disregard this aspect altogether. There is no compelling reason why the *timar* should appear more often than the *iltizam* in *fetva* collections. The *timar* was not such an important and respectable Islamic institution that collection editors would have been obliged to include it as often as possible. Moreover, Uriel Heyd has shown that in the seventeenth century there was much less ideological commitment than previously displayed by the *ulema* to the *kanun* system (of which the *timar* was a cornerstone).[34] By the same token, of all the references to the *timar* only one or two were from the nineteenth century.[35] Thus, the large number of references to the *timar* in the seventeenth century was a rough indication that at the time it was still the major avenue through which land taxes were collected and the major institution controlling the land regime in the Ottoman Empire.

Therefore, in the seventeenth century the *timar* system as a state institution remained basically what it had been previously. *Sipahi*s were still expected to report to the sultanic flag in time of war, and they probably did so, by and large. A number of *fetva*s preserved correspondence between the sultan and guardians of minors who had become heir to *timar*s but were still too young to join the ranks of the army and therefore had to supply substitutes.[36]

As a land regime in the seventeenth century, the *timar* system hardly differed from that of the previous century. Although the *kanun* system rapidly fell into disrepute, this found no expression in the land law of the empire. A number of *fetva*s indicated that *sheyhulislam*s in the seventeenth and even nineteenth centuries still viewed the old *kanun* and customs based on it as perfectly valid law.[37] In the seventeenth century the legal system and the central Ottoman authorities were resolute upholders of the old, primeval land system of the fifteenth century, as evidenced by a long list of *fetva*s in which the old privilege was upheld by the law. In these cases both peasants and *sipahi*s (mostly the latter) wished to enlarge their share at the expense of the other side. The *sipahi* would try to exact more taxes from the peasant by various means or would attempt to change the basis of the tax. He would try to exact a tithe from the processed product instead of from the raw product, or he would force the peasant to bring the tax revenue to his granary at the peasant's expense.[38] However, there were no *fetva*s on attempts made by *sipahi*s to evict peasants from the land unlawfully, either by demanding excessive taxes for *mahlul* (vacant) land or by violating the peasants' rights to the land in other devious ways. We can interpret this absence of records as evidence that such deviousness was not common practice. Indeed, if there had been a threat to the security of peasant tenure and to the classical regime of small landowners, it did not emanate from the *sipahis*. The legal barriers to such a process were too strong, and the *sipahis* were an integral part of the Ottoman establishment and also lacked the stability of tenure. The prospective material gain was not big enough to stimulate such a process on a large scale. Thus, legal and political barriers were important factors in preventing the abuse of peasants' rights of ownership.

We have seen that the land rights and privileges of the peasant remained unchanged. The same was true regarding the restraints upon him. Thus, according to the classical *kanun*, the peasant was not permitted to construct buildings (such as mills, kilns, or burning installations) on *miri* land without the consent of the fiefholder. The same restrictions remained in full force in the seventeenth century.[39] There was also a restriction that prevented the conversion of arable land into vineyards or orchards without the prior consent of the *sipahi*; this, too, remained in full force.[40] Peasants could not legally seize vacant land (*mahlul*) and use it for their own purposes; the granting of such land to individuals was and remained the prerogative of the *sipahi*.[41]

The evidence discussed so far is from *fetva* collections of *sheyhulislam*s and therefore chiefly concerns the core area of western Anatolia. It is also interesting to look at other areas. One important source was the collection of documents of Khayr al-Din al-Ramli, a famous religious scholar in seventeenth-century Palestine. The importance of this source transcends the limited scope of the documents contained in it. We have here the opinion of an important jurist who was not part of the Ottoman establishment but belonged within the orbit of al-Azhar, the great Egyptian center of learning.[42] Indeed, al-Ramli's attitude toward the Ottoman agrarian institution was somewhat ambivalent, for reasons still to be elucidated by much needed research. The ambivalence was implicit rather than explicit and was reflected in a hazy attitude toward various aspects of Ottoman agrarian *kanun*. Thus, the old agrarian *kanun* contained a law by which a *sipahi* could force a villager who had deserted his land to return to it unless fifteen years had elapsed. When such a *fetva* was presented to al-Ramli, he ruled that a Muslim was entitled to move at will.[43] Al-Ramli may have been suggesting indirectly that the above *kanun* contradicted Muslim orthodox law and was therefore illegal. The same document contained another of al-Ramli's ambiguities. He Arabized the technical terms of the *kanun* that pertained to agrarian matters. The *sipahi*'s share of the dues was equivalent to the warrior's share in the *ata* (soldier's pension) of the *diwan* ([pay] register) in early Islam, and the *chift bozan akchesi* (the fine due the *sipahi* from a peasant vacating his land) was rendered *kasr al-faddan,* a literal translation that in itself is meaningless in Arabic. In all likelihood this was not fortuitous, and al-Ramli had probably wearied of Ottoman agrarian law and the *kanun* in general. On the other hand, the system was there and could not be sidestepped or disregarded because it was the law of the land. Therefore, apart from the examples cited above, there was no question that al-Ramli accepted the Ottoman agrarian system and saw it as valid. His collection was further proof that the agrarian *kanun* did not lapse after the sixteenth century and that it was accepted as valid law by orthodox jurists who were independent of the Ottoman authorities. Possibly the most eloquent example of this acceptance was al-Ramli's opinion about the law of succession regarding agricultural land. He unequivocally endorsed the *kanun,* although it contradicted the orthodox Islamic law of succession. He justified his approach by stating that this was the "general agreement" (*ijtima*) of the jurists.[44]

The large number of documents contained in al-Ramli's collection that dealt with the *timar* system were a major proof that the classical Ottoman land law did not fall into abeyance in seventeenth-century Palestine. This number is particularly noteworthy when compared with those relating to the *iltizam* (the latter category contained only three documents,[45] the former, more than one hundred). The documents pertaining to the *timar* system in al-Ramli's collection were noticeably different in character from those in the collections of the *sheyulislam*s. They revealed a continuity between the classical *timar* system and the one system prevalent in sixteenth-century Palestine. In Anatolia, the basic tax imposed was the tithe (*ushr*), while in Syria and Palestine the system in vogue was the *qasm* or *muqasama* (division [of taxes]),[46] whereby the tax paid was one-fifth, one-quarter, or one-third of the produce. This terminology also was employed by al-Ramli, which confirms that he was a realistic source.[47]

In Anatolia, as in Palestine, the most prevalent context in which the *timar* appeared was in arguments between *sipahi*s and peasants about taxation. *Sipahi*s would often try to extract more taxes from their peasants by trying to bargain with them for an agreed global sum in lieu of a share of the produce.[48] The fact that peasants had the ambition and political power to actually address a mufti with a complaint against a fiefholder was highly significant. However, al-Ramli cited some examples in which excessive tax extortion by *sipahi*s and *waqf* officials led to the ruin and abandonment of villages.[49]

Iltizam

Tax farmers constituted one of the main social groups that had close ties with the land in the seventeenth and eighteenth centuries. Gibb and Bowen argued that with the decline of the *timar* by the end of the sixteenth century, the tax farmer effectively assumed the role of the *sipahi*.[50] It is generally believed that the tax farmers soon became an effective landed elite. However, a study of the documents relating to this question revealed that there was in fact little material on which to base such conclusions and that the conclusions that can be drawn are at variance with the accepted version.

An early source on the functioning of the tax-farming institution was Ongan's collection of documents of court records from late sixteenth-century Ankara.[51] Taxes were collected from several villages around the town through taxfarming. Here, tax farming was restricted to one year, or at most to three. Tax farmers were not local strongmen but were state officials who were themselves villagers. In one of the cases Ongan cited, *iltizam* was given on one or two, and only rarely on three, villages. There was no instance of a tax farmer going beyond the levying of taxes. In short, tax farming was not a form of superior/subordinate political relations.

Another area where the *iltizam* can be investigated on the basis of genuine documents was eighteenth-century central Palestine, about which Ihsan al-Nimr published an invaluable and unique collection. Here the *iltizam* did not conform with the usual image of that institution. Taxes were not given to the highest bidder and apparently were not intended to be a source of profit for the collectors. Rather, they were assigned to the local shaykhs, the natural leaders of the society, who would hand over the sums collected to the authorities. Nimr stated further that in this system of taxation there was no excessive extortion,[52] which came only in the wake of the Egyptian occupation (1832–1840) when the principle of selling the *iltizam* to the highest bidder was introduced.[53]

Amnon Cohen's book on eighteenth-century Palestine also contained hard facts on which various conclusions can be based.[54] This book described the career of Ahmed al-Jazzar, governor of Acre (1785–1805). He was the tax farmer supreme of all the areas under his rule and concerned himself only with matters of state and the revenue aspect of land. The extent of his power, however, was such that under his aegis no would-be landowners could possibly emerge.

The case of al-Jazzar leads naturally to a discussion of the concept of *malikane* (tax farm awarded for life). This is often viewed as a natural development of the *iltizam,* destined to culminate in the establishment of full property rights by these grandees. Again, there was little data to help scientifically elucidate this question, except in the case of Damascus and its valley region, which had been documented.[55] Here a number of families received several villages as *malikane* and held them for several generations, which could conceivably be viewed as large-estate formation par excellence.[56] It appeared, however, that this line of development was not quantitatively significant. The other kind of *malikane* seemed to be more representative, and here al-Jazzar's case was illustrative: Al-Jazzar was not merely a tax farmer of his province; he was the holder of *malikane* over it. By the late eighteenth century, many of the provinces were so held.[57] In al-Jazzar's case this had no connection whatsoever with real landownership; the term *tax farmer for life* was not really significant because it was an outcome of power relations between the center and the provincial governor. Al-Jazzar was to lose the right as soon as he was unable to enforce it.

Some rare nineteenth-century documents also cast doubt on the age-old image of the *iltizam* as an omnipotent institution. Thus, in one of them a tax farmer sued three inhabitants of a village near Sophia on the grounds that they refused to pay the tithe owed. The villagers for their part claimed that they had paid the tithe but were unable to produce proof. The *multezim* was required to swear, but refused, and consequently lost the case. This is somewhat surprising. The *multezim* in question was a retired *nizami* (Ottoman Reformed Army) soldier, hardly a local strongman. Not only was he a low-ranking army officer, he had to go to the court in order to have the law enforced.[58] The same pattern emerged in other documents in this collection.[59]

Some interesting information about the tax-farming institution during these centuries also can be culled from the *fetva* collections. About fifty documents relating to *iltizam* were found in the *fetva* collections used for this study, most of them relating to the seventeenth century. These documents made clear that tax farming coexisted with the *timar* system and did not necessarily replace it. In many documents *timar*holders farmed out the taxes due from their fief to *multezims*; in fact, the documents did not contain a single example of *iltizam* in a village that did not constitute part of a fief or a *waqf*. Coupled with the larger number of *fetvas* dealing with the *timar* system, this is probably another indication that the pace of the decline of the *timar* system should not be exaggerated.

Another question to be raised in this context is why there is so little information on the farming out of *timars*. A partial explanation can be found in the documents. Such farming out was undertaken entirely on a private basis, without the consent or the knowledge of the central government, which had no reason to be involved in it. All the documents refer either to legal conflicts between the tax farmer and the fiefholder or between one such party and the heirs of the other. The documents in question concerned the farming out of *timars*[60] as well as *zeamets*[61] and even *has*.[61] In one rare case, the *has* was farmed out for the huge sum of more than one million akche a year.[63]

The *fetva* documents revealed that tax farming was a far less powerful and prodigious institution than is usually believed. Although the *multezim* did supervise the succession mechanism of the land, the documents reflected the pervasive insecurity of tenure. The *multezim* could be evicted at will and in fact, was often dismissed by the *sipahi* or the *waqf* manager.[64] In addition, the lease was drawn up on an annual basis, and there was no indication that *multezims* entrenched themselves in their positions for years.

The usual image of agricultural tax farming in the Middle East in this period is one of an entirely risk-free undertaking—the peasants were at the mercy of the *multezim,* who could extract from them whatever sum he wished. Although there was nothing in the *fetva* documents to squarely contradict this view, there was much that throws doubt on its validity. For example, there was considerable evidence that tax farmers terminated their leases because they were unable to collect even their pledges.[65]

Ayan

The major social group closely connected with landed property in the seventeenth and eighteenth centuries was the *ayan,* that strata of provincial leaders and rulers that virtually monopolized control of the countryside in many provinces.[66] One wonders how this previously unknown group came to be renowned in the eighteenth century. Recent studies indicated that the group may have always existed, but as long as the central government remained firmly in control, its power to assert itself was minimal.[67] However, when the central government was weakened, the *ayan* rose at its expense. It is not our task in this study to investigate the career of the *ayan*s, an institution that reached its zenith with the agreement of 1808, but rather to explore the possibility that they represented the rudiments of a landed upper class in the true sense of the term.

It is evident that wherever the *ayan* ruled their power was immense. But was it sufficient to change the legal status of lands under their political control? This question cannot be answered definitively, for it seemed that in fact they made no attempt to do so, and only went as far as levying taxes. Exactly why is not entirely clear. G. Veinstein's study on the *ayan* of Izmir in the eighteenth century did shed some light on this dilemma.[68] The study addressed itself to the problem of the connection between the *ayan* and the export of cotton and grain in which this region was involved at the time. Veinstein reached the conclusion that although these *ayan* were extremely wealthy, the source of their wealth was mainly taxation and not ownership of large-scale *chiftliks* employing numerous serfs.[69] He found that the grain sold to the Europeans was actually supplied by small producers.[70] Veinstein also concluded that the feudalization process found extensively in the Balkans was not in evidence in the Izmir region.[71]

Another study bearing on this question was M. L. Meriwether's archival study of eighteenth-century Aleppo and its region (northern Syria). She claimed that the thirty *ayan* families she studied derived their original wealth from urban economic activity. Later they also penetrated the countryside, but this only marginally involved real land ownership. To cite Meriwether:

Because of the advantages which could be acquired from control of rural resources, many of these families, although they had emerged out of the urban social estates with their economic base in the city, had extended and diversified their economic interest by investment in the countryside. Investment in the countryside through purchases of land was limited, however, by the structure of land tenure and the method of controlling agricultural production in the Ottoman Empire.[72]

Meriwether's entire discussion of the economic activity of the notables in the countryside near Aleppo was limited to their involvement in fruit orchards, which was only a peripheral agricultural activity in the sense adopted in this study. Control of such assets, for example, did not impart much political power to the incumbent because no peasant villages were located in this belt.

In the Middle Eastern context the establishment of religious endowments revealed much about the attitude of a specific group toward landownership and about the legal status of the land. Ottoman Muslim society viewed with favor the donation of property as *waqfs*. However, Ottoman law forbade the creation of *waqfs* out of *miri* lands because these were not private property. However, when an area managed to retain autonomy vis-à-vis the central government (Egypt was a case in point), groups within that area would completely disregard this state prohibition. Against this background it would be interesting to investigate the record of the *ayan*. In recent years many founding deeds of *waqfs* established by *ayans* have been published.[73] Investigation has shown that none of the *waqfs* contained arable land, a finding that tallied with an earlier study of mine on the *waqf* institution in the Bursa region of Anatolia in the seventeenth century; no case was found in which arable land was converted into a *waqf*.[74] Nor was there a single instance of such a conversion cited in an extensive collection of documents from the court records of Ayntab (south central Anatolia) in the nineteenth century (which included a large number of founding deeds of *waqfs*).[75] B. Yediyildiz's contention to the contrary can in all probability be taken to mean that such cases nevertheless existed but were few and far between.[76] Undoubtedly, Jabarti's claim that by the beginning of the nineteenth century one-fifth of the arable land in Egypt was made *waqf* by individuals was unparalleled in any other Ottoman province.

It is quite possible that a very large proportion of Anatolia was indeed under the institution of the *waqf*, but this could be ascribed to the founding of *waqfs* by the sultans themselves or by senior members of their retinue. I am firmly convinced that this factor constituted a strong, additional bulwark against large-estate formation, especially in Anatolia. Thus, if we take the case of Bursa as an example, we find that most of the villages around the city constituted properties of sultanic *waqfs* established in the early days of the empire. The taxes from these villages supported the wide social strata of the town as well as a whole series of institutions, such as schools, *medreses,* and soup kitchens. These institutions formed a complicated network of checks and balances that together worked to leave the village undisturbed, except for the extraction of taxes.

Temliks

A major avenue to the creation of full private property in land as well as large estates was ostensibly through the sultanic grant of land to various favorites. Mustafa Nuri, for example, told us that from a modest start under Murad III (end of the sixteenth century) this practice soon assumed immense proportions.[77] The picture that emerged from the documents, however, was less decisive. In fact, we have information on only a few *temlik*s (land grant—the term also describes the act of turning a piece of land into *mulk*). Thus, in 1005/1596–7, the sultan's mother received various assets in the form of property from his private estates in three areas. She also was assigned the taxes pertaining to the said properties and was given permission to sell them and convert them into a religious endowment. This was, as we have seen, an important criterion for deciding whether a piece of property was really considered private or not.[78] The source for this document, Feridun Bey's collection of documents, included ten recordings of legal transactions of this nature. The phenomenon, therefore, certainly did exist. But some of the cases in Feridun's collection were of a special nature and were not simple land grants. The chief question is how widespread was this phenomenon. There was a conspicuous lack of evidence to support the conclusion that these land grants occurred on a large scale. Apart from the odd ten cases registered by Feridun, I have not come across many incidents of *temlik.* In the entire court archive of seventeenth-century Bursa I came across only one example. In nineteenth-century Palestine, no cases were encountered at all, not even of those inherited from the past. A revealing piece of evidence in this context was British Consul Werry's 1845 report from Aleppo.[79] Among the five hundred villages in the vicinity of the town not one had *mulk* status. Therefore, the importance of the phenomenon has probably been exaggerated, and consequently, grants by the sultan were not an important breeding ground for the formation of large estates.

Sharecropping

The presence of large estates should have entailed widespread sharecropping and other forms of hired labor, a phenomenon that should be reflected in the *fetva* collections. In the twentieth century sharecropping on the large estates took the classic form of *murabaa,* which was studied extensively in a monograph by Yaacov Firestone.[80] Under *murabaa,* as the name implies, the tiller of the land received one-quarter of the produce. Wherever there were empirical descriptions of *murabaa,* I found that the sharecropper typically supplied only his labor. As in the classical theory, the sharecropper, the *murabi,* invariably had no property or supplies. He had only his bare hands. No mention was ever made in the *fetva* of the term *murabaa.* Was it in use without coming to the attention of the muftis? It is extremely doubtful, because we know that several customary legal terms that were not part of the classical *fiqh* (law) did enter the *fetva* collections. But the evidence was far from conclusive; only rarely were there examples of the classical case of sharecropping in which one side supplied only its labor force. Almost invariably the *muzaraa* was a partnership, in which each side supplied part of the capital needed for production.[81] I venture to conclude from these two facts that if the modern *murabaa* existed at all in seventeenth-century Syria and Palestine, it must have been very rare indeed.

The institution of sharecropping had its equivalent in the orthodox Islamic legal structure. This raises another point of major significance to the question of large-estate formation in the latter period of the Ottoman Middle East. One often hears the contention that the question of formal ownership of the land was neither of interest nor relevance to the satraps of the political elite, such as *ayan,* tax farmers and the like. They were interested in revenue, which was secured through taxation. The institution of *muzaraa* casts some doubt on this argument. It brought to the fore the possibility that by not establishing fully fledged private property these potentates were actually foregoing portions of the obtainable surplus that could be had through *muzaraa* (in addition to the regular taxation).[82] Thus, it is highly probable that formal property did have some meaning in real historical terms.

Nomads and Lawlessness

A major cause of the nonemergence of large estates in the Middle East in the period under study was the prevailing pattern of settlement. With the weakening of the Ottoman authority at the end of the sixteenth century, the subtle balance of power in many areas of the state was tipped in favor of the nomads, whether Bedouin in Syria and Palestine or Turcoman in Anatolia. In all fairness to the Ottoman government, it must be emphasized that the problem of law and order in a Middle Eastern context was more complicated than in most other civilizations. In few other empires was the desert civilization so close to the settled world. A minor weakening of central authority in the Ottoman Empire was enough to let loose a safety valve that had kept the nomads in check. The outcome of such a small slip was vastly more catastrophic than in other civilizations where the weakening of the central authority might entail greater autonomy for the villages. Here it meant desertion of the most fertile stretches of lands, decline of population and the loss of vast amounts of revenue to the government.

The problem of nomads in Syria and Palestine under the Ottomans is well known and needs little elaboration. The vacuum left by the weakening of the government after the sixteenth century (if not before) was a function of the fact that the great bulk of the coastal plain was a roaming ground for Bedouin tribes and was almost totally devoid of permanent villages. In Anatolia the situation was a little more complicated, but the general pattern seemed to have been similar. In fact, the valleys of Anatolia and the Fertile Crescent were only settled when public security increased in the mid-nineteenth century (see Chapter 5).

All these circumstances had far-reaching repercussions for the land regime in existence before 1858. Technically, mountainous regions were (and are) not suited to the development of large, integrated estates and as the population was especially concentrated in the mountainous regions, large-estate formation was greatly discouraged. The outbreak of plagues, which continued unabated until the middle of the nineteenth century, also reduced the population concentrations that might have given rise to large estates.

Whatever the reasons, the failure of large estates to emerge on a massive scale until 1858 was closely associated with the sparsity of the population. A comparison with China could not be more striking. A long period of peace and stability in China from the sixteenth century to the nineteenth resulted in a largely increased population, which created a major pressure on the land. This problem immensely aggravated the agrarian situation and did much to propel China into a total revolution.[83] Nomads, plagues, and a host of other calamities prevented the Middle East from following the same course of development.

Under conditions of sparse population large estates could hardly emerge because a peasant without land could set about acquiring land from the wilderness. The ecological feasibility of obtaining more land is not in itself proof that it was socially feasible, for in many states where the population was sparse, the peasantry was subjected to a politically repressive land regime. This was most probably the situation in czarist Russia. Demographic and ecological factors in themselves were only part of the story, and one has to take into account the political and legal structure of the country. The fundamental tenet of the Ottoman agrarian law was that unoccupied land (called *mevat,* or dead land) was not even considered state land; it was land free for the taking. In an important *fetva* that highlighted this point, there was a discussion between two parties about whether the quarrying of stone in a formerly unoccupied piece of land was sufficient ground to establish

ownership. The mufti ruled perforce that it was not and added that possession of formerly unclaimed land was possible only by preparing it for cultivation and actually cultivating it.[84] We have here in a nutshell a very important explanation for the obstruction of the formation of large estates in the
period under discussion. There was no simple legal way that would-be landowners could acquire ownership of large tracts of land. As we shall see, the
1858 land law was to bring about a fundamental change in this situation.

Pasture Ground

We have seen that an important component of the agrarian system in the
Ottoman Empire in the fifteenth and sixteenth centuries was the pasture
area, which was common to all members of the village. We also have seen
how village lands came under attack from city entrepreneurs in seventeenth-
century Bursa. The *fetva* collections of these later centuries showed that the
common pasture remained all important until the 1858 land law and even
later.

The *fetva* collections of the seventeenth century contained about thirty
documents relating to common grazing ground. These documents indicated that villages had a common herdsman who was an employee of the
entire village.[85] Villages tenaciously guarded their traditional grazing rights
against all sorts of intruders. As in seventeenth-century Bursa, they fought
those who tried to erect sheep pens within their pasturing ground or tried
to plant trees or vineyards there.[86]

One of the most interesting and important aspects of the legal position
of the pasturing ground in the seventeenth century was the precarious position of the *sipahi* vis-à-vis the village community. The right to graze was totally free and not liable to taxation of any sort.[87] Moreover, the villages had
wider rights to this land than did the fiefholder (if he had any rights at all).
This fact was well illustrated in a *fetva* in which one village rented out part
of its pasture to another. The fiefholder's agent claimed he was entitled to
the revenue, but *Sheyhulislam* Ali Efendi ruled in favor of the villagers.[88]
Other documents indicated that the fiefholder was not entitled to till land
belonging to the village pasture[89] and could not confer this right on others.[90]
Nor could the fiefholder confer the right to erect buildings on that land.[91] A
similar legal liability was operative in relation to managers of public endowments when a village constituted part of its assets. Such a manager could
not, without the consent of the entire village community, rent part of the
pasturing ground to outsiders.[92]

The *fetva* collections of the nineteenth century made evident the tremendous importance of the pasture in the village structure and they bore
witness to the great resistance of the peasantry in the face of all sorts of en-

croachment. In this period, too, villages had a common herdsman, and the village community was the sole (or almost the sole) wielder of authority over this land.[93] The village community could and did prevent other villagers from grazing on its land[94] and demolished unauthorized buildings without the builder's consent.[95] In the nineteenth century the community still maintained its superiority over the landlord in all matters relating to the pasture area.

Large Estates

To say that large estates did not appear in the period under discussion is a statement that must be qualified. On a limited scale large estates did, in fact, come into being. A careful investigation of this phenomenon is imperative, for in part it serves to illustrate why large-estate formation remained so limited and to clarify the extent to which the phenomenon represented a break with the former Ottoman land regime. As indicated above, the *ayan* of Anatolia generally stayed clear of commercial agriculture, although there were exceptions. A glimpse into this involvement was furnished by an important collection of documents published by Yuzo Nagata.[96] The documents, found in various Ottoman archives, were published without commentary. The collection included a complete list of the agricultural properties of seven people whose demise occurred in the late eighteenth or early nineteenth century. They were all local governors in the Ottoman hierarchy and apparently all belonged to the *ayan* of western Anatolia. However, the compiler of the collection erred in assuming that the documents were all estates of deceased.[97] This was only true of some. A distinct feature of these documents was that they presented estates with substantially differing characteristics. Some apparently specialized in grain production and others in stock raising; some relied on the labor of sharecroppers. Let us look at these patterns in detail.

There was the case of Yegen Mehmed Agha, governor (*voivode*) of Tire (the document was dated 1788). This man possessed no less than six *chiftliks*. He held a total of 7,900 donums of arable land, most of which were not under plow. He also had 5,000 donums of grazing land.[98] It seemed that the owner's main efforts were concentrated on stock raising, and the same applied to most of the *chiftliks* in this collection. They specialized chiefly in stock raising, with some dairy produce.

The largest land areas in this collection were found in the properties of Hac Mehmed Agha who died early in the nineteenth century. He was the owner of no less than twelve *chiftliks*, whose total land exceeded 80,000 donums. However, from the document pertaining to this man, it was difficult to deduce the exact nature of the agriculture in which he was engaged. This was in contrast to the information in the document (dated 1816) relating to the *chiftlik*s of Kara Osman-zade Mehmed Agha, a former governor of Saruhan.[99] Although most of the other documents revealed nothing about the working of arable land in the *chiftlik*s, here there was copious information. Among other things, the aforenamed owned three *chiftlik*s that were worked by sharecroppers. Forty-one croppers worked a total land area of 1,761 donums, that is, an average of 43 donums each. Some of the plots were actually so small that the peasants in question must have had additional sources of livelihood.

Generally speaking, in only a few of the *chiftlik*s was there evidence of sharecropping, that is, of regular grain production. Rather, most of the *chiftlik*s seemed to have engaged mainly in stock raising, for which they did not need the most fertile stretches of land. They could easily manage, as they surely did, with formerly unoccupied land, which was abundant throughout Anatolia at the time. Such a pattern of agriculture could have existed side by side with small peasant production of the traditional type without necessarily striving to undermine it.

It is doubtful whether these *chiftlik*s were involved in international trade. They probably produced common-type wool and dairy products. Because there was no foreign demand for these products, the *chiftlik*s almost certainly produced for the local market, with its natural limitations. Therefore, what was true for the Bursa region held for these *chiftlik*s as well.

A point of major importance in the documents was the legal status of the arable lands. Were they dealt with as state or as private land? The land referred to in the documents was *miri* (state land) and not *mulk* (private land). Despite some ambivalence in wording, there was no doubt that the arable lands were not treated as private property. The land itself was not assigned monetary value; only the value of the annual rent was listed. Thus, even in the most far-reaching cases, involving *ayan* agricultural activity, the central government nevertheless managed to retain its basic rights to *miri* lands.

Important information on this aspect of the *chiftlik*s also was supplied by the *fetva* collections. There were about one hundred documents relating to *chiftlik*s, and many made it quite clear that they referred to full-blown estates, and not mere tracts of land. The question that concerns us here is whether the land was usurped by individuals and its status changed. The answer derived from available sources was quite clear. A very strict separation between *mulk* (which was orchard land and village land on which buildings stood) and *miri* (wheat-growing land) was preserved. This was not surprising for the seventeenth century; however, a long series of *fetva*s from the first half of the nineteenth century revealed that muftis still clung tenaciously to the tenets of the traditional law.[100] An additional source enables us to widen the scope of the discussion and to present a more realistic picture—

Chavush-zade Mehmed Efendi's *Durr al-Sukuk,* a large collection of court documents from the first half of the nineteenth century contained several references to *chiftliks.* Here, too, complete separation was maintained between the land and the buildings.[101] All these documents concerned the Turkish cultural zone of the empire. The far-reaching developments in this respect in the Balkans, as reported in all sources, were irrelevant for the *chiftliks* of the Turkish zone.

Egypt

Egypt constitutes a special case from the point of view of this study. In the final analysis, it was a part of the Ottoman sociopolitical system and as such needs to be considered within that framework. However, politically Egypt cannot comfortably be included with the other Ottoman dominions in a model where the sultan is the center and the remainder the periphery, a dichotomy that was only partially accurate for Egypt. In very early days a meaningful center was formed in Egypt, so that the real locus for center-periphery relations in Ottoman Egypt was Egypt itself, and one can trace the emergence of a semiindependent Egypt during the course of its history. Egypt was treated as a single political and administrative unit from the beginning. The reason for this was probably to be found in the exceptionally homogeneous nature of the country and the complete dependence of its constituent parts on the flow of the Nile. Egypt was also the main granary of the empire and thus had to be considered one administrative unit. In most areas of the Ottoman Empire the surplus (the land tax) was disposed of locally; it was assigned either to *timar*holders or to *waqf*s. Only in the case of Egypt was the governor of the province entrusted with the task of handling that surplus centrally and redirecting it to other parts of the state. This was a decisive factor in the transformation of Egypt into a semiindependent (and eventually independent) country.

Largely as a result of these circumstances, Egypt developed a political system substantially different from that of the other provinces of the Ottoman Empire. After a short period of obscurity, the old Mamluk households again rose to predominance in the course of the eighteenth century. This separate line of development reached its peak with Mehmed Ali at the beginning of the nineteenth century. The same trend was reflected in Egypt's agrarian structure.

Originally, Ottoman law provided that the peasant be holder of his own viable lot and enjoy complete security of tenure and total control in decision-making concerning agricultural production.[102] But this state of affairs was maintained in Egypt during the sixteenth century only as long as there was firm Ottoman authority in the country. From the beginning of the seventeenth century the status of the peasant declined rapidly.

> As Ottoman authority in the provinces weakened, its land laws became increasingly irrelevant, while intermediaries gained increasing control of the land at the state's expense. By the early eighteenth century, they had acquired landholding rights in Egypt that established them as landlords in every sense of the term. These included: (1) life-time possession of the *iltizam,* as long as taxes were paid; (2) inheritance of it by descendants, wives, or white slaves; (3) the ability to convert land into *waqf,* thereby guaranteeing the family's continued possession of it; (4) the ability to mortgage the land, (5) to pawn it, or (6) to sell it outright.[103]

Indeed, in contradistinction to other parts of the Ottoman Middle East, tax farmers in Egypt were able to exploit the legal device of *isqat* (relinquishment of a debt) and to turn tax farms into veritable private property.[104]

A fundamental element of the *iltizam* in Egypt was the *usiya* or *vasiyye,* "bequeathed" land, a sort of demesne given to the tax farmer in perpetuity for his personal livelihood. Tax farmers, however, regularly coerced the peasants of Egypt into cultivating this land as *corvée* (forced labor). This part of the *iltizam* became private property in a more pronounced way than the rest.[105] Here, too, there was a vast difference between Egypt and the Fertile Crescent, where no comparable development took place. Turning tax farms into religious endowments became a major avenue to large-estate formation. Jabarti noted in 1813 that about one-fifth of Egypt's cultivated land was in fact *waqf.*[106]

The difference between Egypt and the Fertile Crescent also was reflected in the issue of peasants' rights to the land. In Egypt these rights were much more restricted. A case in point was the right to transfer land to heirs. A seventeenth-century document from a *fetva* collection stated that although the right of transfer was safeguarded and accepted in Syria, this was by no means the situation in Egypt, where such land reverted to the state and was allocated anew.[107]

Cuno maintained that the establishment of private ownership of land in Egypt was causally connected with economic developments that had led to a general rise in prices.[108] This interpretation may be true, but should be considered provisional for the time being. Several questions remain unanswered. How do we know that the development was more pronounced in Egypt than in Syria or Palestine? As Egypt was the only area in the Middle East to experience this phenomenon, one is tempted to ask at what stage of economic development does a trend toward private property emerge. These questions must await further research.

Distribution of Landownership
in the Nineteenth Century

In the period 1600–1858, no regime of large estates was being created in the Fertile Crescent and Anatolia. Evidence in support of this contention came from an excellent study published recently by Issawi.[109] The material, culled from British consular correspondence, concerned the year 1863, at which time the 1858 land law (see Chapter 5) had not as yet come to exert any influence. So, unquestionably, Issawi's information was a reflection of the Ottoman land regime in what may be called the second Ottoman period.

Issawi's information left no doubt that on the whole, the land regime remained one of small independent owners. Thus, for the Izmir region, which was more affected by international trade than were other regions, "by far the largest proportion of cultivated land is owned by peasants in farms of 3–20 acres."[110]. For the region of Gallipoli, "75 percent of farm land is in small properties tilled by owners without outside help"[111] This appeared to be the true picture for most of the regime, with the exception of eastern Anatolia where private ownership on a large scale was predominant. It therefore seems that my contentions throughout this chapter are well substantiated. Of all the great empires in history, the social evolution of Ottoman society unfolded in such a way that the peasantry remained relatively free. This was bound to push the area to a path of development that was necessarily different from that of other civilizations, but before we reach that discussion, we should assess the importance and effects of the 1858 land law.

CHAPTER FIVE

The Ottoman Land Law of 1858
and Its Consequences

In 1858, the Ottoman government enacted a land law as one of the chief laws of the Tanzimat.[1] It was destined to become one of the main pivots on which most of the agrarian issues in the Middle East turned in the subsequent century, and it heralded the opening of a new chapter in the agrarian history of the region. In my view this law has given rise to a great many misconceptions emanating from the dichotomy in the historiography of the Middle East between the study of the nineteenth century and that of the preceding centuries.

For the most part, the land law divided the state's lands into five distinct legal categories: *mulk*, land held in absolute freehold; *miri*, state land held on lease; *waqf*, land that belonged to pious foundations; *metruka*, land earmarked for public purposes; and *mevat*, waste and unused land.[2] The major differentiation was between *mulk* and *miri*. The difference, of course, was commensurate with what we have seen in the preceding chapters. *Mulk* land was supposed to be restricted to orchards adjacent to the built-up area of the village, and *miri* land was supposed to be equivalent to the outlying arable land. Doreen Warriner expressed some wonder at the ostensible meaninglessness of this law.[3] *Mulk* and *miri*, she correctly observed, amounted to much the same thing insofar as the actual use of the land was concerned.

> Another surprising fact is that these different divisions do not cover the leasehold tenancies between landlord and cultivator which are by far the most general form of tenure, and which affect the actual tillers of the soil more closely than do any of these muddled and rather meaningless legal categories. The Ottoman Land Code apparently does none of the things that a land-tenure code ought to do. The question arises therefore what the purpose of these categories of land really was. So purposeless are they at first sight that it is easy to conclude that they represent simply some oriental attitude unintelligible to the West.[4]

G. Baer put forward another theory. He claimed that the purpose of the Ottoman land law was to reassert the state's right to its agricultural lands, supposedly usurped in part or in toto by feudal or semifeudal local forces in the provinces. "In the Ottoman Empire vestiges of feudalism still survived, the State was weak, and . . . its rights over its lands were still challenged by local powers. Therefore, the Ottoman law aimed at consolidating these rights of the State, mainly by imposing severe restrictions on holders of *miri* lands and by listing exactly and in detail all rights held by them before its enactment which could not be denied them."[5]

The challenge Baer described was really only a challenge to Ottoman political authority.[6] As has been previously indicated, neither *multezims* nor local rulers ever truly came to the point of wresting *miri* lands from the hands of the government, changing its status in theory or in practice. It is sometimes even suggested that the land law was enacted in order to halt the process of converting *miri* land into *mulk* land. Thus, Tute contended that

> at that time [before the 1858 law] it was easy to convert Miri land into mulk by building or planting. This transferred the rakaba from the State to the individual. On becoming full owner in this way, the individual was under considerable inducement to pass the land into the Wakf class by dedication. . . . The process was one of breaking the control of the State in two stages. Its result was the progressive deprivation of the State of very valuable rights. One of the main objects of the Land Code was to put a stop to this process.[7]

This quotation reveals the fallacy inherent in the whole argument—that is, tying the enactment of the land law to an attempt to prevent state lands from gradually falling into private hands. Whatever our opinion of the consequences of the law, no one has claimed that following its passage in 1858 the state was compelled to or actually did demolish houses or uproot trees and vineyards in order to recapture control of its own lands. Yet with all the changes that occurred in the late Ottoman period (early twentieth century), only a tiny fraction of the lands were still in the *mulk* category after World War I.[8] The inevitable consequences of this supposed "usurpation" simply do not exist. This whole thesis has been erroneous. Apparently, it originated from a basic confusion between the modern (both Western and Middle Eastern) concept of state land and the concept of *miri* land (alas, often translated as state land, too). State land, in the modern sense, is land that the state wishes to keep out of individual use, such as forest land. Such a legal category did not exist in the Ottoman Empire and came into being only in the new states. *Miri* land was not state land in this sense. There was never really a question of usurpation of such land; at the most it could be misused.

Many of these misunderstandings were created by a failure to place the 1858 land law in its historical perspective. In fact, this law was no more and no less than a reenactment of the classical fifteenth and sixteenth-century

Ottoman *kanun*s relating to agrarian matters, with some minor modifications. These were partly a response to some small changes that had crept into the customary land laws of the empire in the intervening period, and partly, but to an even lesser degree, they were true innovations. Seen from this vantage point, the law is perfectly intelligible.

Even a cursory perusal of the land law indicates that in its essentials it closely resembled the classical Ottoman land laws, and in fact, the basic differentiation into five land categories was identical. Moreover, the legal definitions of *miri* and *mulk* land in this law were precisely the same as they had been since the fifteenth century.[9] Thus, according to Article 78 of the land law, land was acquired (other than through purchase or inheritance) by possession for a ten-year period. This accorded exactly with tradition,[10] as did the most important ruling whereby land not worked for three consecutive years became *mahlul* (of lapsed ownership).[11] Basically, the same applied to the right of succession to sown lands. The land law specified that both male and female offspring could inherit in equality and without payment of *tapu*.[12] Although the classical *kanun*s were not entirely systematic on this point, in many the same ruling was valid—equality between sons and daughters and the total exclusion of all other relatives[13] (many of whom might otherwise inherit according to the Islamic laws of succession).

In the preceding chapters I have emphasized the great importance of pasture in both the economic and sociopolitical life of Middle Eastern society in the classical Ottoman Empire. In this respect, the 1858 land law (Article 97) also followed in the footsteps of the classical land laws. Thus, there was historical and legal continuity between the old agrarian laws and the 1858 land law. Provided the law was put into effect, it indicated that the village community was still a very meaningful legal and political institution in the nineteenth century. (As is demonstrated later, this point is of the utmost importance to the thesis advanced in this book.)

However, the 1858 land law also reflected the changes in the land laws of the empire that were begun early in the seventeenth century. A pertinent example is contained in Article 3, which stated that "possession of such [*miri*] land was formerly acquired, in case of sale or of being left vacant, by permission of or grant by feudatories [*sipahi*s] of *timar*s and *ziamet*s as lords of the soil, and later through the *multezim*s and *muhassil*s." Here we have explicit mention of a relatively new element. But the major historical development that found expression in the 1858 land law was the large estates, the *chiftlik*s. As a rule, the institution was not referred to in the classical agrarian *kanun*s; however, it did emerge in the 1858 land law. In one of the few instances where reference to *chiftlik*s was made (Article 131), the clause explicitly mentioned the historical evolution of this important term. However, owing to mistranslation of this article, this point has been obscured in all the extant translations of the land law, thereby obliterating the only intimation that the architects of the 1858 land law had had in mind the classical agrarian *kanun*.[14] The accurate version of the article is as follows:

> *Chiftlik*, according to the *kanun*, means a tract of land such as needs one yoke of oxen to work it, and which is cultivated and harvested every year. Its extent is, in the case of land of the first quality from 70 to 80 donums; in the case of land of medium quality about 100 donums, and in the case of land of the lowest quality about 130 donums. The donum is 40 ordinary paces in length and breadth, that is 1,600 pics. Every portion of land less than a donum is called a piece (*kita*). But ordinarily *chiftlik* means the land itself, the buildings thereon, as well as the animals, grain, implements, yokes of oxen and other accessories, built or procured for cultivation.

The article then went on to state that in questions of inheritance the *chiftlik* did not enjoy a special status; the arable land was inherited according to the rules of inheritance of ordinary *miri* land, while movables were inherited according to the Islamic law of succession. That this point should be explained at all was an indication that it was not always clear to all concerned. We find here, then, the type of association between the land and the farm buildings that is identical to our findings for seventeenth-century Anatolia. The reference to the land—"land possessed and cultivated as subordinate to the *chiftlik*" (*ol chiftlighe tabaiyet ile ziraat ve tasarruf olunan arazi*)—was identical to references to *chiftlik*s in the court records of Bursa. But the surprising and important point is that the degree of association remained more or less what it had been in the seventeenth century. Contrary to what we might expect, *chiftlik* lands did not, through usurpation of rights, become fullfledged *mulk*, and we can be sure that this was not just a matter of theoretical law. I have shown that the whole discussion of the *chiftlik*s means taking into consideration developments in the real world.

In another article of the law one method for creating *chiftlik*s was described.

> The lands of an inhabited village cannot be granted in their entirety to an individual for the purpose of making a *chiftlik* but if the inhabitants of a village have dispersed, as mentioned above, and the land has become subject to the right of *tapu*, if it is found impossible to restore it to its former state by bringing new cultivators there and settling them in the village and granting the land in separate plots to each cultivator, in such a case the land can be granted as a whole to a single person or to several for the purpose of making a *chiftlik*.[15]

If I am right in my assumption that the articles on *chiftlik*s reflected reality, then it follows that in the period before 1858 there were no *chiftlik*s that controlled villages in a truly feudal way. A third article that dealt with *chiftlik*s further supported this view. It also elucidated another important point connected with the *chiftlik*s.

Whatever number of animals of *chiftliks* within a town or village have grazed *ab antiquo* in the common pasture of a town or village, such number cannot be prevented from continuing to graze there. Pasturing grounds, other than common pasturing grounds of towns or villages, special to such *chiftliks* exclusively *ab antiquo,* are not considered as *metruka* land, as pasturing grounds left and assigned *ab antiquo* to the inhabitants of towns and villages are considered. In such a *chiftlik* pasturing ground the possessor of the *chiftliks* to whom it belongs can alone pasture his animals.[16]

According to the classical *kanun* (and to the land law), grazing land was the common property of all the village inhabitants. This article of the law indicated that there was an exception to this rule—namely, grazing lands that constituted part of *chiftliks.* The classical agrarian *kanuns* made no mention of such lands, yet the 1858 law referred to these rights as "old." It stands to reason that this was an example of legal rights being confirmed by the law rather than created anew.

Moreover, as we have seen, in the pre-1858 period rights to arable land could be acquired only by actual working of the land. This article showed that an exception was made in the period after 1600, in that grazing land forming part of *chiftliks* could be owned even though it was only used as pasture. In addition, Article 99 specified that a constellation of a number of *chiftliks* in a village was perfectly normal. All in all, then, the allusions to the *chiftlik* institution in the 1858 land law signified that this was the same institution that emerged from the Bursa documents.

The Ottoman land law was thus conservative in nature. It was intended neither to reduce nor to augment anyone's rights to the land. The answer to Warriner's query cited at the beginning of this chapter is thus obvious. The Ottoman land law did not deal with landlord/tenant relations because such relations were rare in the years spanning the sixteenth and nineteenth centuries. The implications, so widespread in the literature, that the state was trying to reassert its rights are as baseless as the opposite claim that it was trying to confer augmented ownership rights on individual owners. Some scholars have even maintained that the state was trying to transfer ownership rights from absentee landlords to actual occupiers. No article of the land law implied such an interpretation. On the contrary, at least one (Article 23) stated the opposite almost explicitly—that is, that actual occupation was immaterial; what counted was theoretical ownership. Article 23 also stated that occupying land on lease for any period of time did not affect ownership in any way.

It seems, therefore, that the 1858 land law was a rather accurate reflection of the actual agrarian law prevailing in substantial parts of the Ottoman Empire in the seventeenth and eighteenth centuries. It did not indicate that a great revolution in landholding patterns had occurred after the sixteenth century. *Chiftliks* did make an appearance, and sometimes whole villages were turned into such estates, although the latter development was not far-reaching and was quantitatively restricted. There was no change in the actual status of the land.

All this notwithstanding, the land law did contain some legal innovations. These did not appear to serve any particular element connected with the land, but merely to regularize and modernize the whole matter of land-holding. Yet these measures did have unforeseen consequences of a very important nature. The innovation that eventually proved to be the most important was the obligation imposed on every landowner to register his or her land in the government land register and receive a title deed attesting to his or her rights.[17] Apparently, this innovation was not intended to produce revolutionary results, and it was only accidental that it did. The crucial point here is that the state could issue title deeds to formerly unoccupied land. Before 1858, such lands simply could not be owned. In other words, land could, for the first time in Ottoman history, be owned on paper. Herein, I believe, lay the focal point of the 1858 land law. For the first time it enabled the creation of truly vast estates in the Middle East.

There were two kinds of registration. One was registration of land formerly held by the accepted legal methods, the other, registration of newly acquired land that was formerly unclaimed. Registration was to be gratuitous for those peasants possessing land for a long period (at least ten years). Article 78 of the land law was unequivocal on this point. Only the acquisition of new, vacant land required payment. Warriner's suggestion that the land law was enacted with an eye to monetary gain was therefore at least partially correct.

Before we plunge into the topic of the socioeconomic consequences of the land law, let us review first the views expressed by the extant literature dealing with its consequences. Conventional wisdom has it that the outcome of the land law was exactly the opposite of what was intended. Instead of bringing about the registration of land in the name of the smallholder, it resulted largely in the transfer of the lion's share of arable lands to a few landed magnates. This came to pass for several reasons.[18]

1. The villagers needed the city notables to protect them from the Bedouin menace and to represent them in their dealings with the government. In lieu of these services they were willing to register their lands in the names of these powerful urbanites.
2. Peasants were chronically in debt to city moneylenders and often could redeem their debts only with their lands. Such peasants would then remain on the land as serfs of the urban landlord.
3. The peasants were afraid to register the lands in their own names, lest this bring down on them heavier burdens of conscription, taxes,

and exactions. They preferred to have the land registered in the name of a city notable.

4. Sometimes they acted out of ignorance because the whole business of registration was beyond their understanding.

5. Bedouin shaykhs played a major role by registering tribal lands in their own names rather than in the names of individual tribesmen; their actions proceeded from the shaykhs' total political superiority over their tribe.

These are probably the most common reasons advanced. When the empirical evidence was checked carefully, however, I found it impossible to substantiate many of these claims. True, the fifth explanation was found to be entirely correct, but no evidence whatsoever was found that peasants were afraid to register land or to appreciate the value of registration. Neither could I find any instance of a peasant begging a city strongman to register the land in his name. I would not, however, hazard the conclusion that all the supposed "causes" of such land amassment are entirely baseless. Rather, I suppose they do contain a certain measure of truth. The claim I do make is that no scholar dealing with this subject has assembled all the empirical evidence and related it in a specific way to a specific explanation. Instead, scholars again and again go back to the old studies of Jack Weulersse about the Alawite and Hamah regions,[19] which in itself raises the suspicion that there is, in fact, a certain shortage of other examples.

Above all, the old theory can be indicted for failing to include any assessment of the evidence in order to discover quantitatively what actually happened to lands in the Middle East. How much exactly did pass into the hands of large landlords? Why? Was this phenomenon universal, or was it circumscribed by other circumstances? We can learn a great deal about all this once we penetrate beyond the realm of generalities into the various geographical zones of the Middle East. For it seems that many of the consequences of the Ottoman land law were closely connected to preexisting patterns of human geography.

Iraq

The position of nineteenth-century Iraq within the Middle East from the viewpoint of the topic at hand was the most peculiar.[20] According to the available sources, there were few villages in Iraq's countryside, and most of the rural population consisted of seminomadic tribes. Haider remarked that "in the irrigation zone the tribe rather than the village was the social and economic unit. Only in the vicinity of the main towns and in the areas irrigated by lift or perennial canals where the tribes had disintegrated, could landholding be said to be individualistic. In other parts tribal tenure was predominant."[21]

This extraordinary mode of settlement was apparently one result of the deterioration of the canal system in postclassical Iraq, which led, among other things, to rapid salinization of the soil.[22]

> The small *mallaks*, landowners, were largely to be found in the areas that had long been intensively cultivated, such as the water-wheel region in the upper middle Euphrates around the towns of Hila, Hadithah, and Anah; the Khalis valley, and the lower Diyalah, where some of the ancient canal works had survived; the fertile tracts between Kirkuk, Arbil, and Mosul, which had been contiguous to the guarded old post road to Istanbul; the district of Abu-l-Khasib, the celebrated gardens of Basrah . . .; and, finally, the regions of the Hidayya and Shamiyya Shatts of the mid-Euphrates which, in contrast to the regions of the southern Tigris, were very thickly settled due to the fact that the waters of the Euphrates could always be more easily distributed.[23]

In the tribal areas, which comprised most of the territory of Iraq, the situation was entirely different. Here the land was owned by neither smallholders nor by large landlords, but rather by the tribe as a whole. "The tribal land was in general communal property, and the chiefs, though in name and in relation to the government they were the lessees of the land and the tribesmen were the sublessees, according to local practice they were the representatives of the tribe and trustees of the land, and not the landowners."[24] The general consequence of this situation, which remained the status quo until the 1858 land law, was that in Iraq, as in other parts of the Middle East, large estates did not come into existence until the middle of the nineteenth century.

A new page in the history of Iraq began with the land law, a law that was entirely incongruous with the area's particular conditions. The law was intended to deal with individual ownership; it provided no solutions to problems of communal ownership. Indeed, Midhat Pasha, Baghdad's governor from 1869 to 1871, who dealt with the application of the land law to Iraq, tried to introduce individual registration, but he achieved little, and what he did achieve was largely nullified by his successors.[25] Under the conditions prevailing in nineteenth-century Iraq, individual registration was inconceivable. Beyond the question of administrative inefficiency, there was a total contradiction of interests between tribes and their shaykhs. Moreover, even the land right of the tribe as a whole was problematic. Following an age-old tradition, the land law accepted the consecutive ten-year possession of the land as sufficient to entitle the holder to a title deed without payment. But tribal agriculture in Iraq was nomadic, and the condition of a ten-year possession period was rarely met. Acquisition of title deeds in Iraq, therefore, meant buying vacant land. This fact alone prevented most of the tribe from acquiring land individually.[26]

As a rule, the governors who followed Midhat did not work toward individual registration. In order to enlist the cooperation of the heads of the tribal confederations, the governors preferred to have the land registered in the names of these tribal leaders. In this way, the Sadun family of the Muntafiq (lower Iraq) acquired title deeds to vast tracts of land in that area.[27] But such a policy was not always successful; heads of tribes sometimes refused to cooperate and declined to register the lands, which they considered theirs anyway. An inevitable consequence of this refusal was that title deeds were acquired very cheaply by city businessmen, who thus became theoretical landlords. One of the biggest purchasers of this type was Sultan Abdulhamid, who thus became the private owner of a substantial proportion of Iraq's cultivated land.[28] These absentee landlords rarely knew where their lands were situated, while the tribes continued to behave as if the title deeds never existed. Needless to say, this situation was an unfailing source of friction and bitterness, which ultimately was to add fuel to the conflagration in Iraq in the mid-twentieth century.

Even in the context of the traditional theory of the consequences of the Ottoman land law, the case of Iraq was quite exceptional. The law was inadequate to solve the agrarian problems of the country. The outcome was the creation of the first wave of large landlordism, to be followed later by the accelerated development of the same trend. Although the first large estates were mainly created at the expense of tribal rights, the later foundations of large estates more characteristically consisted of vacant and unclaimed lands. "As a rule, the large *mallaks* predominated in the areas that, through the introduction of pumps and the building of barrages, had been relatively recently put to the plough, and where at the same time tribal influence was still or had been potent."[29] In this regard Iraq shared in a process that was common in the Middle East. But as far as the nineteenth century was concerned, it would be a mistake to draw general conclusions from the case of Iraq. The tribal problem was nowhere so pervasive as here, and Iraq was certainly the most backward region of the empire.

Palestine

If nineteenth-century Iraq was the exception, then Palestine was far more the rule. Due to a weak central government, the principal plains of the country, the coastal plain, and the Plain of Esdraelon were virtually void of a permanent, settled population. This void was a result of the terror perpetuated by the Bedouin, who roamed the plains entirely unmolested, and the marshes that covered substantial areas of the plains. The provincial government that did exist did not concern itself with either the Bedouin or the marshes. This situation prevailed until the mid-1870s, by which time the Ottoman government had managed to irreversibly increase its control of the provinces at the expense of the local forces. Thus, the Bedouin were increasingly driven from both the plains and the vicinity of the main towns. It was partly for this reason that these very same years witnessed an unprecedented demographic boom throughout the area.[30] This population growth resulted in a greatly increased demand for foodstuffs, especially grain. Simultaneously, industrializing Europe was fervently seeking grain supplies for its own expanding population, and this factor also played a role in the growing awareness of the agricultural potential of the plains. All these factors combined to exert a heavy pressure that fed the region's disruptive forces.

At the same time, an entirely different pattern was in force in the central mountainous region of Palestine. Here, a densely settled population existed throughout the period of Ottoman history, with no known appreciable decline.[31] In this region there were neither Bedouin nor marshes to trouble the population, which could defend itself without the need to resort to the central government. Consequently, the lion's share of Palestine's rural population in Ottoman times was centered in this hilly region, which apparently was settled to the point of overcrowding. This vast difference in geographical and settlement conditions led to totally different agrarian relations at the outset and to entirely different consequences from the 1858 land law.

To date, the Ottoman period in Palestine has been only lightly touched on by scholars, and those who have dealt with the subject (Abraham Granott is a good example) have based their work on their observation of mandatory Palestine.[32] They often have projected back into the Ottoman period hastily arrived at conclusions based, in fact, on conditions prevailing under the mandate and not under the Ottomans. For example, by the interwar period much of the settlement pattern detailed above had changed, and the hilly land was no longer as predominant as it had been. In order to locate the true effects of the 1858 land law on the country, we must distinguish between the law's consequences in the plains and in the hill country. Elsewhere I have written a detailed study of developments in this latter area of the country, and here we may content ourselves with a summary of the main facts found therein.[33]

The effects of the Ottoman land law on agrarian relations in the region of Jerusalem invalidate much of what has traditionally been said about the law's consequences. If true, these findings about Jerusalem at least serve to raise the possibility that the law's supposed consequences were not universal. The archive of the Administrative Council of Jerusalem for the beginning of the twentieth century contained several hundred documents connected with problems of land registration.[34] It transpired that a very substantial proportion of the villagers of this region registered their land at the government land registry. Requests of this nature were signed by the village headman, and upon receipt of same, the council would appoint a small committee to check and verify the details relating to the land and the owner. Requests were accompanied by a cadastral map of the piece of land in question. In fact, several specimens of such cadastral maps have recently come to light.[35] We should not assume from this that the Ottoman administration of Jerusalem conducted a fullfledged cadastral survey, but we can conclude that there were some material changes in the government's approach to the orderly administration of lands and that the black picture painted by scholars until now concerning this question was overly pessimistic.

If a fullfledged cadastral survey was beyond the capabilities of the late Ottoman Empire, the government nevertheless did conduct a land survey, albeit of a much more modest nature. This exhaustive survey of immovable property was carried out for the purpose of imposing a new tax, the *vergi* tax. Three surveys of this nature were mentioned in the documents—in 1878, 1886, and 1907. In these surveys all agricultural land was supposed to be included, and apparently most of it actually was. Upon presentation of a request for registration of land (*tapu* registration), the details of the land would be crosschecked and compared with the details of the *vergi* survey; only rarely did the documents indicate that such land was missing from the *vergi* survey.

If we go one step farther and check the identity of those requesting land registration, we find that all the cases concerned smallholders who were simultaneously occupants of the land and inhabitants of the village where the land was situated. There was not a single case of a registration in the name of a city notable, a moneylender, some kind of absentee landlord, or any other type of land engrosser known from the literature.

One of the aims of the 1858 Ottoman land law was to bring about the end of the *musha*, or communal tenure of land.[36] The significance of the *musha* had been unduly stressed in the past. Apparently, the geographical extent of the institution was far more restricted than was formerly believed. The institution never existed in Anatolia and apparently was not universal in the mountainous area.[37] Because the plains were very sparsely settled, the *musha* could never have been as widespread as we have thought.

The *musha* system was in rapid decline in the mountainous region of Jerusalem in the late Ottoman period. People came to the council to register land that was not in the form of so many shares of the total but rather was clearly demarcated and owned individually. This was true of all the registration requests in the documents under investigation. Therefore, if the *musha* existed at all, it could only have been of marginal importance. It stands to reason that to a certain extent this situation derived from the activities of the Ottoman government itself, a fact that was at least partially borne out by available secondary sources. Samuel Bergheim, a resident of late Ottoman Palestine, observed:

> The Turkish laws which have been introduced within the last few years in Palestine with reference to land tenure, and which are being rigorously enforced, are changing all these ancient laws and customs [the *musha*], much against the will and the wish of the people. The lands are divided by an Imperial Commissioner into various portions and given to individual villagers. They receive title deeds for individual ownerships, and each one is at liberty to sell his portion to whoever he pleases, either to a member of the village or to a stranger. The villager then sells his . . . right of cultivation in the land . . . the object of the government being to break down the old custom of *musha'a* [sic]. When the government will have attained this object, which it is doing fast, in spite of the resistance of many of the village communities, the old customs above referred to will die out and be forgotten.[38]

It is possible that the *musha* in the Jerusalem region was already far from universal long before the early twentieth century (the period to which the documents of the Jerusalem Council related). The documents indicated that plots of land throughout the area were individually owned for years on end before registration requests were filed. This might mean that the *musha* system was, in fact, never universal in the central mountainous area of Palestine and/or that it was declining as a result of general modernization in the village, not as a result of efforts by the Ottoman government to force the system into decline. In either case, the familiar notion that the land law was not truly enforceable because of the stubborn persistence of the *musha* system of tenure is untenable as a universal generalization.

The present study of the effects of the 1858 land law on agrarian relations in the Jerusalem mountains is apparently the first detailed examination of an area other than Iraq. It would be difficult at the present stage to draw conclusions from these two areas that are applicable to the entire Ottoman state, but we may hazard a few guesses—namely, that the disastrous consequences of the land law were by no means universal; that the peasant in many places had the will and the power to stand up for his or her rights far more vociferously than has hitherto been admitted; and that although the law was woefully inadequate and inappropriate for Iraq, it did suit the existing social structure and landholding pattern in Jerusalem, and consequently, its outcome was beneficial.

Was the case of Jerusalem exceptional in any way? I see no reason to suppose that it was unique. The Jerusalem pattern, in fact, may well have been true for all regions where the power of the government was relatively stronger, such as Anatolia, mountainous regions in other provinces, and areas in the vicinity of at least some major cities. Although no proof of these assumptions is presently available, I show in Chapter 5 that there is at least indirect supporting evidence.

In the coastal plain and in the Plain of Esdraelon development was of an entirely different nature. Until the last three decades of the nineteenth century, it was almost impossible for permanently settled populations to achieve prescriptive rights to lands in this region, but then it did become more feasible and much more economically attractive. Indeed, circumstances were rapidly changing, as Lawrence Oliphant described so well:

> Readers will be surprised to learn that almost every acre of the plain of Esdraelon is at this moment in the highest state of cultivation; that it is perfectly safe to ride across it unarmed in any direction, as I can testify; that, so far from plundering and despoiling villages, the few Bedouins, whose "black tabernacles" are now confined to the southern margin of the plain, have in their turn become the plundered and despoiled, for they are all reduced to the position of being subject to inexorable landlords, who charge them exorbitantly for the land which they occupy, and for which they pay in hard cash, under penalty of instant ejection, which is ruthlessly enforced, so that the inhabitants of the villages, with which the plain is now dotted, live in perfect security.[39]

Until the middle of the nineteenth century many hill villages bordering on the empty coastal plain exploited such land through the extension of "tentacle," offshoot villages (*khirbas*), which existed for only a small part of the year. Peasants from the parent village would put in an appearance to sow and harvest their grain, but as a result of increased security, the need to return to the parent villages became less and less pressing, and thus in the late Ottoman period a whole new series of villages sprouted up along the coastal plain of Palestine.[40]

In contrast, there were other factors at work that generated large, rather than small, landlordism. The opportunity, which was newly created by the land law, to purchase land on paper at the offices of the government and to make a profit from these lands (a previously unheard-of activity) whetted the substantial appetite for landlordism of the autochthonous Arab elite of Palestine. Before long, the plains of Palestine, still mostly unoccupied and unclaimed, were owned in ever-increasing measure by large-scale landlords. The largest and most famous of these was Alfred Sursoq, head of a Christian family from Beirut. In 1872, he purchased from the Ottoman government a vast tract of land in the Plain of Esdraelon said to be somewhere in the vicinity of 200,000 donums.[41] The transaction was regarded with considerable suspicion at the time. It was alleged that the land was bought for 120,000 Turkish pounds and earned the entrepreneur an income of 12,000 Turkish pounds a year, a fact that has been interpreted as evidence that Sursoq's deal was fraudulent and corrupt. But those who so claim ignore the special conditions prevailing in the plains of Palestine in the early 1870s. The Plain of Esdraelon was still marshy and largely uninhabited. There was no line of eager, would-be purchasers. In fact, the very idea of buying land from the government was unprecedented, and such purchases were probably at the experimental stage.

Viewed from this realistic angle, the Ottoman government most likely made an excellent deal. It sold worthless land to an energetic entrepreneur who not only paid a price for it but undertook to put it under cultivation (as in fact he did), thereby increasing not only public security and the general volume of business in the country but also cash revenues through the tithe paid on the produce.[42] Moreover, under existing conditions, only an extremely energetic entrepreneur could have produced such results. Hence, the selling of desolate tracts of land in the low-lying plains to the highest bidder, whomever he or she might be, was the most rational course of action for the Ottoman government, serving as it did the interests of both the Treasury and the country. After all, land for which a price, however modest, was paid was more likely to enter the production cycle than was unclaimed land.

This argument is bolstered by another piece of evidence. In 1871 the Ottoman government appointed a committee of inquiry to conduct an exhaustive land survey in the district of Acre. This committee investigated the status of all agricultural lands in the region. Land that was occupied by villagers was registered as such, and the occupiers were apparently notified that if they failed to pay the proper tax and have their land registered, it would be put up for public auction. The committee also recommended that unoccupied land be sold by auction. It is most likely that the main purpose of this survey was to find buyers for unexploited, vacant state land; some of the entries in the register relating to this survey actually indicated that such land was put up for auction.[43] All in all, there was sufficient evidence to suggest that a policy of large-scale sale of unclaimed lands was implemented.

To my mind, it was basically in these ways, rather than in the ways presumed in the traditional literature, that the major large estates of nineteenth-century Palestine came into being. In fact, there were surprisingly few empirical examples of the transfer of entire villages into the hands of urban notables in illegal or suspicious ways or at all. There probably were some cases of this, but they must have been exceptional. The case of the Sursoq estates in the Plain of Esdraelon was precisely such an example. In the 1920s, the Sursoq family sold to the Zionist movement lands in the Plain of Esdraelon that included entire villages.[44] There was conclusive evidence that at least some of the villages predated the Napoleonic wars.[45] How could Sursoq have acquired these villages? We have no exact details about this at present; however, Oliphant's claim that Sursoq was originally the tax farmer and moneylender of these villages and as a result eventually came to own their lands seemed credible.[46]

Some revealing details about landholding patterns in pre-1914 Palestine can be gleaned from listings of major landlords who emerged after the 1858 land law. One detailed list dated back to the 1920s, although the estates were definitely created during the later Ottoman period.[47] This list included a number of very important Christian landlords (Sursoq was the most prominent but by no means the sole example). There was apparently nothing particularly notable about this fact in later Ottoman Palestine, but when placed in the context of Ottoman history the novelty is striking. In Ottoman Anatolia and the Fertile Crescent, Christians could never have belonged to a social stratum in any way connected with land control; this would have been equated with political authority over Muslims, which *dhimmis* lacked. Thus, we never find Christians as *mutlezims*, holders of *malikanes, ayan,* or the like. Therefore, the phenomenon of Christians as landlords of significance was new.

The names of some of the most important figures (and families) in Ottoman Palestinian history are missing from the list—for example, the Awamir family of the village of Dura and the Abu Ghosh family from Qaryat al-Inab. These two families ruled the Palestinian countryside with an iron fist in the decades preceding the enactment of the land law.[48] If there were anyone in those days who could register entire villages in his name and so turn himself into a large landowner, it was the head of either of these two families. Yet, apparently, this did not happen.

By the same token, this autochthonous countryside elite ruled the Hebron and Jerusalem mountain area in such a way that the creation of a large-scale landed estate was beyond the reach of any Jerusalemite, including members of the city's elite. Indeed, this point deserves special emphasis. Before the Tanzimat, the countryside of Jerusalem was so fraught with danger, replete as it was with warring, armed bands, that the urban elite was totally powerless outside the city walls; the powerful regional figures were village notables. Concomitantly, the urban elite had no dealings whatsoever in arable land outside these walls.[49] (This point invalidates Weulersse's famous generalization that the Eastern village was almost by definition entirely subservient to the neighboring city.[50]) The fact that the names of some of the elite families of Jerusalem (especially the Husaynis) were included in this list can only mean that once again we are dealing with a phenomenon that could have emerged only in the wake of the 1858 land law. On the other hand, it was quite natural that most of their lands were situated in the coastal plain.

One special case on the list calls for particular attention: that of the Abd al-Hadi family of Nablus. This was the only family formerly numbered among the rural elite of Palestine that figured prominently on the list of large landowners.[51] It is possible that this family is an exception to my analysis, but only in a minor way. In this case, too, the massive quantities of land at the disposal of the family in the 1920s were mainly in the Plain of

Esdraelon and were undoubtedly another example of the new type of land-ownership (by way of purchase of waste land from the government). The Abd al-Hadis began their rise to prominence as agriculturalists and landhold-ers. In their original stronghold village (Arabeh, in northern Samaria) they did not establish a feudal pattern of control in the sense that they did not own all the village lands; the village had a long tradition of smallholder inde-pendence.[52] This point is of crucial importance. If there were a village that (according to the traditional theory) ought to have been registered in the name of a strongman, this was it. Yet this did not happen. Apparently, again, peasants in the traditional Middle East had the motivation and power to de-fend their rights to a far greater degree than has been hitherto realized.

All in all, then, the lists of important landlords support my theory that large landlordism was a novel phenomenon in the Middle East, which came into being only, or mainly, in the wake of the 1858 land law, and that the major avenue for creating these large estates was to purchase formerly un-occupied lands from the government. The latter was apparently more true in Palestine than in Syria, as we see shortly.

If we seek additional proof to support this thesis, it can be found even within the annals of the two national movements that struggled for Palestine. It is not by chance that the pre-1967 map of the country showed that the Palestinians occupied the hilly regions of the West Bank and constituted a majority in the Galilee. In contrast, the Jews predominated throughout the plains. The reason for this was embedded in the pattern of agrarian relations that came into being in the wake of the 1858 land law. The land purchasers on behalf of the Zionist movement would not and could not purchase land on a massive scale in the hilly regions where small peasant landlordism pre-vailed. But in the plains the Zionist land purchasers encountered an agrarian situation that for their purposes was most propitious. Vast expanses of land were newly purchased, in the main by the urban rich, who bought them ex-pressly to earn an easy profit. Hence, they were quite ready to sell the land for a good price and did so at the stroke of the pen. Small wonder that the Zionist land purchasers concentrated most of their efforts on this part of the country and that consequently the hilly country remained in the hands of the Palestinians.

Syria

The consequences of the Ottoman land law in Syria are still not entirely clear, and source materials are too few to enable us to form a coherent pic-ture of what actually took place. The twentieth-century consequences of the law are clearer (see Chapter 6); for the present we concentrate on the short-term, nineteenth-century consequences. We may hazard the general conclusion that, on the whole, the consequences of the 1858 land law suggested by the traditional literature were especially applicable to Syria (in its present-day borders). A reliable source gave the following description as early as 1891:

> In the Buqa, and about Hems [sic], Hama, Damascus, Hauran, and the other great plains, the property is partly owned by the freeholders of the villagers, but more usually by large capitalists, who let the land to the cultivators of the villages on the metairial principle. Although the metayers are nominally engaged only by the season, and might be legally ejected at its end, in point of fact this is hardly ever done, and the villagers look upon the lands they thus occupy as a permanent resource for themselves and their descendants. Of course they cannot give any legal transfer of their immunities, but they can share them with their children and relatives.
>
> The peasant cultivators are a shiftless class, and seldom lay by anything in good seasons, and so are almost to a man in debt. Capitalists in the cities are always ready to lend their money at extravagant rates of interest . . . In this way, as individual capitalists favour certain villages, they gradually absorb all the property of the peasants, and the villagers become their metayers.[53]

This generalized description was amply substantiated by many empirical facts gleaned from other sources. Thus, there was an excellent description by Gertrude Bell of the famous large landlordism in the Hamah region in the year 1906. To cite the main sentences of this description:

> The chief interest of the day at Hamah was supplied by the inhabitants. Four powerful Mohammadan families are reckoned as the aristocracy of the town, that of Azam Zadeh, Teifur, Killani and Barazi. . . . The combined income of each family is probably about £6000 a year, all derived from land and villages, there being little trade in Hamah. Before the Ottoman government was established as firmly as it is now, these four families were the lords of Hamah and the surrounding districts; they are still of considerable weight in the administration of the town, and the officials of the Sultan let them go pretty much their own way. . . . I went to the house of Khalid Beg Azam, which is the most beautiful in the city, as beautiful as the famous Azam house in Damascus. . . . The Killani I visited also in their charming house by the Orontes, the Tekyah Killaniyyeh. It contains a mausoleum, where three of their ancestors are buried.[54]

This flowery description gives the impression that we have to deal here with something deeper, culturally more refined, than just a group of post-1858 landmongers. This group may well have appeared long before the mid-nineteenth century, although the new law probably augmented its legal strength.

Landlordism in Hamah was a unique phenomenon in the nineteenth century and was to remain so in the next century. However, large landlordism, albeit on a much smaller scale, was quite widespread in many places. In traveling from Hamah to Aleppo, Gertrude Bell had occasion to speak of this phenomenon more than once. Thus, when around Qalat al-Husn, she had the following to say on the landholding pattern in the vicinity: "Few of the fellahin own land of their own; they work for hire on the estates of richer men. The chief landowners around Kal'at el-Husn are the family of the Danadisheh, who come from Tripoli."[55] When she passed by Qalat al-Seijar, she explained that the fortress belonged to Shaykh Ahmed Seijari, whose family had occupied it for three hundred years. He also owned one-third of the land in the village; the rest was owned partly by the Killani family of Hamah and partly by nomads who lived there part of the year.[56]

Large landlordism also was mentioned quite often by M. Refiq and M. Behjet in their descriptions of the northern parts of the province of Beirut in 1915. Large landlords were said to top the social hierarchy in the town of Tarsus, with one family owning as much as 10,000 donums.[57] The same was said about the towns of Babna in northern Syria[58] and Ladhiqiya.[59] One family from Jibla was said to own most of the 150,000 donums of the plain of that town.[60] The plain of Akkar was also entirely owned by large landlords.[61] Not many details were given on the agrarian relations in these areas, but sharecropping and absentee landlordism predominated. In Syria sharecropping is now called *murabaa,* a term that, as we have seen in the previous chapter, was never encountered in the traditional literature on the pre-1858 period. I believe the institution may nevertheless have existed before the middle of the nineteenth century, although its geographical extent must have been very limited indeed.

Anatolia

Sources on Anatolia in the post-1858 period are no more satisfactory than those on Syria and Palestine. We are therefore obliged to exploit every piece of evidence at our disposal. For Anatolia this means that we still have to investigate the value of the *responsa (fetva)* literature. One major collection, the *Ilaveli Mejmua,* contained a great many questions on agrarian matters that were addressed to *sheyhulislam*s after 1858. What can we learn from this source? Now, as formerly, it should be emphasized that the documents reflected reality and were not merely theoretical. Thus, one major innovation regarding succession of *miri* lands expressed in the collection—that is, the Law Relating to Broadening the Right of Succession in *Miri* and *Waqf* Land which was enacted in 1867.[62] The following *fetva* exemplified this law:

> Zeid, while in possession of a piece of state arable land (*miri*) through payment of *tapu,* died, and this prior to the announcement of the Imperial

Law Relating to Broadening the Right of Succession, which extends the right of succession to grandsons. Of those having a right of possession he left only his son Amr. After Amr occupied the land in accordance with the right of "simple succession" (*intikal-i adi*), cannot Beshir, son of Bekir, the other son of Zeid, who predeceased his father, and Hind, Bekir's daughter, now say: "We too shall take part of the said land, on the basis of the late issuance of the said law"—and this notwithstanding the fact that they admit their grandfather Zeid had died before the promulgation of the Law? Answer: They cannot.[63]

In addition to the methodological value of this document, it also must have been of some practical importance. The law must have made an enormous contribution to the maintenance of small landholding by extending succession rights in a way that bridged the gap between the Sharia and the *kanun*. It also was true that under the new law the rights of daughters of sons precluded other degrees of successors. But until 1867, only first degree offspring could inherit from their fathers in the true sense. Other types of relatives enjoyed only the right of priority to pay the *tapu* and retain the land. Because this *tapu* was expressly supposed to be the nearest possible equivalent of the value of the land, such relatives were in effect buying the land rather than succeeding to it. Naturally, in many cases they could not afford to pay the required sum; however, in accordance with the new law they were exempt from payment and could therefore inherit the land at no cost. Their succession became *intikal-i adi*, "simple succession," exactly like that of offspring since the days of the classical *kanun*. There was sufficient evidence to indicate that this new law was implemented, at least to a substantial degree.[64]

As before 1858, the *responsa* collection showed that the salient characteristic of governmental policy was the defense of the rights of the smallholder against encroachment. It would be naive, however, to ascribe too much importance to this policy, but neither would it be wise to dispense with it altogether. Thus, there were many examples of *responsa* handed down in favor of holders of rights of *intikal-i adi* against attempts to usurp such rights backed by all manner of arguments.[65] The *responsa* showed that some articles of the 1858 land law that seemed theoretical in nature may have been much more than that. Thus, many documents attested to the intense involvement of women in matters of land ownership. From the variety of situations in which these involvements appeared, it was evident that these were real life descriptions and not mere theory.[66]

Another possible article in this category was the ruling that specified that land that remained vacant (*mahlul*) should be first offered to a needy person belonging to the same village community. These documents proved that this ancient ruling of the fifteenth-century *kanun* was still implemented to a certain degree in the second half of the nineteenth century.[67]

In regard to settlement patterns, Anatolia underwent developments similar to those in nineteenth-century Palestine. There were grounds for believing that the major agrarian pattern in Anatolia was analogous to that of Palestine. Major estates were formed on wasteland, often situated in swampy plains, while the statistically predominant form of ownership in the old and established settlement areas continued to be smallholding. In Anatolia throughout the period of Ottoman history many of the fertile plains were actually devoid of permanent settlement for the same reasons as observed for Palestine. The plains were marshy and malarial and inhabited by nomads in the winter cycle of transhumance. Thus, Peter Benedict, who studied the town of Ula near the coast in the southwestern corner of Anatolia, discovered that the plain between the town and the sea was unoccupied in the nineteenth century. "The region's entire expanse of coastal lowlands was, in the nineteenth century, malaria-ridden. Life was tolerable in the coastal towns only under a form of transhumance in which most of the town residents spent the summer in highland summer settlements or *yaylas.*"[68] The valley of Ula became relatively more populated only with the eradication of malaria in the 1930s.[69]

East of Ula, the Plain of Antalya was likewise almost totally void of permanent habitation, as we learn from Planhol's study of this region. Here the crucial factor seemed to have been solely the power of the nomads. The focal point for the beginning of the ensuing change occurred after the Napoleonic wars. At that time, the area was discovered by the European market, and the strong European demand for grain began to make itself felt. The central government substantially increased its power, which brought about considerable improvements in security. This sequence of events led to the beginning of permanent occupation of the plain and sedentarization of nomadic tribes.[70] This periodization, if correct, would have made the Plain of Antalya one of the first regions to stir from its lethargic sleep.

Farther to the east, in the region of Mersin, a similar pattern emerged. The town of Erdemli, studied by Joseph Szyliowicz, was not founded until 1865 because the maritime plain was without a permanent population and served only as a winter habitat for nomads.[71] Soon after its settlement, a number of large-scale Greek landlords settled in the region, which was unusual because non-Muslims had few known connections with large landlordism at any time in Ottoman history. Probably those Greek landlords were of the same type as the Sursoqs of Palestine, and it is likely that their presence was evidence of the same phenomenon—the purchase of uncultivated and unclaimed land from the government.

The Plain of Çukurova also experienced a similar settlement pattern. Today one of the better agricultural regions of Turkey, it was entirely deserted until the period of reform in the nineteenth century. What did exist was a combination of nomads and poor drainage, which also was characteristic of nineteenth-century Palestine. To cite Mübeccel Kiray, who wrote a fine study of this valley:

> Although at present a fairly well-developed agricultural area, the Çukurova was, at the beginning of the nineteenth century, no more than a badly drained, fever-ridden, thinly populated country. Apart from the very mixed sedentary population of a number of permanent settlements along the caravan route connecting Anatolia with the Arab world and the Armenian settlements at the foot of the Taurus mountains, the plain was inhabited by nomadic tribes, mainly yörüks. During the winter season, these tribes used the plain as a grazing area for their animals, and during the hot season they moved up to the pastures in the Taurus mountains.[72]

During the course of the nineteenth century the Çukurova plain became one of the classic areas for large estates in Anatolia. By the use of all sorts of inducements, including sheer force, the government brought about the rapid şedentarization of the nomads much earlier than anywhere else in the Middle East. In the course of nomad settlement in the area the chiefs obtained low-level government positions and became governors of the areas allotted to their tribes. A pattern appeared here that was quite similar to what transpired in Iraq on a grand scale. The case of the Mursaloghlu family from Reyhaniye appeared to have been a common example in this area. As late as the mid-twentieth century this family owned twenty-one villages. One family member detailed to Eberhard the agrarian relations between these landlords and their peasants.

> These are former tribal leaders or members of the tribal nobility. They own villages inhabited either by "fellahs," i.e., immigrants from Syria, or impoverished former tribes people. Relations between landowners and these hereditary tenants were rather feudalistic: the farmers got permission to build straw huts (*hug*) on the owner's land, thus creating a village of it. . . . The landlord supplied land, seed and collected fifty percent of the harvest.[73]

Sources for other regions spoke more generally of the predominance of smallholding. Thus, alongside his statistical figures, E. F. Nikoley presented some impressionistic information. He said, for example, that there were "three systems of exploitation in . . . Turkey, (a) direct cultivation, (b) working on shares, (c) renting. Direct cultivation is practiced the most."[74] Concerning landholding patterns in the region of Izmir, it was observed that "as regards the distribution of landownership, the following may be said: the predominant form is small ownership, of about 20 to 30 hectares."[75] Even in the region of Adana, generally regarded as the classical region of large landlordism, small landownership was quite widespread. In 1910, "there were a few large landlords who owned estates of one thousand to, exceptionally, five thousand hectares. Of these, however, only part was cultivated. There were medium landowners with 200 or 500 or 600 hectares and a much higher number of small owners with only 10 hectares. Overall, one third of the land was held by large owners."[76] If correct, this information implied that most land was held by small and medium landowners. Certainly, most of the units of ownership in this description were small and independent of large landlords.

There are sufficient grounds to generalize from these examples and to conclude that as in nineteenth-century Palestine, large estates were mainly created on waste land in nineteenth-century Anatolia. A recent study came to much the same conclusion.

> In most of Anatolia...such Adana-type estates remained isolated phenomena and existing social relationships tenaciously held sway. Inalcik...remarked that plantation-type big *çiftliks* were exceptions, occurring only in certain regions exposed to special conditions....Most new *çiftliks* in Anatolia and Rumelia, he argued, came into existence on *mevat* land—either waste areas or lands abandoned by cultivators. Plantation-like structures were formed on such newly-exploited lands beyond the already cultivated *miri* lands with their traditional small-sized units.[77]

Moreover, available descriptions of *chiftliks* generally depicted them as isolated farms, not farms dominating villages. This impression was created, for example, by the description of the mode of operation of the large estates in Anatolia given by the *Handbook of Asia Minor,* a description that seemed to be generalized.

> The larger estates have part of their land worked by labourers hired by the year, who get £6–7 a year and their keep; in harvest day-labourers are engaged as well....Another part of the land is let to "ortakjis" (literally "partners" or "tenants"); the landlord provides buildings, seed, implements, one or two pair of oxen or buffaloes and 50 or 100 donums of land, and the tenant hands half of the crop.[78]

The salient point in this description was that landlords did not take over a village, but rather established a farm in an uninhabited place and then recruited laborers. This was quite in line with Inalcik's generalization. All in all, then, it seemed that Anatolia and Palestine were alike in that (1) large landlordism emerged only after the 1858 land law; (2) such estates were created mainly through the sale of waste lands by the government to whomever was willing to buy them, probably in public auctions; and (3) this last process of large-estate formation must have been more important quantitatively than the explanations adduced by the traditional research on this topic indicated.

It is worthwhile pointing out at this juncture that technically the formation of large estates through the purchase of wasteland could be problematic from a legal point of view. Estates in marshy regions, or for that matter in any area, were bound to include large pieces of uncultivable land or land not actually owned. Indeed, the marshy lands of the Gökova plain near Ula were owned by the *aghas* of that town, notwithstanding the fact that the lands were not worked until the 1930s.[79] The problem here was, of course, that the Ottoman land law included a clause to the effect that land left unworked for three consecutive years reverted to the state as *mahlul*.[80] We have seen that this law effectively prevented the appearance of large estates before 1858, and the question is why it did not do so afterward. The answer is unquestionably that the government applied the law at its convenience, and as I have not encountered any case of a land tycoon actually losing his land as a result of the *mahlul* law, we must conclude that the phenomenon of large landlordism of waste land (*mevat*) was probably to the liking of the government, which intended to bring under the plow as much land as possible.

Barrington Moore, in relation to both India and China, described a process of commercialization of agriculture and increasingly close ties with the world market in the nineteenth century.[81] In both countries the process found expression in growing pressure on the small, independent peasant and a concomitant growth in the importance of landlords, moneylenders, and similar social elements. Such commercialization occurred in at least some parts of the Middle East as well. D. Quataert studied in detail the case of Anatolia, which may have been the most notable case in this regard in the Asiatic provinces of the Ottoman Empire. Wheat was the means through which this linkage to the world market occurred, and the major reason for this was the construction of railroads in Anatolia after 1890. Large quantities of grain began to be exported from Anatolia to Europe. "As cereal shipments from the Empire as a whole apparently were declining at the end of the century, rail induced grain exports from Anatolia as much as quintupled."[82]

The second major staple was cotton. The Adana region emerged as the most important cotton-producing region in Anatolia, and production in the Çukurova valley rose by leaps and bounds until World War I. In fact, it might well be said that in Adana cotton—and in this alone—late Ottoman Anatolia experienced something akin to a minuscule agricultural revolution.[83]

Nonetheless, the social consequences of this process seemed to have been much less devastating in Anatolia than in either China or India. Quataert tended to conclude that in Anatolia the trend toward large-estate formation and peasant subordination was very limited: "Few scholars would support the view that the development of commercial agriculture in Anatolia required the presence of a proletarianized agrarian work force laboring under slave-like conditions on vast overseer-run estates."[84] Production and marketing were carried out by the peasants individually. Either Istanbul merchants bought the grain from peasants on the spot and saw to its transportation or (and this procedure was probably more widespread) peasants brought their marketable surplus to the railroad stations, where agents were waiting for them. Commercialization could thus take place within the traditional economy. "This kind of mechanism, that gathered a very large surplus without transforming the land system, minimized the disruption of traditional life inherent in the expansion of commercial agriculture and may well have been the more common manner in which the Anatolian economy responded to foreign market opportunities."[85] Only in the Adana region was this capitalistic spurt possible because here there had not been any previous settlers and hence no social relationships to disrupt.[86]

The above explanation, although sound in itself, poses a problem. Was Anatolia an exception to the worldwide rule of disruption of the traditional modes of peasant landholding by the process of linkage to the world market? If so, what made it exceptional? Anatolia may well have been an exception, and the likely explanation for its status seems to be closely connected to the main thesis I have been arguing up to now. In most of the world, land usually belonged to large landlords, and when a commercial opportunity presented itself, the landlord reaped the benefits, usually by tightening his grip on the occupying peasant. But in Anatolia this simply could not take place because the land was effectively owned by the small peasant. Anatolia thus missed the opportunity to transfer its surpluses to industry (as happened in some countries in the nineteenth century such as Japan). On the other hand, it was spared the devastating social consequences of such a transfer, which in other countries severely diminished the position of the peasant, often with disastrous results for the peasantry and the entire social system.

CHAPTER SIX

Agrarian Developments in Turkey, Iraq, Syria, and Egypt in the Twentieth Century

The evolution of the agrarian trends that were latent in the late Ottoman period reached fruition in the course of the twentieth century. The far-reaching political repercussions of these developments have played themselves out to the full. My task in this chapter is to present the main developments in each of the countries dealt with in this study.

Iraq

We have seen that in the late nineteenth century the Ottomans exhibited renewed interest in the provinces; more than ever they cherished the idea of their metamorphosis into a state that would resemble other modernized states. This implied tribal settlement and individualistic landownership. At this time there was a rapidly growing demand in Europe for grain, which according to John Batatu was the most important factor in eroding the viability of the tribe as a social organism.[1] But in the period following World War I this process of deterioration was largely arrested. The tribal chiefs, who had voluntarily been accepted by their tribes in the Ottoman period, became semifeudal landlords and imposed chieftains under the monarchy. Throughout the first half of the twentieth century there was a massive process of large-estate formation in Iraq. In 1958 tribal chieftains owned a vast proportion of Iraq's arable land, and together with the ruling elite of ex-Sharifian officers they formed a tangible landed upper class that completely controlled Iraq both socially and politically. What concatenation of circumstances brought this about?

In the last half-century of Ottoman rule in Iraq the power and authority of the tribal chieftains were on the wane. Under the monarchy this trend was reversed as a consequence of the policy adopted by the British rulers. The British interest lay in finding a local social pillar upon which their rule might rest as cheaply and effectively as possible. This they found in the tribal shaykhs.[2] Indeed, the tribal shaykhs soon became the principal local medium on which the British administration was based.[3] Sometimes Britain helped to curb the decline of tribal authority by providing armed support (for example, in cases of revolt against the chiefs).[4] In addition, the notable chieftain in each confederation was made responsible for all legal matters in his area. The British also were supportive in getting tribal chieftains elected to the Iraqi Parliament. Thus, in the 1924 Parliament there were thirty-four tribal delegates out of a total of ninety-nine delegates.[5]

By way of exchange these chieftains supported British rule, for which they also were compensated economically. An example of such compensation was a light tax load, as disclosed by one British official in the following remark:

> It is well known that shaikhs are now rolling in wealth owing to the cheapness of their farm rents under our administration. . . . We have pursued a policy of generosity hitherto which has probably repaid us by inducing the shaikhs to help us to the best of their ability. But where we reduce, the shaikhs do not always reduce for their *sirkals* [supervisors] and peasants. . . . The policy of backing up the big shaikhs is incompatible with the principle of a wide dispersion of wealth and prosperity.[6]

Britain also secured the loyalty of the tribal chieftains through direct payment of financial subsidies.[7]

It might be asked why the decline in the chieftains' authority did not continue after Iraq's independence in 1932. In fact, by this time there was an alliance of interests in Iraq between the tribal shaykhs and the central elite of ex-Sharifian officers who were by now large landowners themselves. By what means did these shaykhs control their estates? The *hushiyye,* or armed guard, which most of them founded in this period, was one of the most important control mechanisms.[8] These guards were small private armies composed of mounted armed men, usually several hundred strong. They were often composed of criminals who thus gained protection from the arm of the law. The existence of such private armies implied that there was a real need for them—proof, if any was needed, that the authority of the tribal chiefs at this period needed the backing of an extremely strong and repressive apparatus. Even in the late Ottoman period it was clear that the transformation of the chieftains from traditional social leaders into modern landlords was not going to go unprotested by the tribes. Thus, Batatu cited evidence to the effect that even before World War I tribes in the south had purchased rifles and had begun to violently oppose payment of their land dues.[9] In 1921, one British official in the Amara region wrote that "Shaykhs have on more than one occasion told me that in order to maintain law and order among their tribesmen they must thoroughly frighten them, mitigating this treatment by occasional rewards."[10] Furthermore, when the British vacated the Muntafiq area during the 1920 uprising, the chief shaykhs of the area went with them.

Iraqi development in the first half of the twentieth century was characterized by dynamic economic growth, attributable to improved health conditions and a growth in population. The inevitable result was a rush to acquire vacant lands. The anarchy that had characterized the Iraqi land regime in the late Ottoman period accentuated the process. The status of more land than in any other Middle Eastern country was legally obscure, and under the mandate these lands devolved to the state. In 1932, the Iraqi state enacted a law destined to finally settle these problems, but its execution greatly favored the wielders of political power. Batatu calculated that an overwhelming proportion of privately owned land in Iraq in 1958 was acquired by its owners in the wake of the 1932 land law.[11] Vast tracts of land were granted to chief shaykhs for the express purpose of settling their tribes, as in the case of Shaykh Agil al-Yawer, leader of the Shammar. Instead, to quote a British source, "what he did . . . was to farm the land for his own profit with hired labour without attempting to settle the Bedouin Shammar."[12]

The true ruling elite of the country was an additional factor in the power equation of monarchical Iraq. This elite comprised a small group of ex-Ottoman officers of Iraqi origin who had taken part in the Arab revolt of Sharif Husayn during World War I and had returned with King Faysal upon the latter's accession to the Iraqi throne. They are usually referred to in the literature as ex-Sharifian officers. Their rise to power in Iraq is easily explainable. The center in the Iraqi polity in the wake of the capitulation of the Ottoman Empire was not very strong. Faysal, in effect crowned by the British, entirely lacked local support; the ex-Sharifian officers who came with him from Damascus were his natural local allies. In this way they became the hard core from which most top political officeholders in monarchical Iraq were drawn. The officers themselves were a minute group, and they, too, needed social allies, whom they found in the tribal shaykhs. This unwritten alliance was boosted by the fact that in the 1930s the Iraqi state needed large sums of money to finance development projects. Its ability to raise these sums through taxation was limited, but it had one major economic resource that could be tapped—large reserves of land—which it was willing to sell quite cheaply. The lion's share of these lands was acquired by the tribal shaykhs or the officers. Yasin al-Hashimi, one of the most prominent officers, was a case in point. As minister of finance he helped his friends and himself by distributing jobs, contracts, lands, tax exemptions, and the like. "By the mid-1930s he had become a large land-owner and investor, the possessor of sixteen estates, each of which was between 1,000 and 2,000 acres."[13] By the middle of the twentieth century the elite of ex-Sharifian officers had clearly become an integral part of Iraq's landed upper class.

The agrarian regime that came into being in this political context was extremely coercive and repressive. It was quite close to feudalism, on the one hand, but entirely devoid of the element of peasant consent, on the other. The peasant received an extremely small portion of the produce, and in addition, owed services in the form of *auna*, or "forced labor." A 1933 law forbade peasants who were indebted to their landlords to abandon the land, and for a large number this meant actual serfdom. There is no doubt whatsoever that this agrarian regime produced ever-growing bitterness, which resulted in the large-scale desertion of the land and emigration to Baghdad and other big cities. In 1957, there were in Baghdad alone four hundred thousand such migrants, or one-third of the total population of the city.[14] Most of them hailed from Kut and Amara where the brutal aspects of the Iraqi land regime were particularly pronounced.

Contemporary evidence of the public's disaffection with the regime is hard to come by. Even in Batatu's most detailed account, he presented only one such example, a remark made in 1937 by a soldier who was formerly a peasant, to an Iraqi MP, who was explaining to him the importance of serving one's homeland. The soldier fired back: "Uncle, what homeland? I have no hut to live in and no one allows me to graze my buffalo even in the marshes."[15] Batatu, in fact, went so far as to blame the existing social conditions for the pronounced deterioration in the productivity of soil and even for the reduction in the area under plow. "This state of affairs and the low and declining productivity of the land in the country generally, no less than the primitiveness and wastefulness of agricultural methods, flowed, in an essential and ultimate sense, from the unwholesome social conditions of the peasants."[16]

In this context, Robert Fernea's study of the ecological problems connected with the Iraqi land regime before and after the July 1958 revolution is pertinent.[17] Fernea elaborated and publicized an agroeconomic study by the Dutch agronomist Poyck. Poyck found, surprisingly, that on the average the meager proportion of produce allowed by the large landlord to his tenant was nevertheless slightly more profitable to that tenant than was a piece of land of the same size owned by an independent peasant. Fernea also found that the agriculture of large estates was more rational, in that it could more easily avoid Iraq's perennial danger: overworking of the soil, which led to salinization and the land's total depletion. These are hard facts that Iraq's administrators would be well advised to heed if their drive to economic development is to succeed,[18] but our problem here is a different one, which is to explain how the harshness of the land regime was a source of extreme, widespread discontent. Poyck's subtle and sophisticated calculations were evidently not known to the hundreds of thousands who fled from the landlord-dominated region. There was ample evidence, supplied by Fernea himself, that the Iraqi rural masses saw the landlords as the chief source of their troubles (and obviously these masses were not influenced in this view by Western models). If anything, the social and class structure was perceived as the major source of evil, even though objectively this was untrue agronomically.

Not surprisingly, Iraq's agrarian structure was reflected in the country's power structure. Although four-fifths of the population was propertyless in 1958, 2,480 people owned 17.7 million donums and 49 people owned 5.4 million donums (55 percent and 17 percent of all private lands respectively).[19] There was far-reaching harmony between large landlords and governmental officers. Forty-one of the 49 large landowning families were the chief suppliers of prime ministers, ministers, senators, and deputies. Even as sober and obviously impartial an observer as Doreen Warriner passed a grim judgment on this regime: "No legislation which would infringe on the property rights of the large landowners can secure parliamentary approval. The parliament is composed of the landowners, who secure election by means of their dominance over the cultivators; and this dominance is unquestioned by any internal political force."[20]

I believe that the July 1958 revolution in Iraq was mainly a revolt against this agrarian regime. It involved more bloodshed and violence than any other coup or revolution in the Arab world, and some scholars therefore concluded that Iraqi politics (and possibly the national character) was inherently brutal and cruel. As I have little confidence in terms like "national character," I am more inclined to believe that the excessive violence was scaled to the yawning chasms, tensions, and alienation embedded in the history of Iraq's class structure. It is not simply that the chasms and deprivations were considerably wider than in the other Arab countries—in Iraq the deterioration in the position of the tribal peasant was the most degrading. The chief, once a father figure and leader of a familial structure, became a heartless landlord surrounded by armed bodyguards. The transformation could not have been more potentially explosive.

Syria

The famous French human geographer Jack Weulersse, for all his greatness or probably because of it, is to be blamed for creating a misconception about the twentieth-century Syrian agrarian regime. He contended that large estates were universal and small landownership all but nonexistent. Moreover, he even claimed his findings were valid for the entire Middle East without producing any empirical evidence whatsoever. Not content with this, he turned this picture into an old and immutable characteristic of the Orient by connecting it to Islam in general. His theory has so influenced scholarship in the field of socioeconomic history of the modern Middle East that we should attempt to weigh its true scientific value. This is best done with the geographical area where it was conceived—Syria.

To start with, Weulersse made some exaggerated remarks about the role of large landlordism in the interwar period. "A major fact . . . which dominates all peasant life is the overwhelming preponderance of large and even very large landownership. The Near East is essentially a region of large estates and their owners; the big landlords, whom the peasants reverentially call *aghas,* play the first and foremost economic and social role."[21] What was the geographical extent of this generalization? Weulersse was unequivocal about this: "One essential point remains: it is that large land ownership is present everywhere, in all the regions of the country, from the shores of the Mediterranean to those of the Persian Gulf and that it constitutes the basis of the landed regime of the Near East. Medium-sized and small ownership are never more than exceptions."[22]

The reason for the total supremacy of the landlords, Weulersse claimed, was rooted in two characteristics of Islam—the sociopolitical supremacy of the city over the village and the restraints imposed by Islam on the free pursuit of financial activity. As a result, village lands remained the only outlet for urban investments. These historical facts are, however, disputable. We know today that far from being averse to economic activity, the urban elite in the Ottoman city was greatly interested in international commerce, manufacturing, and finance and interest-bearing loans.

The truth about Syria's agrarian structure in the twentieth century is substantially different from Weulersse's account of it. The trends that began with the promulgation of the 1858 land law continued unabated into the next century until the agrarian reform launched by the Ba'th regime in the 1960s. Large landlords dominated an ever-larger proportion of Syria's agricultural lands. This occurred primarily when new, unclaimed lands fell into the hands of this group and only secondarily when former peasant lands were transferred to these landlords. Indeed, the major means of large-estate formation in mandatory Syria was the acquisition by Bedouin shaykhs of unsettled and unoccupied lands. The process was greatly encouraged by French policy in interwar Syria.

This development already had started in the late Ottoman period. In exchange for sedentarizing their tribes, Bedouin shaykhs received large tracts of lands as private property. This trend continued into the mandatory period. The process of Bedouin sedentarization proceeded vigorously, with Bedouin shaykhs and urban notables entering into close relationships and forming alliances and partnerships in order to exploit marginal areas for market production. In the early 1940s, the Jazira area of northeastern Syria was unfrozen by the government for agricultural exploitation, which brought about the formation of vast estates, many of which were owned in part or in total by the major Bedouin shaykhs.[23]

The Jazira area also attracted more modern agricultural entrepreneurship, as Doreen Warriner has shown. Urban entrepreneurs approached the challenge in supercapitalistic ways reminiscent of what had taken place in more highly developed countries. Indeed, this chapter in Syria's economic development casts some doubt on the argument that lack of entrepreneurship is at the root of underdevelopment in the Middle East. However, this issue is beyond the scope of the present study.

Thus, Syria became a country dominated by large landlordism. Yet this fact should not be exaggerated (see Table 6.1). Table 6.1 points out Weulersse's greatest mistake. The greatest concentration of large estates was not in the immediate vicinity of the great urban elites; on the contrary, it was far from their reach. Where the urban elite was strongest, we also find important centers of small peasant independence. The region of Hamah was an exception to this trend; it was the region where one could actually speak of a feudal regime. A small number of families in Hamah owned whole villages. The Dendashli family owned as many as sixty villages; the Barazi family, forty-nine villages; the Killani family, twenty-four villages; and the Azm family, twenty-five villages.[24] The conditions in which the villagers of this region lived were truly desperate.[25] They were a destitute rural proletariat who owned nothing around them, including the houses in which they lived. Between these villagers and their landlords there was deep animosity, which often deteriorated into violence and rebellion.[26] However, Hamah was an extreme, unique case. It is the only case cited again and again as the quintessential example of large landlordism in Syria, but it would be quite erroneous to consider Hamah representative of a larger pattern. Weulersse's account made clear that Hamah's exceptional status was a function of ecology. The area was agriculturally marginal, bordering the desert, which only al-

Table 6.1
Distribution of Privately Owned Land in Syria in 1955
(Percentage/Hectares)

Province	Under 10	10–100	Over 100
Damascus	19	44	37
Aleppo	14	40	45
Homs	8	59	33
Hamah	2	42	56
Latakia	32	30	38
Euphrates	15	47	39
Jazira	7	58	35
Hauran	47	46	7
Jebel Druze	30	58	12

Source: Adapted from Warriner, *Land Reform*, p. 83.

lowed for very unstable agriculture. In such conditions it is not surprising that peasants were unable to subsist without recourse to urban support, the consequence of which was often loss of independence.[27]

The Bedouin also posed a very real and present danger to the region's population. The villages were often in need of real help. Paradoxically, the influence of the Bedouin life-style on the settled villagers was pervasive and resulted in a meager enthusiasm on the part of the peasants for their own way of life.[28] All these reasons seem to constitute a sufficient explanation for Hamah's exceptional condition.

More generally, G. Baer has remarked that the process of large-estate formation in Syria remained within far more modest bounds than in either Iraq or Egypt.[29] That this was indeed an apt remark can be gauged from a number of available rural case studies, the best known of which was Louise Sweet's study of Tell Toqan, a village in northern Syria. In the mid-1950s, the village contained fifty-six families, of whom only seven owned any land at all. Of these, twelve *feddan* (amount of land that could be ploughed by a pair of oxen in one ploughing season) were owned by one of the village founders' descendants; ten *feddan* were owned by Shaykh Nuri, a tribal chieftain who had settled in the area; seven *feddan* were owned by another descendant of the founders; and the remaining seven *feddan* were owned by four other villagers. This meant that forty-nine village families were landless and had to work either as laborers or sharecroppers on the land of the grandees.[30] Tell Toqan was thus an example of the feudal regime that prevailed in Syria before the rise of the Ba'th. But what kind of feudalism was it? It was of recent origin, going back no further than the second half of the nineteenth century. Moreover, the land owned by the large landlords here was not usurped from the peasants but was awarded by the government, probably because the landlords agreed to cultivate it.[31] The land was formerly unclaimed and unsettled. This was probably the story of the feudal regime in Syria—it was young, inexperienced, and did not sink deep roots. In addition, it was probably not based on appalling injustices as was the case in so many other countries.

As noted previously, Tell Toqan was a prominent case of excessive land concentration, although other land settlement patterns also were in existence. Several of these have come to light in two studies by Raymond Hinnebusch, who collected basic details on the socioeconomic structure of eight Syrian villages.[32] The first village he mentioned was situated in the Hamah region. In light of what we have said about the excessive land concentration in this area, it is small wonder that prior to the agrarian reform enacted by the Ba'th regime, the villagers here were landless sharecroppers on the estates of Hamah's landlords.[33] Another village studied by Hinnebusch was situated in the Alawi region of northwestern Syria. Here, too, urban landlordism was the general rule, and this applied to the village in question.[34] A third village was a Bedouin settlement 12.5 miles west of Raqqa, where the tribal chief managed to have all the land registered in his own name, thereby turning the villagers into penniless sharecroppers or laborers.[35] These three cases represented, it seemed, the three areas where large landlordism in Syria was massively concentrated. In the five other cases Hinnebusch studied, the situation was considerably more complex than in any of these three.

The first of the remaining cases was a village in the plain of Damascus. Here the author's (widespread) tendency to exaggerate the feudal ingredient of the agrarian regime in question was quite distinct. Hinnebusch spoke of the rule of large landlords, but in point of fact it seemed that their role was much more limited than in the former cases. The author also contradicted himself. At one point he maintained that "even here most land was owned not by peasants, but by Damascus civil service, professional and commercial families."[36] But further on he said that "unlike Hamah, land reform here had only a modest impact. Only one-third of the village was owned by outsiders and not all of this was above the land reform ceiling."[37]

Hinnebusch also studied a village in the Hauran. He remarked that the pre-Ba'th agrarian regime here was predominantly a smallholding one.[38] He also reached the same conclusion regarding one village situated 12.5 miles southeast of Aleppo[39] and another the same distance east of Homs.[40] Hinnebusch also studied a Druze village situated in the Druze mountains that was composed basically of smallholdings. Here he went one step farther and asserted that this feature characterized not only this village but the entire region and was a result of the rough nature of the terrain, which allowed the peasants to retain their independence.[41]

While on the subject of Syria, it may be of interest to digress and consider Jordan (or, more correctly, Transjordan), which ecologically and geographically resembles Syria and which from an agrarian viewpoint may vividly highlight several points in our discussion. Transjordan was a very marginal area throughout the entire Ottoman period. It did not become a true part of the Ottoman Empire until the second half of the nineteenth century. As a result of improved public security and a decrease in the belligerence of the nomads, more agricultural settlements came into being, and towns began to develop. Although Ottoman law and rule in this area were never firmly established, the basic characteristics of the agrarian regime inherited by the Amirate of Transjordan in the interwar period were a mixture of late Ottoman legislation and local traditions. Thus, *musha,* or communal ownership, constituted the major basis of most, if not all, of the villages in the area, at least in the first decades of the twentieth century.[42] On the other hand, the basic land classification in the state of Jordan was principally that which had been embedded in the classical Ottoman land law and changed by the 1858 land law and subsequent regulations.[43]

A general picture of the land distribution in Jordan in the middle of the twentieth century can be obtained from a study by G. Baer in which he analyzed the 1953 census of agriculture in Jordan and came to the unequivocal conclusion that

> it shows that a major part of Jordan's land is held in small and medium size farms. In this respect Jordan differs considerably from other countries of the Middle East. According to the figures published in the *Statistical Abstract* of 1950, 36.3% of the privately owned area in Transjordan was owned by proprietors of less than 100 dunums, 49.5% by proprietors of 100–1,000 dunums, and only 14.2% by owners of large estates (1,000 dunums and above).[44]

This conclusion was partly corroborated by information given by G. E. Walpole, a senior civil servant of the Kingdom of Transjordan, who stated that before World War II an agricultural survey was conducted in the northern province of the country, and it was found that "the villages covered were populated by small landowners working their own land; big landlords were conspicuous by their absence."[45]

The case of Kafr al-Ma, the only Transjordanian village case study available, was a fine illustration of all these points. The land distribution in this village was quite equitable. The author of the study remarked that this point was notable because until the 1930s the *musha* system prevailed, which discouraged the purchase of land. But, surprisingly, once the *musha* was eliminated and the possibility of rapid land agglomeration presented itself, nothing of the sort actually took place. "The remarkable fact is that despite the revolution in land tenure and despite the increase of occupational mobility, so little change has occurred in the village whether in the actual alienation of land outside it or the agglomeration of land within it."[46]

How are we to account for this situation? To my mind it represented the original Syrian and Palestinian conditions that were erased in Syria by later developments. By the middle of the twentieth century Syria was already well ahead in its capitalistic development, while Transjordan was still at the beginning of the road, with many areas probably entirely unpopulated and many others still subject to traditional conditions. Without resort to this kind of argumentation the Jordanian case seems incomprehensible. But if my argumentation is correct, then the Jordanian case is an important affirmation of the thesis I propose in this book—namely, that the situation whereby smallholders prodominated was a legacy that the Ottoman land regime bequeathed to the modern Middle East.

To return to Syria, although Weulersse painted a one-sided, exaggerated picture of the Syrian land regime, the political repercussions of large landlordism in Syria nevertheless were far-reaching. In fact, in the interwar period, Syria was ruled by a landed oligarchy. Thus, R. B. Winder, who studied the social background of Syrian deputies before the rise of the Ba'th, found that the most prevalent occupation among them was landownership. The landlords were not only the biggest group in Parliament, but they were sometimes also twice as big as the second group. In addition, if we add the tribal shaykhs, we may conclude that in most parliaments in the period more than 50 percent of the deputies were landlords by occupation.[47] Hourani exclaimed in the same vein, and quite prophetically, "The dominant social class is still that of the landowners, who continue to possess a semi-feudal status. No other social class is strong or self-conscious enough to stand against them. . . . Although the power of the landowners has not yet been challenged, almost certainly the coming generation will see its decline."[48]

Egypt

The agrarian regime in Egypt in the nineteenth and twentieth centuries differed in certain details from the regime's development in the Ottoman Empire proper, which, as we have seen, was mainly the result of the 1858 land law. Because the agrarian regime in modern Egypt has been thoroughly studied by G. Baer and by many others, there is no need in the present context for more than a short summary of these findings.[49] The land regime that prevailed until the nineteenth century was thoroughly wiped out by Mehmed Ali, Egypt's ruler, in the early years of that century. He realized that the extant agrarian system ran counter to his plans, which basically were to exploit Egypt's resources in order to advance the country's military and economic might. The tax farmers completely controlled the Egyptian countryside; not only did they divert a substantial portion of the surplus raised as tax from reaching the state's coffers—they also served as the basis of a powerful political group that undermined the state's central authority. Members of the *ulema,* Mamluks, and Bedouin chieftains all served as tax farmers, many of them for life. The realization of Mehmed Ali's plans necessitated the abolition of these groups.

The destruction of tax farming in Egypt took place gradually and was finally attained by the mid-1820s. The process included mounting pressure on the tax-farmers, physical extermination of the Mamluks in 1811 and the confiscation of their tax farms, imposition of taxes on the *usiya* (demesne) held by the tax farmers, and so on. Because the holders of tax farms were in effect Egypt's landed oligarchy, the measures taken by Mehmed Ali to ruin them amounted to a sort of agrarian reform whose initial step was the nationalization of Egypt's landed wealth.

Mehmed Ali put into motion a significant process that was to characterize the land regime in nineteenth-century Egypt—the bequeathal of state lands to a variety of social groups, with concomitant full rights of ownership of these lands. He started the process by granting unclaimed and unworked lands, which were called *ibadiya,* to state officials, who undertook to cultivate them. He also coerced wealthy state officials into paying the taxes due from villages whose inhabitants had fled to avoid the heavy tax load. In exchange the said officials were awarded far-reaching ownership of these lands, which were called *ubda* lands. Thus, large-estate formation in nineteenth-century Egypt began in earnest. Ali's successors continued this practice, which was considerably accelerated in the second half of the century when Egypt became ever more heavily indebted to foreign creditors. The government of Egypt saw its lands as a disposable asset of which it could make the best economic use. In fact, Egypt's rulers allocated extensive tracts of land to themselves and members of their families, thereby creating the largest estates of that time. The purchase of extensive tracts by foreign capitalistic companies and individuals, who flocked in large numbers to Egypt, also contributed to large-estate formation. There is no doubt that Egypt was becoming a sort of El Dorado because of the country's cotton, which became the chief source of the country's wealth. Nineteenth-century Egypt was a classic example of large-estate formation generated by growing foreign demand for agricultural commodities.

The outcome of these developments was that by the late nineteenth century Egypt had a land regime that was extremely inegalitarian. The situation was aggravated still further by the growing complexity of Egypt's capitalistic economy. An ever-increasing number of peasants found themselves heavily in debt and eventually were dispossessed of their land. In this way an alarmingly increasing proportion of peasants in Egypt became landless. This phenomenon was exacerbated by the fact that in Egypt (unlike in other areas studied here) population growth had caused demographic saturation by the early twentieth century. This meant that while in other regions a landless peasant could still take hold of an unclaimed piece of land, in Egypt virtually all the land was under cultivation.

This land problem also was aggravated by a shift to the production of a supercapitalistic commodity (cotton) destined exclusively for the world market, which led to far-reaching change. The reference is to the institution of the *izba,* or "large estate," something akin to the Turkish *chiftlik.* The *izba* was an estate "in which the tenants were housed in mud dwellings grouped around the central stores and the residence of the owner and of his *nazir,* or overseer."[50] The institution did not seem to exist before the nineteenth-century cotton boom.

> The word *izba* itself first had the meaning of an encampment of temporary straw huts put up for labourers working at some distance from their village. But by the time of the 1882 census it had already been given its modern meaning of "hameau, bourgade-groupe d'habitations construites pour des ouvriers agricoles sur des terres de culture," a small, artificially con-

structed community which unlike a village, generally took the name of its proprietor.[51]

Although in 1882 there were about five thousand *izba*s in Egypt, by 1913 there were about twelve thousand five hundred ownership units of more than fifty *feddan* each, and most of these units contained *izba*s.[52] By 1914, the *izba* institution controlled as much as one-half of Egypt's cultivated land.[53] Contrary to the situation in pre–nineteenth-century Egypt and the Fertile Crescent, *izba* peasants lacked all property rights whatsoever in the estate. "Property rights to the lands were concentrated in the hands of the estate owner. The peasant had no claim whatsoever to the land; they occupied their land parcels entirely on the sufferance of the lord."[54] The conditions of the fellahs who worked on these estates varied greatly. Sharecropping of some sort predominated, and wages were paid only for special jobs, usually in connection with cotton growing. This meant that every peasant received a plot of land that he or she worked independently. The capitalistic conditions of production, where they appeared, were thus only partial. "The result was a system which, though capitalist in some of its aspects, stopped short of the reorganization of production along more capital intensive lines using a combination of wage labour and machines to allow a steady increase in agricultural productivity."[55] (The question of why this was the case is beyond the scope of the present study.)

As the twentieth century unfolded, more and more Egyptian peasants became landless or were owners of small plots inadequate for the sustenance of their families. The agrarian problem became Egypt's foremost problem. Yet, as in most countries controlled by a landed oligarchy, the road to reform, especially agrarian reform, remained blocked and was rarely discussed openly. In turn, not surprisingly, the demand for agrarian reform became the chief issue in the platform of the regime's opposition, including the group of officers who eventually succeeded to power.

Thus, despite certain variations, the landed regime in Egypt in both Ottoman and modern times fell into the same category as it did in Syria and Iraq. It is true that we do find traces of large-estate formation prior to the nineteenth century in Egypt, but these traces were on the whole insubstantial. Those who controlled the land did not have security of tenure. The holding of *iltizam*s remained extremely precarious. Many of the tax farmers were Mamluks, whose tenure was, by definition, unstable. A Mamluk group once removed from office was not likely to maintain its control of the land. As a consequence, the form of large landownership in Ottoman Egypt never went beyond the so-called "prebendal domain"—that is, it never involved more than collection of taxes. Peasants did not become serfs, either legally or practically. It was true that in the nineteenth century the ruler of Egypt bequeathed vast tracts of land in a manner reminiscent of the czar in Russia, but the czar bequeathed land and people, while in the Egyptian case only the land was subject to bequeathal. It would seem, then, that large landlordism in the true sense only came into being in Egypt in the course of the nineteenth century.

Turkey

Turkey differed substantially from Egypt, Iraq, and Syria. The agrarian situation here remained basically what it was in the classical period; large estates were of much less importance than in Arab countries. Here I take a stand that diverges from the current view of Turkey's landholding patterns in the twentieth century. The old view was apparent especially in some excellent quantitative studies. One such study is that of A. Güriz, who presents detailed global tables of landholding patterns from which he concluded that "it is generally seen that in underdeveloped countries the distribution of land ownership is unbalanced and unjust. A priori, this can be said to be the case in Turkey also. There are a number of statistics which prove the point."[56]

Güriz was of course correct when he claimed that the statistics reflected an inequitable distribution of agricultural lands. The top 1 percent probably owned more land than the bottom 60 percent. Unquestionably, his tables contained important information on large-estate formation; however, they failed to note other important aspects that were not evident in the global statistics. For example, how many of the large estates were in fact out of cultivation? What proportion of the Turkish peasantry was dependent on landlords for their livelihood, and what proportion was economically and politically independent? The well-known global figures are inadequate to answer these questions. One has to refer to other sources of information, such as village monographs. Such evidence radically changes our image of the overall landholding patterns in twentieth-century Turkey, as at least one important scholar has already realized.[57] On inspection it appeared that there were numerous village studies on Turkey, more so than on any other Middle Eastern country. Most of these studies revealed that the dominant pattern of landownership was the small, family farm that was part of a lively, viable village community.

According to Bedriye Denker, who studied the rural geography of the Bursa plain in the early 1960s, the land regime at that time was based on the small, independent family farm. Most of the village population owned between 20 and 40 donums. Larger estates were rare. About 20 percent of the peasants were landless (the same percentage as in the seventeenth century). Thus, most land was worked by family labor; sharecropping and other semifeudal arrangements were rare. On the whole, then, the land regime in the early 1960s was remarkably similar to what it had been in the seventeenth century. In the earlier period there might have been more land at the disposal of individual families, but this may have been due to reduced population pressure on the land. Nevertheless, the land regime in the Bursa region was still centered on the small family, which owned its own land and was free from the control of a large landowner, be he villager or outsider.[58]

A long series of studies on Turkish villages indicated that a situation in which a ruling landlord dominated an entire village in a feudalistic manner was the exception rather than the rule. Such a situation was revealed in a study by O. Ozankaya, who headed a research group that compared the social structure of two villages in northeastern Anatolia with two villages in the central plateau.[59] Villages C and D (the central villages) in the group were in fact dominated by *aghas*. Village D was established by five *agha* families—the small peasants arrived later. In village C there was one dominant *agha* who owned one-quarter of the village lands and was the village strongman. In Villages A and B small ownership predominated. In fact, even villages C and D did not conform to the simple feudal model because the *aghas* did not completely control the villagers. Many were independent, and there was little land leasing.[60]

The other clear example of feudalistic domination of a village was the village of Sindel, situated 3 miles from the city of Bergama.[61] In Sindel, sixteen families were landless, and all the others had tiny, inadequate plots of land. The *agha* of the village had no more than 40 donums.[62] In fact, the villagers earned their livelihood by sharecropping lands owned by Bergama inhabitants at the outskirts of the city.[63] On inspection it appeared that this was not a case of land usurpation or loss through debts; rather, the villagers were former nomads who settled in Sindel in the last quarter of the nineteenth century.[64] They were attracted by the city's demand for woodcutting services and camel transportation, occupations that required little land (both of which are now largely defunct). Thus, the villagers had to readjust and turn to agriculture, of necessity depending on sharecropping or similar subordinate arrangements. It is interesting to note that there were thirty villages around Bergama, a situation similar to that of Sindel.[65] Obviously, however, the pattern revealed here did not conform to the familiar feudal type, although at first sight it may give that impression.

Sakaltutan is a village in central Anatolia (near Kayseri) made famous by Paul Stirling's classic study conducted in the early 1950s.[66] (Table 6.2 reproduces Stirling's findings about landownership.) Thus, we observe a somewhat egalitarian land system based on the independent household; there was a small minority of landless peasants, no dominant landowner, and no semifeudalistic institutions. The marginal role of sharecropping in these two villages was a characteristic feature.

> Those who put their land out to sharecroppers are not necessarily the well-to-do. They include the aged, the sick, the widows. . . . Correspondingly, those who take on sharecropping are not the poorest village houses. To

Table 6.2
Land Distribution in the Village of Sakaltutan

Donum	% of Households
0	6
1 – 10	10
11 – 30	9
31 – 60	30
61 – 100	30
101 – 160	11
200 – 300	5

Source: Adapted from Stirling, *Turkish Village*, p. 53.

sharecrop a man needs resources—oxen and supporting manpower. In fact most sharecroppers are middle range landowners who prefer to take on more land rather than supplement their income by other means.[67]

One important component of the Ottoman land regime was the pasture land, the common property of all the villagers, on which only grazing was permitted.[68] This institution existed in sixteenth-century Ottoman land law and was in operation in the Bursa region in the seventeenth century and in the two villages studied by Stirling in the 1950s. These two villages were characterized by small landownership and communities free of the dominance of a large landlord.

Hasanoğlan was probably the most famous village study after Stirling's *Turkish Village*. The author, Ibrahim Yasa, claimed that the subject of his study was representative of many Anatolian villages.[69] This claim is of considerable importance for the present study, with its implication that the data were equally applicable to the land regime in many other villages. The distribution of landownership in Hasanoğlan in 1944 is provided in Table 6.3.

Yasa stated explicitly that most of the landless peasants in the village were new settlers, all of whom were engaged in nonagricultural occupations.[70] Hasanoğlan was not composed of dispossessed landless peasants. Members of the two bottom categories of landowners found some employment as sharecroppers on the larger estates. But the landholdings of even the largest farmers in the village were actually small and obviously insufficient to qualify them as anything more than well-off farmers, so the phenomenon of sharecropping must have been extremely limited. The land system of Hasanoğlan can unhesitatingly be classified as one in which small, independent proprietorship predominated.

Szyliowicz, who studied the small coastal town of Erdemli near Mersin, maintained that "Despite the changes in agricultural processes, farming was still largely a family affair; most households owned and worked a plot of land, usually about five or six donums."[71] There was no mention in the study of large landlords in the region in the Republican era: hence, we can assume that the land regime of the area was one of small owners.

J. E. Pierce's study on a village in central Anatolia only touched briefly on the question examined here. He dealt with the village of Demirciler, about 68 miles southeast of Ankara. He devoted only a few sentences to the agrarian regime, but these contained important information: "The basis of subsistence is wheat farming. Each adult male tills a plot of land as large as he can manage, since all of the villagers own more land than they can till at one time."[72] This was a land regime of small peasant proprietors, among whom no one was dominant; nor were they confronted by any external superior force. The situation was one of an independent village community leading its own life.

This description undoubtedly characterized a village still steeped in subsistence production, as were most villages in the Anatolian plateau during the first half of the twentieth century. Interestingly, the village of Demirciler was no longer at that stage when the study was done (early 1960s). Rather, it was more and more involved with the city market and had begun to produce grain by sophisticated methods, intended undoubtedly for the city market. This fact was reflected in a sudden spurt in population figures after 1950. But the above quotation seemed to reflect a land regime characteristic of a period not yet influenced by the forces of the market, for we find here a situation where land had practically no price and yet the villagers were extremely poor. These two facts, however, are not incompatible, and they explain how poverty can result from factors other than human exploitation. Given the traditional level of technology, there was a very definite limit to the amount of land a villager could work by him- or herself, and because land had no price, a villager was unable to find sufficient labor. Thus, an equitable agrarian regime was totally commensurate with abject poverty,

Table 6.3
Land Distribution in Hasanoğlan, 1944

Category (Donum)	% of Households
0	8.8
5 – 39	41
40 – 69	26.6
70 – 119	12.8
120 – 349	9.3
500 – 549	1.1

Source: Adapted from Yasa, *Hasanoğlan*, p. 66.

even without the presence of land starvation or the effect of land division through inheritance.

Pierce's description was one of an agrarian regime prior to the impact of massive marketing and was corroborated by the description of Demirciler's pasture. As described by Pierce, the situation so closely recalled the Bursa region of the seventeenth century that it could have been taken from the *kadi* records of that city.

> Much of the subsistence of the village also comes from sheep and goats. These animals feed on the sparse grasses in the hills and are slaughtered for food, sheared for wool, and sold for cash. A shepherd comes to the village each morning and collects all of the sheep. These are grazed during the day on land that is held in common by the villagers and called empty land. No one can break this land for farming under any circumstances, so they say.[73]

The village of Harran was a similar example. It was a poor, desert-fringe village situated on the site of the ancient city of Harran in southeastern Anatolia. W. C. Brice, who studied this village in the early 1950s, found an Arabic-speaking population of about five hundred that was semitribal in its social organization.[74] The land regime in the village was not much different from those previously examined. "Tenure is usually freehold, and most of the farmers are peasant proprietors. Individual holdings are normally in scattered plots."[75] Part of the village land belonged not to individuals but rather to the village community as a whole and was used as common pasture.[76]

An especially revealing case study was conducted by Richard Scott of a village near Ankara.[77] This village underwent an economic revolution analogous to the growth of Ankara when it became Turkey's new capital. The villagers immediately realized the potential inherent in their close vicinity to the city and started marketing their dairy produce with ample profits. Later it was discovered that the village soil was clay-rich, which led to enormous economic benefits for the village. Although Scott did not deal with the land system fully, one gets the impression that before the boom started the system was egalitarian and based on household ownership of land. Moreover, it would appear from the description that the system remained egalitarian during the period of economic prosperity, although no exact details are given, and that the prosperity was widely shared by all the village's inhabitants. There was no indication of monopolistic ascendance by an urban or local strongman or entrepreneur of any sort. On the contrary, the new economic opportunities were enthusiastically seized by the formerly dormant village, resulting in vigorous productivity. This clearly contradicts the assumption that in a capitalistic system the small household and traditional village community must lose out to the city capitalist. We return to this important topic later.

A similar, although much less obvious, example was the case study of a strongly market-oriented group of rural communities near Antalia conducted by John Kolars. He hinted at landownership but did not give a global breakdown of the pattern. Thus, when describing the area chosen for research, he said that "the area finally chosen for investigation lies about fifteen kilometers west of the city of Antalya, and consists of the Boğa Çay Ova and the mountain slopes above it. Within this area are located eleven villages which occupy both the coastal plain and the mountain slopes. . . . Their inhabitants, with the exception of only one village, Ingiliz Kavak, may be generally classified as village small holders."[78]

One of the first village studies carried out in Turkey was written by Niyazi Berkes, in the early 1940s, about eleven villages around Ankara.[79] The author, who was better known for an entirely different study he wrote many years later, was renowned for his sensitivity to issues of class structure. It is this point in particular that makes this study important for our purposes; such a scholar would be careful not to draw too idyllic a picture of the rural class structure. Berkes devoted some attention to issues of landownership; however, he was able to obtain exact figures for only one village, which indicated that the village was a regime of small, independent landowners. There were a few larger farmers, but they coexisted with the smaller ones. Berkes did not dwell on the question of the extent to which this village was typical, but his study did confirm, however, the previously held picture concerning this particular village. Thus, he mentioned unusually rich landlords, but on inspection it appeared that they owned no more than 300 to 700 donums, and only in one exceptional case as much as 1,000 donums.[80] Berkes referred to the poverty of the peasants but did not attribute it to class structure or its consequences. The chief reason, in his view, for the poverty was the aridity of the soil, which resulted in poverty even in villages where land was plentiful.[81] In some villages, poverty was a result of land shortage, a condition chiefly attributable to the effects of the inheritance law.[82]

The source I considered the most important for this study was a short article written in 1955 by Nicholas Helburn entitled "A Stereotype of Agriculture in Semiarid Turkey."[83] Based on nine months of field work, the article attempted to trace the most typical characteristics of a large number of villages in the central Anatolian plateau and to draw a conclusion based on a large number of case studies. The author emphasized the paramount place of the pasture and common property of the village community, among others.

> All the land is grazed except the vineyards and vegetable gardens. About three-fifths of the grazing land is natural pasture held in common by the whole village; the remainder is in small plots of cropland owned individually, which are grazed throughout the year when they lie fallow and after the harvest when they are cropped. Communal ownership of grazing rights

and the inability of the village council to control the numbers of stock that any one villager puts into the herd leads to severe overgrazing of natural pastures and low yields of forage, milk, meat and wool.[84]

Exactly as in the Bursa region in the seventeenth century, peasants in the central Anatolian plateau had their arable land spread out over different pieces. "Villagers feel safer from drought and other hazards with their land divided into small plots distributed throughout the village. Having all one's land on a single soil type, in a single location and exposure, is considered risky."[85]

The author gave the following important information about land distribution in a theoretical village of eighty families:

> The wealthy families own a little more than a hundred acres apiece. About 30 acres is average, and several families have less than 20 acres. Ten families may own no land at all, and these, even though they keep livestock, are not considered farm families. One family head may make his living as the village watchman. Another as a cowherd. Of the other eight, six leave the village seasonally to earn an income as construction workers in Ankara and Adana; the remaining two have no apparent source of income. Tenancy, sharecropping, or working for wages on another villager's farm land is not characteristic, though sharecropping among relatives is not uncommon.[86]

These words hardly need further interpretation. They depict a free, independent peasant society whose land regime was still based mainly on the peasant family farm. The average farm size was substantially greater than in the Bursa region discussed by Denker (120 donums versus 40), a function, no doubt, of the great differences in agricultural conditions between the two regions. However, the unity of the land regime transcended these differences. It was still basically the sixteenth-century institution, hardly affected by the historical vicissitudes of three-and-one-half centuries.

The Anatolian plateau yielded another study, the last I shall tap here. Deniz Kandiyoti wrote an excellent small study on the process of modernization in a Turkish village called Sakarya during the twentieth century.[87] This study highlighted all the major points I have singled out as representing the typical Turkish agrarian regime. Before the modernization, which started in the mid-twentieth century at the earliest, land in this village was more or less evenly distributed among small peasant proprietors. All villagers were wheat cultivators with few conspicuous differences in income. Eight to ten households were known to have larger plots of land. However, sharecropping was not common and production relied on family labor only.[88] This general feature was "characteristic of most Anatolian-plateau villages."[89]

One important feature of the agrarian structure of Sakarya at the beginning of the twentieth century, when the village was founded by settled nomads, was that land was plentiful and was in effect a free commodity. The settlers were each awarded a plot, but "land was plentiful and Sakarya villagers opened up new land for cultivation as far as their man and animal power permitted, despite frequent border fights and conflicts over right of pasture with their semi-nomadic neighbours."[90] This land abundance came to an end in this village by the mid-twentieth century.[91] The harshest aspects of an exploitative rural regime, not unexpectedly, are absent in a situation where there is a lack of pressure on the land. Rather than work for someone else, a landless peasant opens up new land. Indeed, Lucien Bianco has shown that the gravest aspects of the Chinese land regime, which bred the biggest uprising in human history, were closely associated with the outcomes of population pressure.[92]

Since the 1950s, the village has entered a period of rapid economic development, which has brought in its wake a much more accentuated class polarization, from which the lowest stratum of the community has suffered the most.[93] This may be ominous for Turkey's future, although in this study I am concerned mainly with the evolution of the present sociopolitical formation.

The *Aghas,* the Landlords of Turkey

The most common term designating the large landlord in Turkey is *agha.* Today this seems to be the chief meaning of the word, although it also may mean "master" in a more general sense. It is important to look at the recent history of the term. A good starting point might be Bowen's article in the *Encyclopaedia of Islam.* However, here we get a partially misleading definition, for it appeared that the original meaning of the term did not include "landlord" as Bowen would have us believe. Those scholars who have worked with Ottoman archival documents would probably confirm the contention that the clear equation between *agha* and "landlord" is a modern usage. It is not by chance that Redhouse's dictionary (first published in 1891) did not give this meaning of the word. Neither is it feasible to claim that the meaning of landlord was at first colloquial only.

The term *ayan,* meaning "notable," also was originally used colloquially, but it was immediately adopted by writers of documents and chronicles. In any event, this was not the case for the term *agha,* which nevertheless was used in a considerable number of contexts, most of them administrative. By the nineteenth century most of these terms had become obsolete, and the chief meaning that remained in vogue in this period was an honorific title for low-ranking army officers. Moreover, some officials, whose posts were semiadministrative and semimilitary, also were designated by *agha.* This was particularly the case for the post of *mutesellim,* an intendant of a governor. Most of those who were known to have filled that post actually bore the title.

It is not known how the term *agha* came to be applied to landlords, but it seems to have occurred as follows. The aforementioned *mutesellims* constituted the main pool of *ayan*—that is, local chieftains and notables who headed local Middle Eastern society in the eighteenth and nineteenth centuries. Although this pattern of leadership declined in the latter half of the nineteenth century, the term may have remained and been applied to landlords, who also became leaders of local society. In addition, it appeared that many of the people who rushed to take possession of unclaimed lands in the latter half of the nineteenth century were Ottoman army officers who bought lands near the places where their units were stationed and often settled on these lands after retirement.[94] In addition, tribal chieftains in Anatolia (many of whom began to settle permanently in the second half of the nineteenth century and thereby acquired ownership of large tracts of land) were often called *agha*.[95] This was probably connected with the fact that chieftains were often assigned minor military duties by the Ottomans and hence accorded the status of low-ranking army officers.

Thus, the meaning of "landlord" attached to the term *agha* only toward the end of the Ottoman period. This was probably further evidence (although by no means crucial in itself) that large landlordism did not emerge before the final phase of the Ottoman period. In some of the case studies in which we can trace the biographies of real *agha*s, we find a very clear chronological connection between the birth of the republic and the emergence of *agha*s.[96] The reason for this may well have been connected with the acceleration of the pace at which unoccupied land was acquired and captured. If the known cases were truly representative of a wider phenomenon, this would confirm the relatively recent origin of the institution of *aghalik* in the sense of large landlordism.

Available materials indicated that one should not exaggerate the position of the *agha*—he was the leader of rural society but by no means its undisputed ruler. Stirling's study finely illustrated this point. Only one of the two villages studied by Stirling had an *agha*, and his position was neither formal nor legally recognized. Indeed, whether or not someone was a true *agha* was debatable—and was in fact debated.

> A certain level of power and prestige, provided it is derived from land, gives a villager the right to be regarded as an *ağa*. . . . This familiar Turkish word was very commonly used in the villages in several different senses. It was, for example, normal in addressing a neighbour to call him "Ahmet Ağa" or "Mustafa Ağa" as the case might be. . . . But a man was spoken of as an *ağa* in a slightly different sense. Thus, Kara Osman . . . has been an *ağa* without any question. One very poor but intelligent informant when speaking of one or two wealthier men whom she personally respected would add this title after their names, but she once remarked that since Kara Osman died the village no longer boasted a true *ağa*, only pretentious nobodies.[97]

Moreover, this *agha* was not in complete political control of the village. He was the largest landlord and owned about 1,000 donums, but he did not control tenures of other villagers.[98] He had no serfs or sharecroppers but merely ten hired laborers.[99] Characteristically, he acquired his land by capturing the lands of Greeks evacuated to Greece in 1923, rather than by usurping local peasant lands.[100]

Another concrete case study that gave a lucid picture of the role of the *agha* came from the pen of John Kolars.

> The usual title of respect given to an older man in the Boğa Çay area is *ağa*. *Ağa* has lost its former meaning of wealthy ruler and landlord except in the case of Akdamlar. There the titular *ağa* is a particularly forceful personality. Although he occupies no official role within the village, his wealth, physical size, many sons, and business acumen have made him the true leader not only in his *mahalle* [quarter] but in all of Geyik Bayiri Village as well. . . . Elsewhere throughout the area many of the older men are addressed as *ağa* much as Americans use "sir" as a term of respect.[101]

Here, too, the *agha* may have been a man of great influence, but he was by no means a ruler. His authority was not based on landownership. Although he had several businesses, he owned no more than 145 donums of land.

What was the extent of the institution of the *agha* in Turkey's villages? The answer, as far as I could ascertain from the available sources, was that the phenomenon was not particularly widespread. I base this conclusion on information supplied by the studies of Scott, Frey, and Roos.

Scott argued convincingly that in the first Republican period (1920–1950) the office of *muhtar* (village headman) was so encumbered by official duties of an administrative nature that no member of the village elite would dream of assuming the job. Although this situation changed in the post-1950 period, even by the 1960s a true village elder was not expected to want the post. It would be too demanding technically and would not leave him enough leisure time to pursue his traditional life-style. It goes without saying that this logic also applied to the *agha*.[102]

Frey and Roos' study on the village *muhtar* in Turkey makes sense only in juxtaposition to Scott's findings. The authors' original idea was to show that the village headman in Turkish society holds a key position that may be conducive as a lever for social modernization, but the study can be employed for our purposes as well. They solicited the opinions of about eight thousand villagers on the position of the *muhtar* in their villages and compared the responses with several other figures in various positions in the Turkish village, including those for the *agha*. Their main conclusion was that the *muhtar* was the most important figure in the village (see Table 6.4). They also found that in villages where there was an *agha* in the real sense the situation was entirely different from that suggested by Table 6.4. In such cases, the *agha* was the dominant sociopolitical figure. One can thus draw

Table 6.4
Leadership Orientations of the Turkish Peasantry:
Headmen Versus *Aghas*

Persons seen as:	Headman	*Agha*
Most knowledgeable	35%	4%
Most prestigious	46%	7%
Most influential	73%	4%
Farming leader	51%	2%
Land dispute leader	47%	1%

Source: Adapted from Frey and Roos, Table 1, p. 8.

Note: It must be emphasized that the original table also included the position of the district governor and other func-
tionaries who are not dealt with in the present study, which is
why the percentages given do not add up to a hundred.

the conclusion that if, in global statistical figures, the *agha* occupied as marginal a position as shown in Table 6.4, it must have been due to the relative
rarity of the phenomenon. In other words, most villages probably did not
have *aghas*.

An exceptionally important study on the *aghas* in Turkey, which posed
serious challenges to my theories, was Benedict's study on the town of Ula
in the southwestern corner of Anatolia.[103] The study was praiseworthy because it is almost the only one that has tackled the true chronological development of this social pattern. The *aghas* here constituted a somewhat
special pattern. Unlike those we have seen so far, they lived in the town itself,
not in villages. Whether this difference concealed other, deeper differences
was not entirely clear.

Benedict reconstructed the historical chronology by which the social
pattern of the *agha* developed in Ula, and this chronology was the familiar
one that I claimed earlier in this work to be, on the whole, incorrect. In other
words, Ula's *aghas*, according to Benedict, were direct genealogical deriva-
tives of the *sipahi*s of the fifteenth and sixteenth centuries and the *multezim*s
who succeeded them in the sixteenth to nineteenth centuries. In this theory
the political pattern of the *aghas*' landownership and political dominance
was assumed to be the major mode that prevailed in Anatolia for centuries.
It is possible that this chronology was correct for a few places, and Ula may
have been one of these. Nevertheless, Benedict's chronology suffered from
certain serious drawbacks—namely, that almost his entire body of evidence
was oral, and most of it was of a highly dubious character. In addition, some
important facts were missing altogether. We do not know anything about the
lands Ula's *aghas* owned or the exact relations between these *aghas* and the

actual tillers. Lacking these crucially important details, it is impossible to assess properly Benedict's historical thesis.

The most unconvincing part of this chapter of Benedict's study was his claim that from the second half of the nineteenth century onward, Ula's *agha*s were in decline, as evidenced by, among other things, the loss of lands to merchants and even to peasants.[104] This seemed to be the sole case on record in the Middle East in which political grandees lost out to peasants, and it is all the more surprising that this should have occurred at a period when everywhere else in the Middle East landlords were on the ascent (as was shown in Chapter 5).

It is quite likely that Benedict had an unduly exaggerated opinion of the status of Ula's *agha*s in former times, and upon finding peasants in possession of land in the later Ottoman period, he interpreted this as a sign of decline in the position of the *agha*s. In any event, Ula's case does not affect the validity of the general theory I have been trying to construct in this study.

Another type of *agha*, and one also of considerable importance to the present study, was revealed by Michael Meeker's study of the eastern Black Sea region of Turkey. The *agha*s here were not village leaders but rather heads of loose groups, each composed of several villages that had in common the fact that they all considered themselves descendants of the same forefather. This was an important and clear case of rural political leadership not based on big landlordism. Meeker was quite explicit on this point.

> [T]he Black Sea districts of the petty valley-lords, especially those between Trebizond and Batum, had no towns; the overland trade by-passed them at Trebizond, and the local markets merely served the people of a particular valley. The local agriculture, perhaps best termed horticulture, held little promise of achieving large surpluses. . . . In light of these conditions, it is not surprising that a feudal system based on social classes and the organization of agriculture around estates never emerged in this region as it did in many other parts of the nearby Caucasus. The Georgians, Circassians, and Ossetes, whose territories included productive agricultural areas and towns, maintained elaborate social systems, with a staggering assortment of social classes in the case of the Circassians.[105]

The simplicity of the politicoagrarian structure in the region contrasted sharply with a Persian case study (cited by Meeker) in which a chieftain "was an estate owner, had tenants, and could raise an army from a section of the population. It is interesting to compare the social complexity of the Iranian case with the relative homogeneity and egalitarianism of Turkish Black Sea society."[106]

To summarize, I have shown that the pattern of agrarian political dominance connected with the term *agha* is of relatively recent origin, and dates back to the beginning of the twentieth century. In addition, *agha*s were apparently found in a minority of Turkish villages; in many cases their dominance was not particularly far-reaching, and in a number of cases *aghas* were not associated with agrarian domination at all. Thus, it is incorrect to view the whole of present-day Turkey as a country of large landlordism. It may be true only of the eastern and southern parts of the country, which have been subject to special conditions.

We have seen how large estates were formed in the Adana region in the second half of the nineteenth century, largely as a consequence of the process of settlement of the nomads. In the course of this process many tribal chieftains managed to become landlords of their former tribal members. In eastern Anatolia feudalistic landed regimes reigned supreme from earlier times, and here the influence of the Ottoman Empire was accordingly smaller. But the land system in the greater part of the country was still the old, classical system of the small community and the family farm.

Why did the land regime in Turkey remain one of small proprietors, while in Egypt, Iraq, and Syria it became one of big proprietors? To a certain degree consideration of these questions started with the important studies of Çağalar Keyder.[107] His analysis suffered from its exclusive focus on Turkey, and so the crucially important comparative perspective was lacking. Keyder suggested an economic/technical explanation relating to cyclical price trends of agricultural commodities as the clue to the dominant small proprietorship in Turkey.[108] Did comparable price trends take place in Egypt, Syria, and Iraq between 1850 and 1953? Obviously they did. Nevertheless, there was a constant and vigorous trend toward large-estate formation. Surely, Keyder's explanation does not suffice.

Following the findings in this study, I tend to think that the purely economic explanation linking large-estate formation to capitalist development holds only in extreme cases. It worked in the case of English wool, Jaffa oranges, and Egyptian cotton. In other words, the pull of the demand would have to be exceptionally strong to revolutionize the landholding regime. Only in the nineteenth century did the European demand for agricultural commodities grow strong enough to exert transformative influences in a more generalized fashion, as we have seen in the connection between large-estate formation and the export of agricultural commodities in Palestine. Nevertheless, distance from the coast and political and institutional barriers could easily restrain such development.

Let us look first at a case, studied by Daniel Chirot, where political institutions greatly facilitated the transformation to a peripheral economy.[109] This was the case of Wallachia, a Rumanian principality that until the beginning of the nineteenth century was under the suzerainty of the Ottomans. In Wallachia there was a landed aristocracy that was extremely weak and dependent on the central ruler until the Ottomans conquered the area in the fifteenth century. The conquerors were not interested in establishing a full-fledged Ottoman administration, but they were content with indirect control. As a result, the institutional format remained unchanged. The landed aristocracy collaborated with the Ottomans (who needed a local ally), thus gaining the immense power needed to become a truly landed aristocracy. This weighed heavily on the peasants, with onerous, newly instituted serfdom and other traits of a typical feudal landed regime. Owing to these circumstances, according to Chirot, the European economic drive into the peripheral areas in the nineteenth century was exceptionally successful here.

> The changes that took place in the nineteenth century reveal the great power of capitalist market forces. Certainly, Western Europe never exerted as much direct political power over Wallachia as had the Ottomans. But its economic influence was sufficient to revolutionize rural life by creating a large class of serf cultivators. This change was, however, greatly facilitated by the fact that the political supremacy of the Wallachian landowning class was well established before 1829. In no other Balkan cases (particularly not in Serbia or Bulgaria) did the nineteenth century produce such a blatantly colonial society.[110]

This situation can be contrasted with circumstances at the end of the nineteenth century in western Anatolia, where an institutional format worked in the opposite direction. Here English capitalists bought extensive tracts of land, hoping to make them profitable by using cheap local labor. The initiative was unsuccessful, however, and the lands were soon sold, for it was impossible to find a cheap labor force.[111] On the one hand, land was plentiful: on the other, it was politically impossible to force people to work other than under free-market conditions. The correct explanation, therefore, ought to combine economic and political factors.

In Turkey there was a rare combination of factors, which was indeed matched only by the rarity of the specific political regime that developed in that country. The main factors were (1) the sheer size of the country and the great distance between the coast and the interior in any direction, coupled with the lack of good navigable rivers, which made it more difficult to develop capitalist agriculture in Turkey than in any other region in the Middle East; (2) the great natural aridity of much of the interior of Turkey, which meant that relatively little produce could be appropriated as "surplus," a factor that further exacerbated the problem for a would-be capitalist or land engrosser; and (3) an extremely powerful political rival to the landowners, that is, the ruling elite, which was heir to a strong tradition of centralism and antiperipheralism. In the nineteenth century it became a middle-class elite. Not only was this elite rather unenthusiastic about sharing power with landlords, it was also unwilling to distribute favors to that group in the form of land grants.

In Syria and Iraq institutional factors (mandatory policy, declining tribal loyalties) immensely favored the position of an incipient group of large landowners. In Egypt these political factors were coupled with the unusually strong pull created by the European demand for cotton. All these factors were absent in the case of Turkey.

CHAPTER SEVEN

The Agrarian Origins of the Modern Middle East: A Comparative Approach

In the Ottoman Empire conditions were not conducive to an industrial revolution. Such a revolution, if it had come about, could have transformed the entire economic structure of the empire into one based jointly on a large, urban industrial sector and a small, but productive, peasantry. This argument is predicated on geographical, ecological, and institutional factors rather than on cultural ones. Fundamental to the Ottoman political system was a combination of total central power and a fair amount of liberalism in the periphery. Until the middle of the nineteenth century one expression of this policy was the central government's constant nipping in the bud of all signs of a landed upper class or large estates. In contrast, lower-class institutions enjoyed extensive autonomy, and the prevailing agrarian regime throughout most of the Ottoman Empire was one of small proprietors. To avoid any misunderstanding, I should emphasize that the failure of a large-estates regime to appear before 1858 was mainly the outcome of a class struggle in which the primary contenders were the central government and the provincial potentates. The central government ultimately prevailed in this mainly political struggle, but the episode should not be viewed as purely political. Had the climatological and geographical conditions been more propitious, the local potentates might have had a stronger impetus to develop commercial agriculture, and the outcome of the struggle might have been different. Consequently, it seems that Ottoman society had few potentially explosive tensions inherent in its class structure—fewer than existed, for example, in states such as Russia and China. Herein, I believe, lies the main explanation for the fact that until the mid-nineteenth century we find no tendency to rebel among the peasants in the Middle East.

Large estates emerged for the first time following the 1858 land law and the beginning of land registration. This new development coincided with a rise in the power of the central government, the beginning of a demographic revolution in the Middle East, and an increasing European demand for Middle Eastern foodstuffs. These conditions naturally favored large-estate formation, but they were not in themselves sufficient, nor were they equally operative in all areas. In Iraq, Syria, and especially Egypt, transportation facilities were superior to those in Anatolia—which was one of the reasons why large estates sprang up much more rapidly in these countries. However, recent studies have shown quite convincingly that the capitalization theory is too simplistic. Small peasant communities are far more resistant to market forces than is usually appreciated. As I show in the following section, only when the pull of the market is unusually strong does it constitute a powerful factor encouraging large-estate formation. This clearly applies to nineteenth-century Egypt. Consequently, we may conclude that in Syria and Iraq the major factors in the formation of large estates were political no less than economic. The political power of the tribal shaykhs, who amassed enormous stretches of land through alliances with the colonial powers, was one of these factors.

The rapid, intensive expansion of large estates and large landlords touched off a process of mounting social tensions, which increasingly found expression in peasant unrest, particularly in the middle of the twentieth century. However, Arab society in Iraq, Egypt, and Syria was not ready then to revolt. On the basis of experience in China and Russia, one is tempted to conclude that it takes several centuries of pervasive agrarian problems to cause a revolution. But the bitter feelings were there simmering beneath the surface, and they were endured particularly by army officers, a group that constituted a major part of the ruling regime in many other states. In the Middle East, however, this group belonged in sentiment among the opposition. In Ottoman times no social stratum of landed upper class existed; therefore, no aristocratic army appeared on the scene. Consequently, army service only attracted members of the lower classes, a tradition that persists to this day. As the ruling regime in the Middle East, based on large landlordism, became gradually less popular, there was little to bind the military to service obligations.

Thus, I reject the suggestion that in the Middle East an army regime is inevitable because "this has always been the case." The idea is untenable, for it seems that in all historical empires the role of the army was of central importance. Even in the British Empire there was no clearcut division between the military and civil authorities, the great magnates of the realm being both military and civilian rulers. On the other hand, the total equation between the military and civil authorities in Islam is grossly exaggerated, at least as far as the Ottoman Empire was concerned in the last two or three centuries of its rule. In neither China nor Russia did the military come to power in the modern formation. In my view, the explanation for the army's unusually important role is to be sought in the army's traditional role. In empires in which a revolutionary situation developed, the army remained subordinate because army officers were well-equipped to lead coups but not true social revolutions. Such a conclusion was reached, for example, by scholars of China.

The army revolutions in the Middle East should not be viewed merely as coups staged by praetorian cliques motivated by their own petty interest. The army elite was a meaningful part of a new ruling class, the lower middle class. Although the major grievance behind the revolution was the agrarian problem, the army officers did not conduct the revolutions in the name of or for the benefit of the peasant. This situation recalls the Bolshevik revolutionaries, who traveled only part of the road with the peasantry. The grievances of the officers, as members of the (mainly urban) lower middle class, were not identical with those of the peasantry, any more than were the grievances of the alienated Russian intellectuals. It seems that different forces with different grievances merged into one opposition, but as the peasantry constituted the great bulk of the population, its grievances were particularly explosive in revolutionary situations—hence, the fact that agrarian reform leads the agenda of the army revolutions in the Middle East.

Here we find an explanation for additional phenomena that have characterized public life in the Middle East in recent years, such as the substantial reduction in the number of military coups. In my view, army coups are generally not (or not only) the outcome of the petty ambitions of the officers involved, but rather are expressions of deep-seated and widespread societal resentment against the ruling regime. Because the last generation was ruled by an elite that socially represented the majority, the former objective reasons for the recurrence of coups no longer exist. In other words, the army regimes of the Arab world have been enjoying a wider measure of legitimacy in recent years.

Another problem that my paradigm tries to explain is why none of the radical regimes in the Arab world has gone as far to embrace communism in its anti-Western stance. Concomitantly, communism has fared no better among the masses. I suggest that communism enjoys a better chance where the ground is ripe for it—that is, in societies with a massive and long-standing agrarian problem. One often hears the argument that mildly leftist social policies (those prevalent in the contemporary Middle East) are simply a matter of fashion in present-day Third World countries. This contention is entirely unconvincing. Current fashion did not prevent Albania in 1944 or Cuba in 1959 from embracing communism. Similarly, fashion did not prevent India or Turkey from remaining at least partially democratic and enforcing a bourgeois social policy. In substance, the argument falls short in far too many cases for it to be considered tenable.

Evolution in Turkey and Lebanon followed a different path. In Turkey conditions were not suited to the emergence of a tangible landed upper class, even in the wake of the 1858 land law. I would argue that herein lies the major difference between Turkey and the radical Arab countries. With the fall of the House of Osman following World War I, a bureaucratic middle class rose to power in Turkey. Atatürk's greatness, in this context, lay in the fact that he did not try to impose his own personal ambitions on the system. Consequently, there was no social ideology to conflict with that held by the majority of the bureaucratic middle class. This was democracy and therefore was ultimately to succeed. Lebanon presents us with a somewhat different version. One cannot minimize the crucial role of sectarian loyalties in Lebanon, but I try to show that this regime was also, in a very meaningful way, the outcome of important relevant social and agrarian factors.

The Absence of an Industrial Revolution in the Ottoman Empire

One of the major characteristics of the socioeconomic structure of the modern Middle East is that it is still largely steeped in a preindustrial era. Most of the gainfully employed are engaged in agriculture, which is still largely primitive. Modern industry is still in its infancy and struggling to establish itself. The question of why no industrial revolution occurred in the Middle East under the Ottomans (which, strangely enough, has not been seriously tackled until now) is difficult to answer. It is an issue that is vital for the elucidation of the problems raised in this book and cannot be avoided under the pretext of insufficient data.

The comparative method appears to be the best way to approach the issue, and I have chosen England as the *locus classicus* of comparative history.[1] According to most analyses, the Industrial Revolution in Britain began about 1760; thus, the revolution's main developments took place in the nineteenth century. There are, however, several reasons why it would be futile to expect an industrial revolution in the nineteenth-century Middle East. For one thing, the great political inferiority of Egypt and the Ottoman Empire vis-à-vis Europe found expression from 1838 onward in free-trade agreements. This meant that Europeans were free to inundate Eastern markets with cheap textiles, while the East was powerless to establish an industry based on modern machinery—a situation that would necessitate high tariff barriers and one diametrically opposed to free-trade agreements.[2] This in itself was reason enough to smother any attempt at industrialization.

But there is another reason why the nineteenth century is the wrong context in which to make a comparison between England and the Middle East. Being of a social nature, the Industrial Revolution had deep historical roots and antecedents; without these it would never have taken place.

The Agricultural Revolution

The Industrial Revolution in England wrought drastic change in the structure of the labor force. In traditional societies the overwhelming majority of members are engaged in agricultural pursuits; this situation was reversed during the Industrial Revolution. Most of the work force now found employment in industry, and only a small minority remained in agriculture. For this reversal to be feasible, those remaining on the land were required to produce sufficient food for the entire population. In fact, an agricultural revolution is a necessary precondition for an industrial revolution, and what we really have to ask ourselves here is why did England experience an agricultural revolution while the Middle East did not. The explanations suggested by certain scholars are unconvincing when seen from an Ottoman perspective. The Ottoman Middle East undoubtedly experienced some combination of all these factors. Our objective, however, is to find the unique factors that were present in England but absent in the Middle East.

Seventeenth-century England underwent a period of great political vicissitudes, which included the deposition and execution of a king, the restoration of the monarchy, and a great social revolution, the Glorious Revolution of 1688. From a social and agrarian viewpoint these upheavals brought about a dramatic rise in the political power and influence of the aristocratic class of landlords, which found expression in the second half of the seventeenth century in the enactment of several laws intended to finally and formally seal the landlords' ownership of their estates. Formerly, the peasants had retained rights that had been carried down since the medieval period. It is for this reason that some historians regard this period as the end of the medieval period in agriculture and agrarian relations.

At this time the landlords started to revolutionize the structure of English agriculture, and the period thus came to be known as the agricultural revolution. Briefly, these changes consisted of usurpation of the commons, that is, the village grazing areas (legally the common property of the villagers), which were tranformed into the landlords' private food-growing estates. The landlords also started to alter the agricultural process itself. The fallow period was eliminated, and in its stead new crops were grown that enriched the soil exhausted by the customary crops.[3] This caused a substantial rise in the productivity of a given piece of land. To cite one study that summarizes these changes:

> An agricultural revolution of unparalleled achievement took place before 1673. Its main components were the floating of water meadows in 1629–65 (these dates are very rough and concern the high point of the movement), the substitution of ley husbandry for permanent tillage or grass (1659–

1660), the introduction of new fallow crops and grasses (turnips, clover, sainfoin, 1650–73), marsh drainage (1590–1653), manning . . . and stock-breeding. These changes had greatly increased production of corn, fodder, meat and dairy products at lower costs.[4]

These improvements did not occur unaided or without planning. They were a product of conscious improvement, accompanied by a burst of agricultural literature. English landlords were by now pure capitalistic entrepreneurs in the field of agriculture.

No such development occurred in the Middle East. Whereas in England the vicissitudes of the seventeenth century led to the entrenchment of the aristocracy, nothing comparable took place in the Ottoman Empire, where the central government remained as strong and as antiaristocratic as ever, thus preventing a total transformation of the countryside as in England. The phenomenon of the *chiftlik* remained a scattered and sporadic one; the traditional village community remained extant and lively, a strong bulwark against land agglomeration on a massive scale. Here we hardly find the pattern of the enlightened landlord. Indeed, agriculture remained backward and traditional, intended mainly for subsistence purposes. The important question is why.

The answer should be sought not in issues of mentality, but in geographical factors and/or sociological arrangements and institutions. In fact, if we take a hard look at the Middle East, we will find that a revolution comparable to the English agricultural revolution did take place, and this revolution was a function of the introduction of cotton into nineteenth-century Egypt. In most other areas of the Middle East geographical reasons precluded such a development. Large areas of the region were arid or semiarid, and the introduction of highly sophisticated and intensive agriculture was, and still is, almost impossible. It is therefore unlikely that an English-style agricultural revolution could have taken place in Anatolia even if other preconditions had existed.

Some areas were clearly exceptional,such as the Bursa plain of western Anatolia, a region richly endowed with fertile soil and water. This area underwent a partial transformation to market-oriented agriculture. The *chiftliks* that sprang up produced substantial quantities of dairy produce for the Bursa market, but even here it appears that no substantial rise in the productivity level took place.

Egypt, however, was one region in which a true agricultural revolution took place, albeit a very different one from the English version. A comparison between England and Egypt provides the key to an understanding of the predicaments of the Middle East. In the English agricultural revolution vast capital investments were necessary, but these were modest in comparison to the massive investments poured into the railway system and other projects constructed in the nineteenth century. The difference clearly was not one of the availability of capital but rather of something more subtle.

A comparison of seventeenth-century England with the seventeenth-century Ottoman Empire reveals that one major and a few derivative factors present in the case of England were lacking in the Middle East. Consequently, I contend that the main reasons for the agricultural revolution in England were as follows: (1) the control wielded by England of vast foreign markets, due to the special quality of English wool; (2) the capitalistic approach to economic factors particular to the English aristocracy since its handling of the "wool revolution" of the late Middle Ages; and (3) the special institutional class structure that emerged in England in the wake of the late medieval depression. All three factors were equally essential for the revolution to take place.

Before analyzing these factors, I would like to briefly discuss the issue of taxation, which at first sight appears to be of primary importance but on further examination is less relevant from the Ottoman perspective. The crushing burden of taxation on the Ottoman peasantry is a familiar theme. E. L. Jones and S. J. Woolf attributed a crucial role in the agricultural revolution in England to the absence of taxation.[5] There is ample evidence that in the nineteenth and twentieth centuries the burden of taxation on the peasantry in the Middle East was eased, yet this development did not result in an industrial or agricultural revolution. Instead, the higher standard of living encouraged the peasants to have larger families. Consequently, the additional income was largely absorbed by growing population pressure. This, however, did not happen in England, and again the crucial question is why not.

The Role of Wool

All the sources agreed that beginning in the late medieval period England started to receive enormous benefits from the exceptional quality of its wool, which was prized throughout Europe.[6] English wool, like Jaffa oranges and Brazilian coffee, was a unique natural resource. However, unlike coffee or oranges, wool was the true basis of the premodern economy. Initially, the effect of wool on the economy was limited. The desperate economic straits of the English kings in the late Middle Ages turned wool into an important historical factor. It was realized at this time that it would be easier to impose taxes on wool than on the areas subject to the rule of the large landowners. Further, if wool were exported in a finished form it would mean greater revenue. Consequently, in the fourteenth century Kings Edward II and Edward III imposed a strict ban on the export of raw wool, which created a demand for English woolen products. This policy was decisive in the foundation of the English textile industry.[7]

By way of comparison, an examination of the situation in the early Ottoman Empire reveals a striking contrast. Ottoman policy did not encourage or favor local industry; it treated export and import alike. In the sixteenth century the Ottomans lavishly distributed trade privileges among the eager Europeans and were entirely oblivious to the long-lasting, disastrous consequences of such a policy.[8] One explanation for this bewildering behavior was that the English kings (unlike the sultans) traditionally enjoyed limited power to impose taxation as they saw fit, while the Ottoman sultans did not have to encourage foreign trade in order to gain access to revenue. For the English kings, however, it was the only way out of their economic straits.

Although the export of wool underwent many fluctuations in the sixteenth and seventeenth centuries, it nevertheless remained extremely important. Thus, C. Hill remarked, "Between 1530 and 1640, income from sheep-farming rose from four-and-a-half to seven times in East Anglia. The biggest profits seem to have been made by capitalist farmers, men who leased land in order to produce for the market, including the rapidly expanding export market."[9] Indeed, exports were growing by leaps and bounds and overcoming all sorts of temporary setbacks.[10]

By the end of the seventeenth century 40 percent of the English population lived in the cities, and the majority was engaged in industrial pursuits.[11] Hence, it is not surprising that as the urban population increased, the rise in agricultural prices topped those for industry. The impact of the wool industry was not confined to the urban population. The role played by rural industries is a topic that in recent years has come to be considered vitally important in the context of the Industrial Revolution. All the sources on the history of England emphasized the unusually important position of rural textile industries long before the Industrial Revolution. For our purposes it is sufficient to quote Lawrence Stone's words: "In few [countries other than England] had there developed such extensive rural industries, as in areas such as Gloucestershire, where a substantial proportion of the work force was engaged, full or part time in industrial and distributive trades."[12]

Only a few of the studies on this topic have sought to explain this fact. It may be that scholars immersed in English economic history viewed this as a natural process. In contrast, in the Ottoman Middle East there were few rural industries. In five hundred villager estates in western Anatolia in the seventeenth century there were few instances of artisan activity. Therefore, the prevalence of rural industry, or protoindustry (as it is currently called), in preindustrial England requires an explanation, and the explanation is that the tremendous world demand for wool attracted many villagers away from agricultural pursuits.[13]

The almost limitless foreign demand for English textiles in the sixteenth and seventeenth centuries fulfilled two major functions. It absorbed the vast number of people evicted from the countryside, and it attracted people who had remained on the land away from agriculture. These circumstances exerted strong pressure to increase agricultural efficiency. Yet those who left agriculture possessed the income to pay food prices, even higher prices. Agriculture was forced to make do with less workers but had to produce as much or even more. The need for greater productivity may be the key factor in the agricultural revolution. Thus, it was neither the spirit of capitalism nor unusual genius that provided the impetus toward agricultural improvement. It is highly likely that had there been this rare combination of circumstances in seventeenth-century Egypt, an agricultural revolution would have taken place there, too, despite Egypt's "oriental" nature and unfavorable political regime or burdensome taxation. Instead of opening new investment channels, the increase in real income of the peasants of Ottoman Egypt in the nineteenth century was counterbalanced by an increase in population. There was no incentive to change traditional methods.

The modern history of Egypt provides prima facie evidence for the feasibility of this theory.[14] Those acquainted with historical and travel literature on Syria and Palestine are familiar with the descriptions of a totally primitive agriculture. However, the situation in Egypt was completely different. Egyptian agriculture was agronomically far from backward; land productivity ranked very high when compared with other countries in the world. Egypt's malaise was not low productivity per unit of land or the Middle Eastern "mentality," for nineteenth-century Egypt experienced an agricultural revolution in many respects quite comparable to that experienced by seventeenth-century England.

Egypt had an excellent starting point.[15] The Nile inundates large areas of land every year, carrying with it mineral-rich silt land that serves as an excellent natural fertilizer. On this basis, during successive Egyptian governments in the nineteenth century a veritable revolution took place. A drastic and costly transformation from traditional basin irrigation to perennial irrigation was effected. Before the nineteenth century water would inundate the land and be "captured" by the peasants by means of small dykes at the fields' edges (hence the term basin). After the land received a sufficient quantity of water, the remainder would be drained back into the Nile via a great number of canals that connected the fields with the river. Early in the nineteenth century it was realized that cotton grown in Egypt possessed unusual qualities, almost unrivaled (especially for its length) by any other country in the world. It was a natural resource, much like English wool, whose quality could never be fully equalled elsewhere. This realization came exactly when the Industrial Revolution was about to terminate the "golden age" of wool and start the reign of cotton as the chief source of the world's clothing. But in order to grow cotton on a massive scale, watering was needed at a time when the Nile was low. Therefore, it was necessary to drastically raise the permanent level of the Nile waters. This was accomplished, beginning in the 1820s, by the erection of several dikes and dams along the length of the river. In this way the water level was raised to reach the level of the canals leading water to the fields. Concurrently, there was additional canal digging, which added vast new lands to the Egyptian agriculture.

The change effected in the system of irrigation enabled the Egyptian peasantry to grow a greater number of crops annually. Thus, scientific crop rotation was introduced, based on cotton. Cotton became the "growth engine"[16] of nineteenth-century Egypt and may be considered the key reason for the revolutionary changes. Another important crop introduced in this period was maize, which was the major grain consumed by the nineteenth-century Egyptian population. In this way Egypt achieved agricultural success of worldwide proportions. Land under cultivation increased, but the land that produced several crops a year area grew even further and reached one-and-one-half times the cultivated land by 1917.[17] The Egyptians successfully executed the main organizational change that characterized the English agricultural revolution, namely, elimination of the fallow.

However, Egypt still remained an extremely poor country, with characteristics typical of underdeveloped countries that had not experienced an agricultural revolution. Most of the population continued to be engaged in agriculture at the subsistence level, although net income did increase somewhat during the century. On the other hand, all efforts at industrialization failed, and with the 1838 free-trade agreement between the Ottoman Empire and England any further possibilities were doomed in advance.

It is important to note the significant difference between wool and cotton. Wool was a labor-saving crop, while cotton was extremely labor intensive. The growth of cotton meant keeping the majority of the Egyptian population on the land, thereby inhibiting the rise of modern industry. This did not mean that cotton was a poor agricultural choice; it was probably the best possible option. It was a tragedy for Egypt that its best resource was cotton, much as it was England's good fortune that its best resource was wool. Today there are labor-saving devices in cotton agriculture, but labor-saving devices cause the equally agonizing dilemma of unemployment for a labor force freed from agriculture. In today's competitive world market it is almost impossible to imagine what a country like Egypt could do to appreciably augment its export of industrial commodities. The situation is exacerbated because today there are masses who need to be fed. Mehmet Ali in 1820 did not have this problem and was probably in a much more promising position to launch Egypt into industrialization. Indeed, it seems that Mehmet Ali is judged too harshly. Were it not for the 1838 free-trade agreement, Egypt could have succeeded, at least partially, in its industrialization drive.[18]

The dynamics of the wool industry imparted to the English aristocracy a capitalistic approach to economic life that no other rural elite in the world possessed. However, other elites would have reacted similarly had they been confronted with such a golden opportunity. This capitalistic approach later exerted a strong influence on the entire gamut of this elite's economic activities.

The foregoing logic may be disputed by some, but it was demonstrated quite clearly in the following statement made by Hill, which incidentally also served to show the deep, far-reaching impact wool had on English history in general.

> Thanks to the early development of sheep-farming in England, wool had become a useful source of taxes. Medieval kings therefore did nothing to discourage its production, and gradually became more and more dependent, in the absence of an army, on Parliament which voted taxes, and on the gentry whom the Commons represented and who assessed and collected the taxes. The fact that the Lord Chancellor sits on the woolsack symbolizes the close connection between wool-growing and the survival of Parliament in England. *Wool also helps to explain the Whiggish predilection of the English landed classes, very early shown, for sending their younger sons into trade.*[19]

One can gain certain insights from Robert Brenner's recent suggested revision of the modernization process of England.[20] Brenner's starting point was the situation prevailing in Europe in the Middle Ages, where feudal lords effectively controlled the land while subjugated serfs worked it. Legally the lords may have been the owners of the estates, but this ownership was far from complete. The peasants enjoyed various customary legal rights that tied the hands of the lords in many ways. Brenner began his discussion with the final crisis that brought an end to this agrarian regime—the demographic catastrophes of the fourteenth century, particularly the Black Death of 1348. The period following this was characterized by a great scarcity of labor. Feudal landlords were struggling desperately to maintain the traditional position of their peasants. The commutation of feudal obligations that followed was a natural consequence of the labor scarcity. In the words of Slicher Van Bath, "The lord of the manor was forced to offer good conditions or see all his villains vanish."[21] But Brenner claimed this was not an inevitable outcome of the labor scarcity. In Eastern Europe the lords faced almost the same situation, but their response was to further tighten their grip on the serfs by all possible means, including brute force. The different consequences of the struggle in these two areas were due to different outcomes of class struggle. In England the lords simply lost the battle: "By 1400 it was clear that the landlords' offensive had failed; revolt and flight which continued throughout the fifteenth century, led to the end of serfdom."[22] Brenner contended that the chief reason for these differential results was the social structure of the village. In the West the village community was much stronger and could face the demands of the lords more resolutely.

Thus, in England all the efforts to maintain serfdom failed, and eventually the status of the peasants rose considerably. They were not very far from the ultimate takeover of the land, which would have turned England into a land of peasant smallholders. However, this far-reaching development never materialized. In the second half of the sixteenth century England entered a period of inflation that continued until the middle of the next century. The landlords were hard hit economically, and there was little they could do under the circumstances. Due to the relatively strong position achieved by the peasants in the preceding period, the landlords could hardly press them for more revenue. The only course of action open to them was to take advantage of a loophole in the existing law that entitled them to charge entry fines as they saw fit. In this way they could raise rents whenever the land changed hands, which led to a massive eviction of peasants holding traditional tenure. This claim was corroborated by other studies. Thus, Hill spoke about the rapid period of inflation between 1530 and 1640, a period that threatened to wreak havoc with the revenue of those lords whose agrarian arrangements with their peasants were of long duration.

There is no question that in China or Ottoman Egypt landlords would have tightened their grip on their peasants in an attempt to make good their losses. Not so in seventeenth-century England, where this simple device seems to have been blocked for good. "As fixed rents and dues were dwindling, it was necessary to get rid of freeholders and copyholders, and to convert long to short leases. Increasing entry fines and racking rents seemed a revolutionary breach with custom: but it was the only means by which landowners could keep pace with rising prices."[23] In other words, the only way for the English landlords to cope with inflation was to clear the countryside of the traditional peasantry and to establish new institutions to make agriculture more profitable. Under these circumstances it is not surprising that they hit upon the capitalist solution. They already had shown a tendency in this direction.

The Scientific Revolution

It has been observed that a prior scientific revolution was a necessary, although by no means sufficient, precondition for the Industrial Revolution in Europe. In the course of this revolution, which was actively underway by the seventeenth century, patents were issued for a large number of inventions, such as measurement tools, navigational devices, barometers, microscopes, telescopes, and the like.[24] Without these implements the major inventions of the Industrial Revolution would not have been possible, and yet their invention was entirely unconnected with the short-term causes often proffered for the Industrial Revolution. Rather, these inventions were related to deeper socioeconomic (and possibly political) factors.

C. N. Cipolla dwelled at length on two fields of technological development in which Europe outdid other civilizations—including the Ottoman
Empire—with far-reaching consequences: artillery and sailing ships.[25] A
technological gap in artillery between the Ottoman Empire and Europe did
begin in the sixteenth century. Official efforts to bridge this gap were half-
hearted and futile. The Turks' initial advantage over the Byzantine and European armies was their light cavalry, which, however, could not overcome
walled cities. It was apparently for this reason that the Ottomans were
among the first to introduce into their army huge guns built especially for
siege purposes. They used this weapon with great dexterity, particularly in
the conquest of Constantinople in 1453. However, huge guns were totally
ineffectual in field battles. In the sixteenth century a new type of gun, the
light gun, which was especially adapted for open field battles, was developed for various European armies. The failure of the Ottomans to adopt
this technological innovation led to their disastrous defeats in the seventeenth and eighteenth centuries. Were the Ottomans more receptive in the
fifteenth century to technological innovations than they were in the sixteenth? Or was the larger, immobile gun more suited to their simpler and
less sophisticated technological capabilities? I favor the second explanation,
but at the present state of knowledge this remains conjecture.

The same was true in the case of Europe's mastery of the use of ocean-
going sailing ships.[26] Both the Ottomans and the Italians established their
navies in the period when the galley reigned supreme. However, in the
sixteenth century the Dutch, English, and Portuguese developed the big,
gun-carrying sailing ship, after which the galley rapidly became obsolete.
However, the Ottomans, like the Italians, could never make the changes
necessary to ensure their survival.

Clearly, societies in various non-European civilizations were structured
differently from those in Europe and found it extremely difficult to adapt
themselves to new conditions. In the case of China we see this quite lucidly;
and there appears to be a basic similarity in the Ottoman case, although to
date there is no hard evidence to support this assumption. Thus, Cipolla
dwelled on the Chinese attitude to imported European technology and cited
the opinion of a knowledgeable observer who sent home the following rec-
ommendation as to what should be exported to China. "One should bring
to Peking especially those playthings that European boys use to amuse themselves. Such objects will be received here with much greater interest than
scientific instruments or *objets d'art*. . . . When Chinese people buy at great
expense some mechanical pieces in Canton, they do it not in order to use
them for the purpose for which they were constructed but rather to use
them as toys and amuse themselves."[27]

What was the origin of the difference between European society on the one hand and the Ottoman Empire and China on the other? It is doubtful whether we possess at present the final solution to this enigma, but Cipolla's analysis seemed to contain at least part of it. The explanation is to be sought in the difference in the sociological structure of the city in both areas. The postmedieval towns in Europe sprang up as refuges from the prevailing social and political regimes. Society in postmedieval towns was established by merchants and artisans and very largely run by them; they certainly constituted the most vigorous and dynamic classes in the towns.[28] In contradistinction, for example, the Chinese invented the printing press, and the Ottoman Empire knew about it, but neither found it unusually attractive; in the Ottoman case it was neglected until the beginning of the eighteenth century. In contrast, European civilization, where utilitarian and practical ideas (the ideas of the merchants and artisans) were pervasive, made skillful use of the printing press, thereby significantly lowering the rate of illiteracy in Europe. While in the medieval and postmedieval European city the merchants and artisans were the leading groups, this was not the case in China or the Ottoman Empire. In China the Mandarins headed the social pyramid, and they were emphatically uninterested in matters of technology; the social gap between them and the artisans was vast and unbridgeable. In the case of Ottoman society the situation was more complicated, for there was no evidence of a negative attitude toward artisanship. I doubt whether this was as extreme as in China, but in the Ottoman city, too, artisans and merchants were not at the top of the social pyramid. This position was held by the *ulema,* the scholars of religion.

David Landes discussed the same topic and arrived at the same conclusions by way of other examples.[29] Both he and Cipolla believed that a passionate interest in science and technology was a powerful and autonomous factor in bringing about the age of modern industry. Landes studied the process of invention of the marine chronometer, a vital instrument for fixing longitude at sea. The idea of such an instrument was contemplated for about two hundred years, until it was finally invented by the Englishman John Harrison in 1759. Spain, which was the pioneer of oceanic navigation, was also the first to offer an extremely generous prize for the chronometer's invention but was forced to abandon such efforts because the social ambience in the country was not conducive to technical inventions:

> Spain, for all its priority in oceanic navigation, was in no position to experiment and invent. . . . It lacked the craftsmen because intelligence and skill gravitated in Spain to other, more honorific occupations. It lacked a base of interest and experience in time-measurement, which was far more important to merchants and manufacturers (as in England) than to conquistadores, encomenderos and caballeros.[30]

In England, however, the atmosphere was right. Why? Landes' query remains unresolved, and he admitted he had no conclusive answer. Yet he nevertheless advanced some fruitful ideas that complemented Cipolla's explanation. One refers to the fragmentation in the political structure of the medieval state and the alliances into which rulers had to enter with autonomous cities. A second important idea is the early recognition of the sacredness of the right to own property in the medieval city, a right that grew inevitably out of the city's autonomy. This atmosphere would indeed have been conducive to innovation.[31] A third idea involves the Catholic Church. The monastic orders constituted closely knit communities, which were highly productive and efficient economically.[32] The reason for such an attitude is ultimately to be sought in the autonomous realm of attitudes, "the choice of activism over contemplative life."[33]

The Industrial Revolution in England was in effect a product of the two trends surveyed above—the constant expansion of the traditional textile industries and the invention and adaptation of machines that facilitated the transformation of the old industry.[34] An extremely developed protoindustry, therefore, was a precondition for generating an industrial revolution.[35] In this context it is also pertinent to mention that C. Tilly and R. Tilly suggested that one of the greatest differences between the industrialization of Western Europe and the developing countries of today stemmed from the earlier "protoindustrialization of the European countryside."[36] This was largely because rural industry helped change the traditional sociodemographic structure of European societies. Youths could now marry earlier and establish independent families, for they possessed independent sources of income and were no longer dependent on family estates.[37] (The role of traditional kinship situations in modernization and its predicaments is an exceptionally promising subject of research in the context of the modern Middle East.) There were additional factors that gave rise to the differences between England and the Ottoman Empire in the context of the Industrial Revolution, such as the role of Protestantism (and in England the equivalent role of Puritanism). However, the chain of developments connected with wool was the key factor that accounted for England's early industrialization.

The Absence of Peasant Revolution

A major feature of the transition of the Middle East into the twentieth century was the region's peaceful nature. In contrast to other great bureaucratic-agrarian empires, notably Russia and China, the Ottoman did not experience anything resembling a peasant revolution. There was evidence, however, of unrest. G. Baer, in a relevant study, listed a number of rebellions in the last two hundred years, with a conspicuously larger number in Egypt than in the Fertile Crescent.[38] Given the background of peasant rebellions in

Russia, for example, the phenomenon was extremely limited in the Middle East. For the Fertile Crescent, Baer mentioned the following instances of peasant revolt:

1. The revolt in Palestine against the Egyptian occupation (1834)
2. Druze revolts in the Hauran (1837, 1877–1879, 1895–1896)
3. The Lebanese revolt against the Egyptians (1840)
4. The Kisrawan rebellion of 1858–1861
5. The Arab revolt in Palestine (1936–1939)[39]

There were no known cases of revolt among the Syrian peasantry. In Palestine there were only two major cases of rebellion. To complete the picture I investigated the relevant literature on Anatolia (mainly Uluçay's books on Western Anatolia).[40] Surprisingly, among the hundreds of cases recorded there was not one instance of peasant rebellion. Rather, in accordance with tradition the villager's role was that of the victim. Indeed, most recorded acts of lawbreaking were committed against the villages. Here it is important to note that the great social upheavals in late sixteenth- and early seventeenth-century Anatolia (known as the Jelali revolts) were not peasant revolts.[41] It might be claimed that some of the rioters were victims of the desperate situation in their villages, but this would be forcing the evidence. Villages as such did not rise up. Moreover, there was sufficient evidence to support the claim that peasant rebellions in Anatolia were extremely feeble and ineffectual. Peasant uprisings in Russian history provide a significant enough contrast to make this point quite clearly. "Between the end of the Pugachev rebellion (1775) and the end of the eighteenth century there were some 300 outbreaks in 32 provinces, and there was never a time when the peasantry was completely quiescent. Between 1826 and 1867, there were 1186 peasant uprisings, showing a steady increase with every five-year period."[42]

It is not merely the small number of peasant revolts, which is so glaringly evident in the case of the Middle East, that is significant but it is also their nature that is important. Many revolts and certainly the bigger ones were not even remotely agrarian by nature. Baer himself noted this fact when he said that not until the 1950s did peasant revolts in this area assume a really agrarian character.[43] Some great social revolutions did start out as (or remained throughout) a struggle for national independence (the Chinese revolution was a case in point), but in the Palestine revolts of 1834 and of 1936 the struggle for independence was and remained the sole issue at stake. In the known records of these uprisings, no social-agrarian motif has ever appeared.

This paucity of peasant rebellions was characteristic of the Middle Eastern section of the Ottoman Empire, but not of the Balkans. There the very opposite was the case. Balkan society after the sixteenth century was in fact aptly described as a powder keg.[44] Indeed, revolts by peasants were frequent enough for the phenomenon to be designated as endemic. The classic rebels against the Ottomans, the *haiduks*, were recently publicized in a study by Eric Hobsbawm, who made of them the quintessential bandit. He called them "social bandits," the lawbreakers who rebelled against the established order.[45]

> Neither royal nor signorial, these free *haiduks* were robbers by trade, enemies of the Turks and popular avengers by social role, primitive movements of guerrilla resistance and liberation. As such they appear in the fifteenth century, possibly first in Bosnia and Herzegovina, but later all over the Balkans and Hungary, most notably in Bulgaria, where a "*haidot*" chieftain is recorded as early as 1454. These are the men whose name I have chosen to typify the highest form of primitive banditry, the one which comes closest to being a permanent and conscious focus of peasant insurrection. Such *haiduks* existed not only in south-eastern Europe, but under other names in various other parts of the world, e.g., Indonesia and, most notably, Imperial China. For obvious reasons they were most common among peoples oppressed by conquerors of foreign language or religion, but not only there.[46]

For Hobsbawm the basis of the *haiduk* phenomenon was fundamentally political: "The definition of the *haiduk* hero is fundamentally political. In the Balkans he was a *national* bandit, according to certain traditional rules, i.e. a defender or avenger of Christians against Turks."[47] In Anatolia and the Fertile Crescent Ottoman rule was not perceived as foreign rule, and it is therefore small wonder that the term *haiduk* and the institution behind it were entirely absent.

We are now in a position to discover why there was no agrarian revolution in the Middle East. Theda Skocpol assumed that any great agrarian bureaucracy was sensitive to such revolts.[48] Moore went one step further and attempted to examine the exact conditions under which such revolts occurred. He suggested first that societies characterized by diffuse, weak centers, such as Indian society, were not sensitive to peasant revolts. On the other hand, those with strong centers, such as China and Russia, were sensitive to peasant uprisings throughout their history. He offered an interesting reason for such a revolution: "Turning to the process of modernization itself, we notice . . . that the success or failure of the upper class in taking up commercial agriculture has a tremendous influence on the political outcome. Where the landed upper class has turned to production for the market in a way that enables commercial influences to permeate rural life, peasant revolutions have become weak affairs."[49] There is no doubt that the examples he has in mind were England on the one hand and Russia and China on the other. "The main areas where peasant revolutions have in modern times had the greatest importance, China and Russia, were alike in the fact that the landed upper classes by and large did not make a successful transition to the world of commerce and industry and did not destroy the prevailing social organization among the peasants."[50]

The Ottoman case was certainly one with an extremely strong center (even in the eighteenth century), where the landed upper class made no serious attempt at a transition to commercial agriculture in the English style. Yet no peasant revolution took place. We might perhaps ask whether the Ottoman Empire averted agrarian revolution for the same reason that India did. In India the caste system worked as a shock absorber by giving a place in the community, modest although it might have been, to the most wretched landless peasant. No such explanation is warranted in the case of the Middle East. Later in this chapter I devote some attention to the Middle Eastern village community. My conclusion is that the village community discouraged rebelliousness to some extent, but the major reason for the failure of a peasant revolution has to be sought elsewhere.

In the final analysis, it seems that the one great difference between the social structure of the Ottoman Empire and the other great agrarian states was that in the Ottoman Empire a crystallized, landed upper class did not emerge. It was in all likelihood this difference that was eventually to prevent a peasant revolution. More specifically, a good measure of the explanation lies in the de facto full ownership of the land by small peasants. A partial confirmation of this hypothesis is to be had from the Kisrawan peasant revolt of 1858–1861, aptly described as the only true agrarian revolt in the modern history of the Middle East.[51] The circumstances that led to the revolt were unusual. At the time, Lebanon was a feudal regime, reminiscent of medieval Europe. The Kisrawan uprising began as a rebellion against illegal taxes levied by the landlords—a widespread stimulus to peasant revolt in this area. However, there rapidly developed a stalemate in relations between the two sides, which were unwilling or unable to reach a rapprochement.[52] As the two sides became increasingly entrenched, the peasants eventually seized the landlords' properties. They went one step farther and established a "republic," which held until 1861. With the eradication of anarchy in Lebanon and the restoration of public order, the feudal regime was officially abolished in the constitution adopted in 1861. In addition, although the confiscated lands were supposed to revert to their former owners, the peasants actually managed to retain them.[53] We see, then, that total revolution took place only where there was total subjugation of peasants to large landowners, even when the immediate source of grievance was taxation. In descriptions of serious peasant uprisings (for example, in Russia) we often find that the specific targets of violence were the landlords and their properties, rather than the representatives of the state. In the case of the Russian Revolution of 1905, "the predominant form of the movement was the attack on the landowner's estate. This often involved the destruction of the manor house and outbuildings, to ensure the 'master' would never return, and the seizure of the estate lands and property by the peasants."[54]

We may pause to ponder the difference between tax appropriation and full-fledged landlord-serf relations. It is possible that there is more than a grain of truth in the suggestion that there is an "ownership" instinct, which, when unfulfilled, may cause deep-seated bitterness. I am, however, more inclined to the following explanation. Rebellion against a tax collector strikes at the individual, not the system; before long the central government is likely to send another tax collector. Different is the case of a revolt aimed specifically against landowners. This implies taking over their properties, evicting them, and sometimes killing them. Such a revolt aims naturally at the very heart of the entire social system and, if widespread, constitutes total revolution.

It would seem, therefore, that peasant revolutions tend to take place in those bureaucratic empires that are based on an agrarian regime in which a large proportion of the land is legally and effectively owned by large landlords. An examination of the evidence in the case of imperial China and czarist Russia reveals that this was indeed the case. A short comparative analysis of these two examples also shows that there were other factors besides the existence of large landlords that fomented opposition in these two empires. To complicate the issue, some of these factors also were missing in the case of the Ottoman Empire.

In the few centuries before the communist revolution, China had no feudal regime.[55] Ownership of the land was more or less equally divided among the small peasants and the large landlords, the latter leasing their lands to tenants, whom they could evict at will. Indeed, most large estates would hardly be considered such in European or Russian terms. The owners of these estates were also the wielders of political clout in the Chinese countryside.

The Chinese peasant who owned no land owed his landlord not only the land tax and other extortions (like the traditional Middle Eastern peasant), but he also had to pay rent, which constituted a major problem. Bianco said that before World War II rent averaged 45 percent of the produce. Students of the Middle East probably consider the taxation mechanism under the Ottomans excessively punitive. It appears, however, that the Chinese had devised more extreme steps, such as the levying of taxes years and even decades before they fell due.[56]

Demographic pressure, which sent rents soaring, aggravated the land problem in China. This pressure was the outcome of enormous population growth in the two centuries preceding the revolution. The most cautious estimate is that between 1651 and 1851 the Chinese population tripled. In the eighteenth century alone, the population doubled in less than one hundred years. Consequently, by the beginning of the twentieth century the land area available to a peasant family was extremely small. Some calculations quoted a figure of 3.3 acres per family. If this is a general average for China, it follows that a large proportion of the peasantry had much less to sustain themselves. Indeed, Bianco found it appropriate to cite one village study carried out around 1940, which concluded that the average family in the village had the use of slightly less than 1 acre.[57]

Popular peasant revolts were rife in Chinese history. Scholars have concluded that there was a direct continuity between the revolts and the great Chinese revolution. It is evident, therefore, that the origins of this final revolution were in past tensions and grievances. According to Bianco, there were many reasons for the plight of the Chinese village. In assessing the crucial cause for the revolution he named the specific ownership problem.

> Objective conditions, i.e. economic and demographic conditions, were in themselves sufficient to make the distress of the vast majority inevitable. But because human actions arouse more indignation, they are more useful in inciting peasant revolt; the excess comfort of a privileged few, their arbitrary and oppressive conduct, seem less bearable than a general scarcity of resources. That is why, in discussing the social causes of the Chinese Revolution, I have chosen to give relatively more extensive treatment to the exploitation of man by man.[58]

The roots of modern Russia lie in the reforms of Peter the Great (1689–1725), which represented an important comparative case for center and periphery relations in the Ottoman Empire.[59] Peter's reforms were not the first in Russian history, but they were the most significant. Militarily, his reign was marked by many foreign wars, a number of which were against the Ottoman Empire, but most of them were fought against Sweden. In 1709, Peter vanquished the Swedish army at Poltava, thereby ending a constant threat to his state and gaining secure access to the Baltic Sea. Concomitantly, Peter made strenuous efforts to modernize his country and transform it from one of the most backward into one of the most powerful states on the Continent. The reforms he introduced were extensive and wide-ranging; he built a large fleet, ports, a new capital city within a marshy area, factories, mines, canals, and bridges. In assessing this enormous effort, Gerschenkron said that "the very magnitude of the effort, its vigor, amplitude, and persistence endow the Petrine reign with unique features. Nowhere else in the mercantilistic world do we encounter a comparable case of a great spurt compressed within such a short period. . . . Nowhere else was the State to any comparable extent the demiurge of economic development. Nowhere else was it so strongly dominated by the interests of the State."[60]

To finance these enormous expenditures, Peter imposed excessively high taxes.[61] Gerschenkron calculated that by the second decade of Peter the Great's reign the tax on agricultural produce raised by the peasants amounted to about 64 percent, "a most shocking result."[62] The heavy tax levied by the czar was only one example of his complete disregard for human considerations. His projects cost the lives of hundreds of thousands of forced laborers. They were restrained for life to fortresslike institutions, under the guard of army units.

We see, then, that the reform movement in Russia was immeasurably more intensive and powerful than the various reform efforts in Ottoman history before or during the nineteenth century. The reason for this was twofold. First, Russia's rise invoked far greater difficulties (in terms of foreign adversaries) than did the Ottoman Empire's. Consequently, in order for the Russian state to expand it had to have a far greater measure of central power, and this was achieved at the expense of the periphery. Second, in contradistinction to the Ottoman Empire, Russia was, in the final analysis, an integral part of European civilization, and as such regarded the Western state as a model to be emulated at all costs.

Russia was familiar with a particular version of the feudal regime—if it could be called feudalism at all. For several centuries preceding the revolution the power of the state was almost absolute, and the aristocracy, whose power was real in medieval Russia, enjoyed only marginal influence on the real management of state affairs. Until the end of the sixteenth century the Russian peasant was free as far as property and mobility were concerned. A decree in 1649 changed all that. A large number of peasants in Russia became enslaved to landlords and were forbidden to leave their land. In turn, the landlords were compelled to serve the interests of the central government. Their loss of freedom never ceased to be a source of bitterness and rebelliousness on the part of the Russian peasant.[63] If the reigns preceding Peter the Great were relatively calm, this changed completely on his accession. Serfdom became an extremely onerous institution.

In the generations that followed Peter's reign, external pressure on Russia subsided, and consequently, in 1762 the landed gentry was released from its service obligations. Hence, the basis for serfdom became ever more tenuous and the agrarian problem explosive. The peasants never came to terms with their downgrading from freeholders paying taxes to the central government to serfs belonging to landlords. After 1762, the peasants were even less accepting of the situation.[64] One outcome of this pervasive discontent was the great Pugachev rebellion of 1773–1775, which threatened to topple the entire regime. The central Russian government came to realize the necessity of finding social support within Russian society and inevitably found such a base in the landed aristocracy. Serfdom thus became even more widespread, with new czars bequeathing thousands of serfs to various aristocrats. Gerschenkron emphasized the fact that the term "serf" was an understatement. "It must be noted that the term serfdom to characterize the peasant's condition in Russia, although conventional, is quite misapplied. With the strong centralized government guarding the rights of the landowners serfdom had long degenerated into outright slavery."[65]

In 1861, serfdom was officially abolished, primarily to forestall the dire consequences that could result from the mounting pressure from the peasantry. However, the process was put into effect in a way that increased peasant grievances rather than alleviated them. For example, the freed peasant would have to pay dearly for the land he acquired. For millions this meant, in effect, continued bondage.[66] Consequently, the agrarian problem in late czarist Russia was as severe as ever.

It should nevertheless be emphasized that the situation in Russia was complicated by the fact that there were other sources of total opposition to the regime, such as religious opposition, which were important causes of the Bolshevik Revolution. The rift between the official Russian church and the Old Believers that appeared in 1666 was more bitter and agonizing than the conflict between the official and popular religions—an open wound in Russian society for centuries.

An important role in the origins of the Russian Revolution was no doubt played by the intellectuals, a group originating in the middle classes and largely marginal to traditional Russian society. The basic and most important flag hoisted by this group was on behalf of the peasants, which the intellectuals adopted as their own. As Isaiah Berlin put it:

> The cause of the oppressed was still at that date overwhelmingly that of the agricultural workers, who formed the lowest stratum of the population, the vast majority being serfs in state or private possession. The populists looked upon them as martyrs whose grievances they were determined to avenge and remedy. . . . The central populist goals were social justice and social equality. Most of them were convinced . . . that the essence of a just and equal society existed already in the Russian peasant commune—the *obshchina*, organized in the form of a collective unit called the *mir*.[67]

The role played by the peasant community in the Russian Revolution is particularly interesting when compared with that played by their counterparts in the Middle East. Theda Skocpol has convincingly analyzed the role of the commune in events leading to the Russian revolution and during the revolution itself. The village commune always existed in Russia, but its position was immensely strengthened in the wake of the peasant emancipation of 1861.[68] The *mir*, or village assembly of all household heads, was placed on a legal footing and given a crucial administrative role in the management of all village affairs.[69] The nature of the traditional village commune in Russia was that of a closed religious congregation; now this body became even stronger in daily life. It became an organization especially suited to peasant rebellion. Indeed, in both 1905 and 1917, peasant participation in the revolution was "most violent and radical" in those areas where the landlords were harshest on the peasants and where the repartitional peasant commune prevailed. In fact, "the organizational basis of the peasant revolution was, so to speak, 'ready-made' in the villages."[70]

In the case of the Middle East, there was no real agrarian problem on the Ottoman scene until 1858, when the Ottoman land law was inaugurated. Large-estate formation began in earnest, but even so, several factors were at work that obviated social bitterness. First, several decades were to elapse until the accumulation of land reached serious proportions. Second, and most important psychologically, it seems to have taken an extended period of harsh agrarian conditions to bring society to the brink of social revolution. In Russia and China it took several centuries. In addition, there were specific factors that prevented social unrest from surfacing. Skocpol has shown that for rebelliousness to come to the fore the peasants had to have tactical space or autonomy. Nineteenth-century Egypt does not seem to have been ripe for revolt in this respect. The most important agrarian development there was connected, as we have seen, with the institution of *izba*, the large estate. It was precisely in such estates that peasant autonomy was at its minimum because peasants were always under the close surveillance of either the landlord or his agent. Richards has shown that in early twentieth-century Egypt peasant unrest remained individual, but it was nevertheless rife and specifically agrarian in nature. Thus, an Egyptian landlord related the following to Russel Pasha, Egypt's chief of police, in a chance discussion: "You don't really think that a landlord in the districts could sit on the veranda after dinner, with a bright light over his head, do you, and not get shot?"[71]

The classic example of peasant rebelliousness being blocked by lack of tactical autonomy in the twentieth-century Middle East was the case of Iraq. I have shown that in Iraq the political and social framework of the tribe remained viable and powerful, notwithstanding that the socioeconomic structure was entirely transformed into brutal landlord/serf relations. The result was a clear break between class structure and the ideological perception of the society. "The cultural model is described by the tribesmen themselves as an equalitarian tribal organization, with the shaykh as equal among equals; the reality is a stratified tribal organization with the shaykh and his family in a clearly superior position vis-à-vis the remainder of the tribe."[72] Although the shaykhs played a role in this repressive class system, they still enjoyed a certain measure of legitimacy. Even when their legitimacy was weakened, the shaykhs did live amid their people, and their control was tight and not easily avoidable. Such conditions were not conducive to peasant-tribe rebellion.

The available evidence indicates that during the middle of the twentieth century a real shift in the course of agrarian relations in several Middle Eastern countries occurred. I have presented evidence on this subject (in relation to Egypt) in the introduction to this book; the same trend was apparent in contemporary Iraq. Batatu has shown that in the 1950s there was an unprecedented increase in the number of rural revolts. The first known case of popular peasant revolt of an agrarian nature took place as late as 1947 in the village of Arbat in northern Iraq. In the nineteenth century the villagers were small, independent landlords. During the course of the twentieth century they were subject to the total and degrading control of a shaykhly family that imposed an extremely heavy burden of taxation. In November 1947, the peasants rebelled and declined to comply with the demands of the shaykh's overseers. After a protracted conflict and much violence, the matter ended with a compromise.[73]

One should not be misled, however, by the fact that this was the only village rebellion in the period. In Iraq most peasants belonged to tribes, and it was the multiplicity of such revolts that should be viewed as ominous. At the end of 1952 and the beginning of 1953, two agrarian revolts, the result of "deep-seated agrarian discontent," took place in Amara and Arbil. In one case the immediate cause was the government's decision to alienate the shaykh from the traditional domain of the tribe. The revolts mainly consisted of a refusal to pay taxes and the expulsion of the landlord's agents. The landlords called in the army, and after a show of force the revolt was easily suppressed.[74] The unique feature of the agrarian revolts in Iraq in the 1950s was their local and sporadic nature. All were of short duration and remained isolated. The country was obviously not ripe for total social revolution, and yet revolts broke out in Iraq in 1947, 1952, 1953 (three cases), 1954, 1955, and 1958 (April).[75] Never in the past had agrarian revolts occurred at such a pace.

Within the context of peasant unrest in Iraq mention should be made of the strong class and peasant element in the Shawwaf rebellion against Abd al-Karim Qassem in Mosul in March 1959. This incident highlighted the tension inherent in the prerevolutionary Iraqi social structure.[76] The Shawwaf rebellion was organized by Ba'thi and Nasserist officers with the cooperation of landlords, who stood to lose most of their lands because of the newly instituted agrarian reform law. Especially noteworthy in this category were a few tribal shaykhs. The revolt was to be started by the Mosul garrison, and it was hoped that it would spread throughout the country. But the whole revolt was organized so carelessly that upon its outbreak the regime's supporters were waiting and ready to strike back. Thousands of local peasants flocked to the town, partially at the instigation of the Communist party. By the end of the first week of March 1959, the situation in the city had deteriorated rapidly to a state of complete chaos, which lasted for three or four days. In the course of its duration hundreds, and some say thousands, of people were killed or "executed."

This tense atmosphere was reminiscent of those familiar descriptions of the atmosphere in Paris at the height of the terror stage of the French Revolution. Distrust and wild rumors were rife. Within the general anarchy there was also systematic violence perpetrated by the lower classes against the rich, particularly the landlords. An eyewitness to the events related to Batatu in 1963 that "as soon as it came to the knowledge of the [crowd] that so-and-so was wealthy . . . there was a beating of drums on the next morning before his house which was then searched and pillaged."[77]

The events that took place in Iraq, Syria, and Egypt in the 1950s and 1960s were more than mere army officers' revolutions. It seems clear that class struggle would inevitably have led to a social, agrarian revolution, but the army movement short-circuited such an eventuality.

The Village Community

The village community, one of the main pillars of peasant society, is intimately linked with the topic of agrarian structure. I have shown that a major source of strength of the Middle Eastern village community lay in the strenuous effort made by the Ottoman government in the classical period to preserve the community of smallholders from infiltration by outsiders. The community as such was not mentioned in the *kanunnames* (sixteenth-century Ottoman state laws), and obviously it had no legal basis because Islam only recognized the legality of the community of believers. But informally the village community did exist, and the Ottoman land laws added substantially to its vitality and strength. I have demonstrated the actual working of this institution in the case of seventeenth-century Anatolia.

The information available to us on the twentieth century, although insufficient, indicates that in this field the continuity between past and present has been remarkable. Egypt may be viewed as an exception to this generalization. Egypt is also the best starting point for the discussion because it is the only country in which the village community has attracted direct research.

G. Baer has made a strong case for the thesis that the Egyptian village community had all but disappeared from the scene by the close of the nineteenth century.[78] He based his conclusion on the fact that the only three formal legal traits of the Egyptian village—communal ownership and periodic redistribution of lands, collective responsibility for taxes, and collective responsibility for the maintenance of irrigation canals—had either declined or entirely disappeared.

This conclusion has drawn considerable fire.[79] Other scholars have claimed that the village community may find expression in less tangible features than those outlined by Baer and that to view the problem through the eyes of the government is incorrect. Nevertheless, Baer's critics dispensed too lightly with his methodology. Shared legal liabilities and privileges may sometimes represent an unpleasant reality. Moreover, such laws often survive the states that have inherited them. The common right of grazing in many Middle Eastern villages in a case in point. Hence, it is probably correct to assume that the Egyptian village community was indeed weakened by the disappearance of these three legal features. Baer's critics were correct in assuming that a village community may find expression not merely in legal traits but also in less tangible ways. Indeed, there is enough evidence to support the thesis that the Egyptian village community remained a moderately cohesive body well into the twentieth century and most likely to the present day. The main evidence for this supposition came from Ayrout's classic, *The Egyptian Peasant*. Baer cited Ayrout's remark that "the Egyptian village is not a community in the social sense, not an organism, but a mass." But Ayrout also provided quite different information, which has been sadly neglected by the disputants. His description is worthy of extensive quotation.

> When the fellah is in barracks, or when he has left for the town to make a little money, he never forgets his village, and homesickness shows in the stolid face. He tries at least to keep up contact with home and to retain some of its habits. . . . When the vital interests of a village are threatened, everyone feels deeply that he is one of the community: men, women and children all grouped together into a single force. The drama of Abu Shadi is an example. In order to better the drainage, the irrigation department had decided to cut off a canal which for thirty years had provided the whole district with water. The entire population rose against the laborers, against the police, even against the military, to prevent the diversion of the water. . . . This is one of the contradictions of village life. Everyone knows everyone else in the village, and no one would ever be allowed to die of hunger. Men help each other in housework. The solidarity shown by the fellahin when working for a common interest, and not under orders or outside interference, can be striking, if it is rare.[80]

Regarding the Fertile Crescent, there are no written sources on the village community before the twentieth century. However, even without these sources, it appears that the strong cohesiveness of the village commune prevailed, dictated largely by geographical and ecological factors. The typical village in the Fertile Crescent was a cluster village—houses were close to each other and surrounded by the village lands, chiefly because of the village's dependence on a single source of water supply and also because security was easier when houses were close together. Whatever the explanation, the close proximity of the dwellings to each other created its own sociological dynamism, and a strong village community was a natural consequence. Indeed, a number of twentieth-century sources confirmed the existence of a strong commune. Sociologist Afif Tannous was one of the first scholars to recognize the importance of the village community; one of his articles was actually entitled "The Arab Village Community of the Middle East."[81] The village in Tannous' analysis was much more than the sum total of its component institutions.

The *fellah* is always conscious of the fact that he is a member of a certain community, and he knows that wherever he goes people expect him to identify himself as such. A stranger is always "placed" with respect to his village, family and church. . . . Marriage within the settlement is preferable to marriage with an outsider. . . . In intervillage competition or conflict loyalty to the local community asserts itself in an unmistakable manner and is expected from every individual.[82]

This analysis was fully corroborated by the findings of Lutfiyya regarding Baytin, a Palestinian village near Ramallah.

As in all folk societies, the villagers at Baytin have a strong feeling of belonging to each other, as well as to their village. They all claim the same ancestral origin and in their daily interaction they tend to relate themselves to one another. "We are all cousins" is a remark often made to a stranger who may ask a villager if he were related to someone in the village who is not a close relative. The villagers refer to themselves as "we," as against all others, who are "they." This community of feeling stems from the biological as well as cultural resemblance that the villagers bear to one another.[83]

This case was all the more notable because there was no communal ownership of land at the time the study was made, as the author related that villagers claimed family ownership of particular plots of land for a period of generations.

Farther north the same conclusion was reached by John Gulick, whose field research was carried out in a Lebanese village. "There can be no question but that the Middle East village is a classic example of the in-group. It is small, physically very tightly clustered, and it tends to be physically isolated from its neighbors."[84]

In contrast, Louise Sweet's conclusions on the village of Tell Toqan (northern Syria) were quite different. Notwithstanding the fact that the village was a *musha* village, the village community was weak, with little or no cooperation between families. Indeed, nothing that concerned the villagers was decided by them. The reason for this must have been the fact that almost everything in the village was decided upon by Shaykh Nuri, who was not a formal village head but the largest landlord and who was at the same time resident in the village itself.[85] This is confirmation of the claim that large landlordism in most small communities in the Middle East imparted overwhelming political power to the incumbent. It also makes the argument that strong internal class divisions wreak havoc with the cohesiveness of the small community.

An important point should be added here. As is evident from the foregoing information, the strength and cohesiveness of the village community in the Middle East is no longer reliant on legal considerations such as collective liabilities. An exception may be the shared ownership of grazing land, a point that I believe is more important for Turkey than for the Fertile Crescent. However, it is clear that in the twentieth century the village commune rested mainly on the foundation of shared ancestral descent (true or assumed) and the social effects of neighborliness. Furthermore, the village is in some sense a community in itself. The material available on Turkey further substantiates this point.

We may start our survey of Turkey with the group of villages in southwestern Anatolia studied by Kolars. Kolars had no hesitation in viewing the villages he studied as having a "corporate identity." This identity found its expression, according to Kolars, in a core, or center, that was the focal point of village activities. Around this center were public buildings such as the mosque, coffee house, and school. Most of the informal meetings in the village took place in and around the coffee house, and much of the institutional framework of the village found concrete expression there.[86]

Paul Magnarella studied a village nearer to the Black Sea region. Having identified the interstrata differences that existed in the village, the author emphasized that unity nonetheless existed. "Intergroup cohesion is continuously promoted by a number of cultural forces, including an ideology of Muslim brotherhood, diffuse kinship ties, and a common identity with Hayriye as a unique village and a Georgian community."[87]

Berkes, who studied eleven villages in the Ankara region in the early 1940s, noted the existence there of a village community and described it in some detail.[88] He claimed that the existence of the commune was felt vividly as soon as one entered the village. The villagers distinguished sharply between their village and other villages or city folk and perceived the unity of the village and its solidarity (*tesanüd*). He sensed a strong in-group/outer world dynamic in all these villages.

Scott's study of a village near Ankara sheds additional valuable light on this topic. In the village he studied, an interclan conflict threatened to undermine village unity and cohesiveness. The cause of the trouble was the *muhtar*'s son, who had killed a madman who had offended his mother. Anxious to contain the conflict, the *muhtar* decided that he did not want his son to return to the village after his release from jail.[89] Clearly, at least outwardly, he was acting for the common good of the village commune rather than for the good of his own clan.

For our purposes Stirling's study of two villages in central Anatolia was the most important source.[90] Solidarity and cohesiveness in the two villages studied by Stirling were quite apparent and found expression in the intensely positive emotion of the inhabitants toward their own village. They were proud of their village and found it natural that the author considered it worthy of research. The people of the surrounding villages, in contrast, found his decision astonishing and incomprehensible. As in the Bursa region in the seventeenth century, the main tangible manifestation of the village community was the common territory of the village, which was tantamount to the pasture area, and the pasture was the sensitive issue about which quarrels tended to erupt between villages. However, cohesiveness and unity were not strongly marked. The situation was one of mixed elements.

> The village as I have described it is a collection of households of different degrees of strength, wealth and prestige, living together in close intimacy, and with enough cooperation and mutual tolerance not only to survive, but to form a strong and stable community. Yet it lacks any effective formal structure of authority, and any undisputed informal leadership. In spite of the truculent independence of most respectable household heads, the existence of innumerable unsettled disputes and quarrels, and constant jockeying for influence and prestige between the leading households, the village leads an orderly life; people are constantly visiting, helping, advising, cooperating and intermarrying.[91]

The same impression was created by Frey and Roos' study of the political role of the village headman in Turkey. Most peasants interviewed by the authors saw the village political structure as a kind of oligarchy headed by the *muhtar*. Nonetheless, they observed that the headman was not a despot with arbitrary powers but rather a figure to whom the villagers had easy access and who was considerate of their opinions and wishes.[92] In other words, we once again have the phenomenon of a village community that was neither democratic nor despotic in the extreme, neither very cohesive nor entirely loose and disparate.

One of the agrarian institutions of central importance to the Middle Eastern village commune was the *musha,* or communal ownership of land. Through this system the arable lands of the village were communally held by the villagers and periodically redistributed to village households. The institution was astonishingly similar to the Russian *mir,* an exceptionally important institution in Russian history, as we have seen. Was the *musha* of equal importance in Middle Eastern history? On examination the answer proves to be emphatically in the negative.

It is surprising how few references there are to the *musha* institution before the twentieth century—despite its presumed antiquity. Samuel Bergheim's account, dating back to the 1890s, is usually considered the earliest clear description of the institution,[93] but the Swiss traveller J. L. Burckhardt described it in the early nineteenth century.[94] Still, this description was relatively late, and the question remains why no earlier account has come to light. Is it possible that the *musha* is not as old as it is assumed to be? The possibility exists, although so far we lack evidence. If it were proven to be less ancient than is generally supposed, the *musha*'s social and psychological roots may not be so deep either.

In the past many scholars assumed that the *musha* was universal in the traditional Middle Eastern village. This is decidedly incorrect with regard to Anatolia, where the *musha* did not exist in the seventeenth century, and as a plethora of twentieth-century sources will attest, it does not as a rule exist in modern times. We also know that the *musha* was never extant in lower Egypt (the delta region), nor did it exist in most of Iraq's rural areas, which were collectively held by the tribes.

Furthermore, I have shown in another study that the *musha* was not, and could not have been, widespread in mountainous regions, for simple technical reasons.[95] On the other hand, we have seen that a sizable proportion of the population throughout Ottoman history dwelt in mountainous areas. Therefore, quantitatively the *musha* system of landholding was unimportant in the Ottoman period. In the nineteenth century it probably spread far and wide with the extension of the low-lying inhabited areas, but by then other factors were at work to undermine it, among them the Ottoman land law, which prohibited the registration of communal land in the land registry. This was possibly one of the reasons for the decline of the *musha*, according to information supplied by Weulersse. He observed in Syria in the interwar period the widespread phenomenon of the "stabilized *musha*"—that is, a *musha* that was frozen and discontinued.[96] Thus, it seems clear that the historical role of *musha* institution in the agrarian history of the Middle East was marginal.

The Class Basis of Army Rule

In recent decades some of the most important countries of the Arab Middle East have come to be dominated by military regimes. The military coup of General Bakr Sidqi in Iraq in 1936 preceded similar events in the 1950s and 1960s in Egypt, Syria, and Iraq where army rule has become the norm. With this, the Middle East joined a large group of Third World states in which army dictatorship is the prevailing form of government. Unquestionably, military control is the single most important feature of the contemporary Arab scene. In this context the first question that springs to mind is why did the army become involved in the politics of these countries. Is there a specific, discernible Middle Eastern pattern that distinguishes this region from other Third World areas?

The Middle Eastern army has attracted intensive scholarly attention in recent years. Be'eri's book may be considered an indispensable starting point for clarifying some of the major problems connected with the subject.[97] However, certain important points still remain unresolved, and they are specifically those points that constitute the focus of the present study. In other words, if we note carefully the main peculiarities of the army-in-politics phenomenon in the Middle East, I believe that an adequate explanation should include a discussion of its socioagrarian roots in Ottoman society.

There are two major questions of concern here. The first is the political involvement of the armies; the second concerns the world view of the officers' elite in the Middle East. In the democratic West, and more so in Latin America, we are accustomed to associating armies with right-wing ideologies and political conservatism, while in the Middle East the army has as a rule been associated with political radicalism.

Why have Middle Eastern armies intervened in politics? After all, state bureaucracies build armies to serve them obediently; an army, ideally, should not have a will of its own but should take orders from its political overlords. This is the case in many states throughout the world. Why do armies obey in some countries, while in others this obedience fails to materialize? This question has given rise to much controversy among certain scholars.[98] I intend to deal with this issue on a practical level in the context of the Middle East.

There is a tendency to differentiate between West European and Middle Eastern armies on the basis of the fact that the former underwent a process of professionalization, while the latter remained essentially a continuation of the former Mamluk armies—that is, cliques of undisciplined officers ever ready to seize and maintain power by force for as long as possible.[99]

> The modern officer corps is a professional body, and the modern military officer a professional man. . . . A profession is a peculiar type of functional group with highly specialized characteristics . . . expertise, responsibility and corporateness. Expertise means technical training for the special kind of job; responsibility is the sense of duty which the army should feel towards its client, that is, the state; and corporateness means group feeling and solidarity of the officer corps.[100]

Be'eri compared the Western European army with the typical Middle Eastern army officer (the Mamluk—a model that includes the Janissary soldier). While the professional modern officer is said to be characteristic only of the industrialized West, in the Middle East the Mamluk pattern remained as the sole representative of the historical heritage.

A theory that places the entire explanatory onus for Middle Eastern armies on the Mamluk system is misguided. Historical continuity cannot be assumed a priori. Certain historical patterns persist and influence the future directly, while others do so only indirectly or not at all. The last important polity that ruled the Middle East before the modern age, the Ottoman Empire, was not, strictly speaking, based on military overlordship. Although some of the early sultans did serve as military commanders, most of the later ones did not. The Ottoman sultan was no more of a military overlord than was the Russian czar, who on more than one occasion also led his troops in the field. It is noteworthy that the sultanic authority in this state survived for six centuries without succumbing to military intervention on the part of army commanders eager to replace the dynasty. The notorious meddling in state affairs by the Janissaries may be construed as intervention on the part of an urban group trying to guard its vested interests, rather than as full-fledged army intervention. Thus, the role of the army in the Ottoman Empire should be seen in its correct perspective and not unduly exaggerated. It was probably no more far-reaching than in most other historic empires where it did not lead to the modern phenomenon of army rule.

The phenomenon of Mamlukism seems to have had little influence on future developments. In Egypt the institution existed until the rise to power of Mehmed Ali early in the nineteenth century. In 1811, he annihilated the Mamluk's main body, thereby putting an end to its existence as an institution. A similar institution existed in Iraq, where it was terminated as a result of Ottoman intervention in 1831. In the main body of the Ottoman Empire no Mamluk institution as such ever existed, although there was something similar—the conscription of Christian boys from the Balkans by the famous system known as *devshirme*. These boys were later made to convert, and after intensive training they were sent to the various administrative and military organs of the state. This institution was the main source of manpower for the corps of Janissaries. Here, too, the institution disappeared early, long before the period of modernization in the Middle Eastern armies. In the case of the *devshirme*, this disappearance occurred at the end of the seventeenth century.

So far I have dealt with the formal side of the Mamluk and quasi-Mamluk institution. But what was its deep-seated historical impact? It is well known that the Mamluk institution had a far-reaching influence on the issue of succession to the throne; a new ruler could establish himself only after intense conflict among the Mamluk *beys*, or leaders. The concept of a ruler nominating his successor was unknown in the Mamluk system. But in nineteenth-century Egypt, accession to the throne took place several times and always in an orderly, nonviolent manner, according to a predetermined rule. It did not differ from the succession process of most distinguished dynasties in contemporary Europe. There was no trace of the Mamluk heritage, no sign of a behind-the-scene influence of the army.[101]

A similar change occurred in another major Mamluk tradition—namely, the conscription of non-Muslim youths from the non-Islamic world; these youths were converted and prepared as replacements for the retiring Mamluk generation. In the nineteenth century this custom fell totally into disrepute. Mehmed Ali, ruler of Egypt between 1804 and 1848, carried out some experiments in the building of a modern army. In the 1820s he began enlisting members of the local indigenous population (mainly fellahs), over whom he placed officers who were remnants of the Mamluk forces of Egypt. The Mamluk system thus faded out naturally. The new Egyptian army was in principle entirely modern; it was conscripted from local elements and was originally trained by French officers who had remained in Egypt after Napoleon's departure.[102] Thus, it availed itself of the most superior military training available at the time in Europe. Although it could justifiably be claimed that the nineteenth-century Egyptian army never attained the level of contemporary European armies, it nevertheless evolved into a professional army.

The Egyptian army had another distinguishing feature. Until the crisis of the late 1870s, it never interfered in politics—a phenomenon to which I refer again. In the Ottoman Empire the Mamlukish elements in the army also disappeared at quite an early stage, and local elements were drafted in their stead. In order to obtain a clear picture of the sociological character of the Ottoman army between the sixteenth and the nineteenth centuries some prior observations are in order. The first concerns the Janissaries and the second, the role of the technical corps, such as the artillery. I have already dwelt on the fact that the Janissaries did not interfere in politics in order to shape policy. Their efforts were restricted to keeping the government at arm's length from their ill-gotten privileges. They never questioned the legitimacy of the House of Osman and its right to rule the empire. In this sense the role of the Janissaries in politics could easily be exaggerated.

Their sociological structure in this period was aptly summarized by Gibb and Bowen in the following words:

> Janissary recruits of the new type were drawn chiefly from the artisan classes of the towns in which *ortas* were stationed, among whom, as among Moslems in general, early marriages were the rule. Consequently it became more and more unusual for them to live in barracks, and more and more difficult to subject them to discipline and training, and more and more common for them to supplement their pay, and occupy the leisure thus created, with industrial or commercial activities.[103]

Moreover, in the sixteenth century the main bulk of the Ottoman fighting forces was not composed of Janissaries. Although there are conflicting figures, the number of Janissaries in the sixteenth century apparently never exceeded twenty-seven thousand troops.[104] The main military force at this period was the feudal army, which numbered more than one hundred thousand troops. The backbone of this force were the *sipahis*, who in the sixteenth century may have also been mostly *devshirme,* but the greater part of the feudal army comprised local conscripts drafted on an ad hoc basis for a single war. These facts indicate that the significance of the Mamluk principle in the sixteenth century may be overstated. Eventually, it was to become even less manifest.

A number of sultans in this period tried to reform the structure of the army, notably Selim III (1789–1808). He promulgated new orders and regulations, appointed inspectors, sent out investigators, and warned and admonished all, but to little avail.[105] Opposition from the grass-roots level was immense. Efforts to amend the situation of the *sipahi* corps failed in the face of fraudulence and bribery. Nor were the Janissaries any less cunning and adamant in resisting reform. "They rioted in the streets whenever any effort was made to give them new uniforms or weapons or to provide them with instructors trained in the new ways. Each effort made to reduce the size of the corps by dismissing inactive members who were artisans or merchants was successfully opposed, and the number of men in the corps actually increased."[106]

Here we have in a nutshell the main problem affecting the Ottoman state at that time. It was neither poor policy nor insensitivity to world affairs nor even a sense of cultural superiority and overconfidence. Rather, the problem was the lack of governmental political power to execute its policies. Here was a bureaucratic state disintegrating along the lines of a patrimonial state. Although this basic situation remained unaltered, it is clear that any attempt at true professionalization of the army was doomed in advance. Similar, but more far-reaching developments were concurrently taking place in some of the major urban centers of the provinces, as exemplified by the case of Aleppo.[107]

On balance it seems that numerically the most important armies in the Ottoman Empire between the sixteenth and nineteenth centuries were private armies, conscripted, trained, and financed by provincial governors at their own initiative. Qualitatively, they must have included some of the best in the empire because a governor's political career was entirely dependent on the army. The best known example on record was the case of eighteenth-century Palestine, studied by Amnon Cohen.[108] The army created by al-Jazzar was a powerful war machine. A large proportion of its members were foreigners from North Africa, Albania, and Afghanistan. Some were Bedouin from Egypt, and a few were local recruits, peasants from the Galilee. The army was not held in high esteem by the local population because of the obvious social and class differences between the two. The Albanians and North Africans were not interested in the misfortunes of the Arab Palestinian society and the hardships it endured at the hands of the provincial governor. Chiefly for this reason, the armies of al-Jazzar were loyal to the governor personally. This loyalty created a veneer of professionalism, but on the whole it was conducive to the political culture of the Ottoman Empire, for it helped keep the troops in the barracks until late in the Ottoman period.

In the nineteenth century the pace of professionalization in the army increased noticeably, facilitated by the elimination of the Janissaries in 1826. The military standards resulting from this reform are not our concern here. Of more relevance is the fact that the Ottoman army in the late nineteenth century was professional, fitting Huntington's definition no less than do the armies of contemporary Europe.[109] A notable feature of the nineteenth-century reformed Ottoman army was that it was apolitical. It returned to political involvement only in the late nineteenth century and then later in the early twentieth century at a time of crisis that eventually saw the rise to power of generals for the first time in the modern history of the Middle East. It might be argued, then, that the real heritage of the Ottoman period to the twentieth-century Middle East is not Mamlukism, but rather a watered-down, bureaucratic army with a substantial component of modern professionalism.

The major flaw in the Mamluk theory of the military phenomenon in the Middle East is as follows. The Mamluk elite was not only a military elite but also a status elite. It regarded itself as superior to the local society and formed the uncontested social elite of the late medieval Egyptian and Syrian city. If the military phenomenon in the modern era were a direct derivation of the Mamluk phenomenon, we would expect the army officer in Arab and Turkish society to enjoy a high social status. However, the most conspicuous feature of the Middle Eastern armies is the low status of their officer class. This low-status phenomenon already was apparent in the Janissary corps of Istanbul as early as the sixteenth century. There was an association between the Janissaries and the Bektashi Order and the artisan guilds of Istanbul.[110]

Again, the same pattern features in the reforms of Selim III. Unable to effect a serious change in the structure and functioning of the old armies, Selim established a new corps, the New Style Army, destined to be the nucleus of nineteenth-century military reform. This new corps comprised a motley assembly—the officers were all Christian renegades captured in war, while the soldiers were an assembly of one hundred Turks gathered "from the streets of Istanbul."[111] Later, to complete the regiment, more recruits were admitted. They came "mainly from among unemployed youths roaming the streets of Istanbul and from the private armies of the leading notables of Anatolia."[112]

Abd al-Karim Rafeq, who wrote a fine study on the armies of seventeenth- and eighteenth-century Syria, depicted these troops as unruly, disorderly, and of obscure social origin, implying a low-class status.[113] They owed allegiance to no one and were ready to mutiny at the slightest pretext. These forces, which were held in low esteem by the populace, constituted a telling example of the decline in bureaucratic standards in later Ottoman history. Against this background it is easy to understand why upper-class families in modern times regard a military career with some disdain.[114]

Eliezer Be'eri provided excellent information substantiating the low-class origin of the officer corps. Surprisingly, he did not attempt to reconcile the differences between this phenomenon and the alleged primacy of the military occupation in traditional Islamic countries. Thus, he quoted the German officer Moltke as saying in 1840 that "the weakest part of the army . . . was the officers. Two of the major-generals came from the harem of Muhammad Khusrau's palace, a third had been a porter ten years earlier and a fourth had been a galley-slave taken off a ship. . . . Often very young men were made majors. They might have been narghileh-tenders or coffee-makers to some pasha, and they were immediately given command of a battalion."[115]

A British traveller at the time noted that students in the military medical school all came from "the very poor. . . . [They were] sons of common sailors, ostlers, pedlars, porters, etc. and no Turk of upper or even middle class would send his son to the school."[116] Similarly, a European source in 1870 noted the narrow social gap separating officers from the ranks in the Ottoman army and went one step farther in differentiating between the Middle East and Europe: "There exists an intimacy between the officers and the men which in other European armies would be contrary to regulations. . . . This unusual state of affairs is explained by the low standard of education of the officers, most of whom are of necessity taken from the ranks, since the educated classes keep well away from service in the army."[117]

With modernization in the twentieth century the profession of army officer gained in importance. However, old habits die hard, and the low-status pattern of Middle Eastern armies has indeed persisted. For example, in twentieth-century Iraq most army officers originated from lower-middle-class urban families. Although Iraq was ruled by a landed oligarchy, there was no recruitment to the officer corps from that class.[118] The same situation obtained in Egypt, where the officers were recruited from the lower middle class and not from the landed oligarchy or the lower classes.[119]

The close connection between the lower classes and politics in Middle Eastern armies was brilliantly analyzed recently by John Batatu. A special feature of the Syrian political system in recent decades has been the dominant role of a group of officers from the Alawi sect, a small religious minority held in suspicion and contempt by the Sunni Muslim majority. This unusual situation had its roots in the period of the mandate, when the French expressed their preference for reliable social elements by recruiting troops mainly from the minorities. However, this is only part of the story. Since independence (1946) the Syrian army has increased considerably in size, minimizing the role of the old recruitment patterns. Thus, the explanation for Alawi involvement in the Syrian army lies basically in the country's class structure. I have shown that the Alawis constituted the most depressed rural population in Syria; their social and agrarian subjugation predated the 1858 land law. One of the consequences of this historic situation, according to Batatu, was that Alawis were among those who could not afford to pay the *badal*, the exemption tax from military service.[120] From this information we may deduce that many of those who could afford to do so paid the tax and gained that exemption. Here we have an important insight into the attitude of Syrian society toward the military profession, one that has led to a situation whereby the representation of the Alawis in the army has been much greater, proportionally, than their numbers in society.

This theory accentuates the importance of the lowly origins associated with the military. Nevertheless, in all Arab countries there are exceptions, with officers from higher social strata serving in the military. It might be asked, then, how upper class families came to send their sons to the army against this background of contempt for an army career. The explanation seems to lie in the fact that such officers were predestined for top army positions, which were often of a combined military/civilian nature. This group formed part of the political elite of the country and presents no serious challenge to this thesis.

Where did this class structure of the military in the Middle East originate? The decline from the peak period of the Mamluks is easily explained. Although the Mamluks were initially the rulers, later this ceased to be so, and the military profession became a profession in name only. In order to understand the Middle Eastern perception of this issue, it has to be compared with other cultures. In medieval Europe the armies were initially feudal armies, with the landed aristocracy the main pillar and value indicator of society. Unquestionably, the conservative viewpoint prevailing in the ranks of European armies today has its roots in the basic medieval structure of the army. M. Janowitz emphasized this continuity, despite the fact that modern European armies are middle-class armies.[121] He described the modernization of the Western European armies in the nineteenth century and the gradual introduction of new social elements and their socialization into the contemporary sociopolitical world view.[122] The new army, although largely of the middle class, was still permeated by traditional values. "The traditional qualities of aristocracy, courage, initiative, independence, leadership," were still vital on the battlefield. Although many new qualities were now demanded of the officer, "the aristocracy could still provide the kind of characteristic leadership which was their traditional *raison d'être,*" and an officer was still called upon to be a "heroic leader."[123]

Compared with the Middle East, Latin America presents a totally different picture—one yet to be explored. The right-wing, conservative nature of the officer corps of Latin America dates back to the colonial period when there was a close association between white colonization and the defending army. Whereas in the case of medieval Europe the style remained aristocratic, in Latin America the colonial nature of the association became dominant. Johnson highlighted brilliantly the difference between Latin America and the Middle East where (as I claim in this book) no landed oligarchy existed until 1858.

> Militarism was constrained in the colonies but force was not. For extended periods of time the mother countries could make their authority felt only within the administrative centers and their immediate environs. Seldom

were they able to provide protection for their subjects on the distant frontiers exposed to Indian forays and inroads by foreigners. In the areas beyond royal protection and royal law, the *hacendado* was left largely to his own resources as long as he recognized the ultimate authority of the mother country. He was free to assume personal responsibility for the welfare of his family and property and, much like a feudal lord, for the protection of those who associated themselves in one way or another with the *hacienda*. In such circumstances the *hacienda* became a social unit whose government was the *hacendado*. In a very real sense the *hacendado* was the colonial equivalent of the local boss of the nineteenth century. Like the local boss he represented unregulated force and violence.[124]

The landed oligarchy in Latin America had too much to lose from government by the intellectuals, and in Johnson's opinion the power struggle in the wake of the War of Independence there ended in an alliance between the military and the landlords. "Marshals turned statesmen tipped the balance of power at the national level, away from the intellectuals and towards the oligarchs. . . . The alliance between the military and the oligarchy persisted throughout the century because landowners and armies leaned on each other much too seriously even when the landowners found the officers uncontrollable allies."[125] Therefore, the rightist leaning of the army in Latin America is anchored in the tradition of the colonial period, rooted in a deep-seated harmony of interests between the military and the landed oligarchy.

This description is particularly accurate for the less developed countries of Latin America. As José Nun has shown in his famous study, in the more developed countries, such as Brazil and Argentina, the army is composed largely of middle-class recruits.[126] Nevertheless, the army strives to preserve the existing socioeconomic order because in these countries a kind of fusion took place between the landed oligarchy and the urban bourgeoisie.

Contrary to the situation in medieval Europe or Latin America, in the Middle East there was simply no connection between the traditional military and a landed aristocracy or oligarchy, for no such group existed until 1858. The army was bureaucratic, whether well organized or in disarray, but it was never entrusted with the agrarian function of safeguarding the sanctity of large landownership. It would be impossible to cite episodes where such a function was performed, for it can safely be postulated that in every society where landed interests take precedence it is the function of the army to safeguard the status quo. Thus, because large landed proprietorship did not exist, the army did not earn the high status conferred on it in states where it was associated with the landed class. Hence, the danger and inconvenience associated with the military profession relegated it to the bottom of the professional hierarchy.

In Turkey and the Arab countries the low-class pattern of the military profession seems to have had some bearing on the profession's modern political behavior. In the sixteenth century the Janissaries, who were recruited from outside the indigenous population, were mostly indifferent to their social environment. By the nineteenth century, however, recruitment was mainly confined to the lower classes of the local population, and inevitably the interplay between class and status groups, or state and society, began to make itself felt. If the officers did not become involved in politics it was probably because they did not constitute a depressed class—that is, they were not ruthlessly exploited by a landowning class. The main expropriator of the surplus was the ruling elite itself. Within Ottoman society the class situation was not perceived in this way. Until the diffusion of nationalism the House of Osman enjoyed a large measure of legitimacy, and the sultan's right to levy taxes was uncontested. This point was recently demonstrated in Percy Kemp's studies on Ottoman Mosul (northern Iraq) in the late Ottoman period.[127] According to Kemp, the House of Osman received massive support from the local populace and represented the sole bulwark against foreign and internal enemies alike.

On attaining their independence, the major Arab countries found themselves under the effective control of a landowning oligarchy whose rule created problems of legitimacy. These problems were the result of cooperation between the ruling elite and former foreign occupying forces—an indictment that is open to confutation. The record of the nationalist leaders in Syria, for example, is impeccable in this regard. There is no overt evidence of cooperation between the nationalist Syrian elite and an occupying force. Their revolts and battles were often doomed in advance; they instigated boycotts of the mandatory authorities and relinquished governmental posts.

It would seem, rather, that resentment of the old elite must be perceived in class terms; the rule of a landed oligarchy cannot help but be a cause of resentment and bitterness. In the Middle East this issue was complicated by the newness of this oligarchy. Its rule was perceived by much of the population as usurpation and was hence illegitimate. This lack of legitimacy can easily be demonstrated by empirical facts (see D. Lerner's chapter on Syria); in Syria extensive social and psychological tensions simmered below the surface years before the Ba'th came to power.[128] Likewise, Patrick Seale asserted that the main ideas of what later was to become the doctrine of "positive neutralism" were widespread among educated Syrian youth long before it became the official ideology of Arab states in the mid-1950s.[129]

After World War II, army officers found that their position was that of a depressed class. They had feelings of class enmity toward the ruling elite, which enjoyed neither legitimacy nor approval in the society. This situation, coupled with a wide measure of social disgruntlement and the unpopularity of the elite, inevitably led to a coup that triggered off army intervention. The professionalism of the army seems to be entirely irrelevant in this regard. It is only against this background that we can understand some of the peculiarities characterizing the social ideology of the officer corps in the Arab world.

Unlike the armies of the West or Latin America, Middle Eastern armies were never called on to defend the privileged interests of a landed ruling elite. Army recruits were not exposed to an educational drive to win them over to a ruling, right-wing ideology. The ideology did not exist because until 1858 there were no landed oligarchies. Moreover, because the Middle East did not experience the extreme exploitation and brutality of czarist Russia, the prevailing social ideology was milder than the totalitarianism of the Eastern bloc. The social and ideological issues of the contemporary officer elite in radical Arab countries are in fact intelligible only within the context of agrarian class relations in the Middle East after 1500.[130]

A point of major importance is illustrated by the armies of Saudi Arabia and Jordan—two of the most backward, conservative states in the Middle East. Yet they are also states where the army is detached from politics and loyal and subservient to civil authority. For theoreticians like Finer this situation constituted an analytical problem, because according to their analysis there is a correlation between the sophistication and modernity of a political culture and the intensity of the political involvement of the army in it. Yet here we observe the opposite situation. Finer tried to circumvent the problem by stating that in Jordan political authority rests on the goodwill of the military. However, there is no evidence to indicate that this assertion is more true of Jordan than of other countries where civil authority is usually considered supreme. The Jordanian king, to all intents and purposes, is not a puppet but is the real locus of political power in his country, and this is certainly so for the palace in Saudi Arabia. It is difficult to avoid the conclusion that these two polities present a major obstacle to models associating civilian supremacy with a sophisticated political system.

The Jordanian army also presents an analytic problem to the Mamlukist theories of Middle Eastern armies. If the contemporary Middle Eastern army pattern is a continuation of the Mamluk pattern, we should expect to find this true especially in polities that are traditional and "reactionary." But Jordan and Saudi Arabia, with their minimal measure of army intervention, least resemble the Mamluk model. The Jordanian army was established with the founding of the amirate of Transjordan in the wake of World War I.[131] At that time the region was mostly desert, and the tiny army was mainly composed of Bedouin. It remained a small, elite army until the beginning of the 1950s, when its large-scale development started. The main body of recruits then came from the settled population, both old and new, that is, the population of the West Bank. The Bedouin component remained the backbone of the army, even though numerically it constituted only 40 percent of the total.

In the interwar period Great Britain was the main pillar of support and training for the Transjordanian army. The situation changed in 1956 when Jordan severed relations with Britain and drew closer to the United States. This is of course a mere sketch of the history of the Jordanian Legion. Politically, with the exception of one hazy incident in 1957, the Jordanian army seems to have remained totally subservient to its superiors throughout this period. P. J. Vatikiotis, who has written the most important study on the Jordanian army, began his book with the strong argument that there is a big difference in the structure of armies in the East and West. In the West the army is strictly loyal to the civil authority, supposedly because the army is a national body and the soldier is inculcated with an attitude of pride in the army. In contrast, this attitude is lacking in the Middle East, due to the persistence of traditional primordial ties.[132] Vatikiotis then carefully documented the history of the one Arab army whose social composition is farthest from that of the European West, yet whose political role most resembles it.

Vatikiotis also has shown how in the 1950s the Jordanian army was transformed from an elite army to one composed of tens of thousands of troops, mostly new recruits from the newly acquired territory of central Palestine. This group was a potential source of disloyalty. Mark Heller has suggested a useful distinction in the structure of the armies of Jordan and Iraq that highlighted Jordan's peculiarity. In Iraq the British authorities were not selective in their choice of candidates for the officer corps; thus, the majority came from the lower classes. But in Jordan the two British commanders of the Legion personally supervised the purging of suspect elements. In other words, it was not the army's professionalization that accounted for the difference but rather the selection of its candidates. Nevertheless, the Jordanian army is by no means free of class questions. As Heller remarked, the Jordanian Legion "was distinguished by no special education or class background, so that, far from being a disgruntled caste, it was the only Arab officer corps whose members 'neither regard themselves nor are they regarded by others as intelligentsia in uniform.'"[133]

I suggest that this attitude is neither fortuitous nor unrelated to our findings on the Jordanian agrarian structure. In contrast to prerevolutionary Egypt, Syria and Iraq, there was no pronounced class distinction in Jordan between peasant and landlord. Rather, the agrarian and class structure was more balanced, and possibly this is why the army did not become a mirror of the class struggle as in other Arab countries.

What, then, is the nature of the new elite that emerged from the barracks? Is it a mere praetorian clique seeking to rule for its own ends until, in turn, it is evicted by another clique of officers? Or is it a vanguard elite of a new ruling class that has emerged in the Arab world? These and other questions have been the subject of heated controversy. It is sufficient in this context to briefly mention the protracted debate between Manfred Halpern and Amos Perlmutter.[134] Halpern contended that army officers were the core of a new, salaried middle class, striving to rise to power in Arab society. He claimed that this elite had a modernizing and transformative potential as the leading force of a whole class.[135] Perlmutter disagreed and argued instead that these officers were merely seeking self-aggrandizement. It appears that Halpern's thesis is closer to the truth. A comparison with Latin America may clarify this point. There is a wide consensus among scholars that most officer groups that rise to power in Latin America have no ideological program and that their real motivation has to be sought elsewhere. This is reflected in the well-known tales of enormous fortunes in the possession of Latin American despots prior to their downfall. No such phenomenon has been observed in the Middle East. Moreover, Middle Eastern officers are characterized by left-of-center, or even radical, ideologies. It is relevant to note certain of these features, such as, the total eradication of the ruling landed oligarchy, land reform in the countryside, and nationalization of big businesses that does not interfere with the sanctity of private property. These policies reflect a consistent trend, which is compatible with the class position of the officer corps as civilians. These officers were simply instituting a lower-middle-class social policy, which created a new class and not merely a new elite.

The decline of military coups in the radical Arab states in recent decades confirms this argument. In Syria there has not been a coup since 1970, and in Iraq the last "real" coup was in 1968. Egypt experienced only the 1952 army revolution and has possibly reached a point where scholars may start pondering whether army politics are still characteristic of that country. In the context of Iraq and Syria the question may be raised as to what caused this radical decline in the number of coups. The conventional reply would have us believe that it is a manifestation of improved measures of repression, combined with the attrition of a potential opposition group.[136] I suggest an additional explanation, more in keeping with my explanatory paradigm. The phenomenon of the decline of the coups is prima facie evidence that the Mamluk theory regarding the army phenomenon in the modern Middle East is deficient. Coups were an in-built feature of the Mamluk system and the only means of grasping power. This issue is the subject of an important study by E. Be'eri.[137] He considered the chief reason for the decline of military coups to be the "failure" of military regimes, which sensitized people to the shortcomings of the officer-turned-politician and made them more inclined toward the technocrat.[138] However, there is insufficient evidence for the "failure" in terms of public legitimacy. The success or failure of a regime is clearly a complex issue, and this is a case in point. For our purposes it is enough to cite Issawi's conclusion that the pace of economic development in the major Arab states in the 1960s was one of the fastest in the world, which suggests that the "failure" thesis is questionable.[139]

The growing politicization of the Arab armies, leading again to the familiar professionalization argument, is also debatable, as I have shown. For example, the Arab armies in the 1960s possessed the most sophisticated Soviet weaponry, which they could not have handled without a certain degree of professionalization. It is appropriate to note the high professional level of the Argentine army in the 1983 Falklands war, at the very time when a military junta was ruling the country—that is, when the politicization of the army was at its zenith. It seems doubtful, therefore, that professionalization and army coups are related factors.

The reason for the waning of coups could be sought in terms of social structure. In Latin America military intervention in politics came in the wake of the armed struggle for independence, at a time when tension and conflict between the landed oligarchy and the middle class reached a peak. The usual analysis for Latin America is that the army was reluctant to retire to the barracks once it had been drawn into politics, and thus the pattern repeated itself.[140] However, in Latin America the old struggle between a strong landed oligarchy and a relatively strong middle class (unquestionably the most advanced in the Third World) has persisted unremittingly since the nineteenth century. Today the landed oligarchy is as entrenched in its old positions as ever, and its success in the field of economics has made the urban middle class even more thirsty for political power. In such a stalemate situation the old mediatory position of the army is of vital importance if bloodshed is to be averted, but the army is ideologically committed to the preservation of the status quo, which effectively freezes the prevailing stalemate.

In the Middle East events took an entirely different course. Here the army was from the start committed to a lower-middle-class ideology. Consequently, its first act upon assumption of power was to eliminate the ruling elite, which was effected with ease and very little bloodshed, thereby demonstrating again that the new landed oligarchy in the Middle East was not yet deeply entrenched. With the overthrow of the elite the class structure of these countries became much more egalitarian, and pockets of discontent, resistance, and potential rebellion were eliminated. Consequently, the army regime enjoyed a relatively high level of public legitimacy. The question of the degree of support that a regime enjoys is crucial in determining if an army coup is to take place.

Communism, Socialism, and Beyond

I have shown that large-scale peasant revolution did not occur in the Middle East because there was no massive agrarian problem in this area until the middle of the nineteenth century. It is my contention that this situation also explains both the meager success of communism in the Middle East and the ideological course adopted by radical Arab regimes. In trying to comprehend why Middle Eastern regimes and populations refrained from adherence to communism, I first discuss the voluntaristic theories of some devoted Egyptian Marxists and their European colleagues.

These voluntaristic theories were forged mainly in the context of a Marxist assessment of the social nature of the 1952 Egyptian revolution and the Nasser regime.[141] Marxist observers were basically sympathetic to the Nasser regime because of its role in the final decolonization of Egypt and the various socialistic measures it took against private capital enterprise. They were, however, critical of the regime for its failure to institute a "true" socialist regime based on massive social mobilization with the help of Communist party machinery. The Marxist explanation for this failure is purely voluntaristic—that is, that the basic ideology of the officers was and remained nationalistic. "The group *refused* to change to universalistic socialism."[142]

This view is too simplistic; it renders a sociological class analysis of the society in question superfluous. Indeed, Egyptian Marxists tended to attribute the failure of their ideology to the wickedness and folly of the ruling elite rather than to objective factors. Yet the impartial analyst should consider the possibility that Egypt was in a sense objectively unprepared for the transition to communism.

Study of the relations between Islam and communism is by now more than a generation old. It may have started with Bernard Lewis' 1954 pioneering article, in which he observed that Islamic societies were susceptible to communism because both Islam and communism adhered to authoritarian (if not totalitarian) principles.[143] By the same token, in parts of the Islamic world, as in communist countries, the state has always played a preeminent role in the economy. Nevertheless, this half-prophecy was not fulfilled, and other than Southern Yemen, which is strictly speaking beyond the scope of the present study, communism has not become a major force in any Middle Eastern country. If Lewis' analysis, despite its theoretical brilliance, has not been substantiated, we probably ought to take into account additional factors other than the structure of the two respective creeds.

Manfred Halpern, in his famous book, *The Politics of Social Change*, devoted a chapter to the prospects of communism in the Arab world.[144] He was much more circumspect than Lewis in considering the various factors favoring or discouraging communism. He reached the conclusion that citing the formal resemblance or differences between the two creeds weighed as much against communism as for it because those who professed Islam also may have identified the potential "danger" of communism. Thus, almost every argument for or against communism was a two-sided coin. According to Halpern, a major factor that hampered the success of communism in the Arab world was the early support of the Soviet Union for the establishment of the State of Israel. This argument is only partially convincing, for soon after 1948 the Soviet Union reversed its policy quite definitively. Clear proof that indeed no trace of ill-feeling remains is reflected in the cooperation and cordial relations between the Soviet Union and several Arab states since the mid-1950s.

While Lewis sought to prove that Islam was receptive to communism, others claimed that Islam was a bulwark against communism. This argument was contradicted by the case of Albania as well as by at least one major political development in the area—namely, the massive support of the Arabs in Israel for the Communist party, which reached 50 percent of the Arab vote in the 1977 general elections. True, it has been claimed that the support of many Arabs in Israel for the Communist party is not so much a genuine commitment to a Marxist-Leninist world view as it is an expression of repudiation of the State of Israel. However, this argument is untenable because there is, in fact, no formal version of Marxism or communism, and in most historical situations where communism suddenly became widespread, formal adherence to Marxism often appeared to be superficial and the real ideological motivation was usually total rejection of the ruling regime.

Consequently, I would argue that Islam as such is probably not a bulwark against communism. Other theorists have made the somewhat erroneous claim that the low popularity of communism stems from socioeconomic backwardness. It is evident that there is a strong association between communism and industrialization in this theory. However, this point is clearly contradicted by all countries that have adopted such a regime. As far as the Ottoman Empire is concerned, the theory is contradicted by the case of Albania, certainly one of the least developed polities to have evolved out of the Ottoman Empire. In the Middle Eastern context this contention is partially contradicted by the case of Iraq, one of the most backward Arab countries, yet the Arab country where the Communist Party has succeeded more than anywhere else. It is worthwhile analyzing this case in some detail.

Tareq Ismael drew up statistics for Communist party membership in 1965. Membership for the main Middle Eastern countries was Syria, 4,000; Jordan, 500; Turkey, 1,000; Egypt, 1,000. The number was notably higher for Iraq—15,000.[145] A general idea of the peculiarity of this phenomenon can be found in Batatu's monumental study, which was largely devoted to the history of the Iraqi Communist party. The enormous attention he gave to that party could create an impression of inflated significance. But the book presented evidence that at certain times the Iraqi Communist party was genuinely strong. Before the 1958 revolution its peak period was the year 1948, when it numbered 4,000 members and was the second largest party in the country.[146] In 1949, the power of the party was estimated by the chief of political police in the following words: "Its doctrines spread so widely in the big towns . . . that . . . nearly fifty percent of the youthful elements of all classes had been carried away by them. It even found its way into the prisons which for a time took much the aspect of institutions of Communist learning."[147]

The finest hour of the Iraqi Communist party was under the Qassem regime, following the 1958 revolution, when the ruler, without a natural social base, found his main support in that party. After the revolt against him in Mosul (March 1959) and pressured by Nàsser's "cold war," Qassem gave the Communists a virtually free hand in forging Iraq's institutions. Thousands of avowed Communists were permitted to appropriate key positions in the army and administration. They included three brigadiers, eighteen colonels, and twenty-seven lieutenant-colonels.[148] But their brightest star was, no doubt, the commander of the air force, also an avowed Communist. Small wonder that the February 1963 coup that toppled the Qassem regime began with the assassination of that very same officer.

According to Batatu, the Communists enjoyed the overwhelming support of the Iraqi public at the beginning of 1959. Their registered membership was estimated at about twenty-five thousand and the number of members in its auxiliary organizations at several hundred thousand.[149] Although these figures are probably exaggerated, they are convincing enough to cite Batatu's statement that "the people who lived through those times still remember with a certain awe the vast sea of men that the party could evoke at a moment's notice."[150]

The considerable public support that Iraqi Communists enjoyed whetted their appetite for power. They made heavy demands on Qassem, which he promptly rejected. In response, the Communists convened a public rally, attended by at least three hundred thousand people. This moment in 1959 was no doubt an all-time high in the influence of the Iraqi Communist party. As Qassem remained adamant in his refusal to submit, the Communists retreated from all-out war against him, a decision some of them were to regret bitterly years later.[151]

Thus, although Iraq is no exception to the general rule of low popularity of Communist parties in the Middle East, it is here that the party had its moments of success, and social historians should seek a far-reaching explanation for this phenomenon. I suggest that the relative success of communism in Iraq lies in the harsh brutality of the agrarian regime associated with the ancien régime, which was harsher than that of any other country in the Middle East. Here there was a gaping chasm between the entirely unexploitative nature of the old tribal social structure and the massive enslavement of tribespeople to their chief that was the norm during the mandatory period and the monarchy.

I may at this point venture to generalize that the success or failure of communism in the Middle East is unconnected with Islam as such; rather, it is related to the general level of class cleavages permeating the society. The low popularity of communism emanates chiefly from the fact that we do not find the centuries-long bitterness and resentment of the masses, mainly peasants, against their oppressors. Therefore, communism, or an ideology of total rejection of the ruling regime, has no real pillar of support; this was especially so after the feeble beginnings of a new ruling class were easily wiped out by the army revolutions. This absence of a natural flag to hoist, I believe, is the real malaise behind the crisis of the intellectuals in the Arab world.

The same reasoning that accounts for the failure of communism in the Arab world applies to the general ideological course chosen by the radical military regimes. This line has been aptly described as left of center, and I believe that this choice was not made by chance nor was it wholly rational. Rather, it was motivated by deep-seated social and psychological factors: such as former social structure and class determinants.

As far as Egypt is concerned, this social policy has often been described, and there is no need to reiterate it. Studies in recent years have shown more or less the same course of development in Iraq and Syria. Good examples are the ideologies of Iraq's rulers Hasan al-Bakr and Saddam Husayn. Hasan al-Bakr was a devout believer and a man of mild social views. These traits found expression in Iraq's 1968 Ba'thi constitution in which we find such phrases as "Islam . . . is the fundamental principle of the constitution"; "the family is the basis of society . . ."; "inheritance is a right governed by the holy law." Socially, the constitution expressed, in J. Batatu's words, "commitment to a mild form of middle class socialism."[152]

P. Mansfield, who studied Saddam Husayn's ideology, saw him as a pragmatic left-wing leader who shunned ideological extremism. He gave Marxism a local, Arab meaning that was substantially different from that ideology in other areas.[153] His personal background was also of relevance in the formation of his ideology, and in this regard Mansfield made the following interesting comment. "His own personal experience derives from central Iraq where, in contrast to the north and south of the country, the humiliating conditions imposed by feudalism hardly existed."[154] It also has been observed that Saddam Husayn's idea of socialism, was expressed only very rarely in public, included very general socialist slogans, and was far removed from the teachings of the founding fathers of socialist doctrine. In practice, as is well known, in Saddam's Iraq, as in the other Arab socialist countries, the main content of that doctrine was really etatism.

The same left-of-center, mild social policy was apparent in Assad's Syria. If we take as an example the land reform policy, we observe clearly that it has been enforced in a strangely mild way. As late as 1976, old landlords were still a force to be reckoned with; they could transfer much of their land to relatives and still enjoyed considerable political influence. Strangely, aside from the expropriation of their lands, they have been left in complete peace.[155] Similarly, the regime's social mobilization policy has been conducted in a mild, even conservative, social atmosphere. A completely modernized party branch leader in a village near Damascus may still veil his wife and seclude her from the outside world. A similar pattern has been found in the economic policy of the regime. Some progress and development have been achieved, but there has not been any really fundamental revolution, especially not in agriculture—the key area of the economy. In short, the Syrian regime, much like the Iraqi, has shunned the Stalinist model of social and economic mobilization.[156] I believe that the underlying cause of this situation and attitude is again the absence of an agonizing historical agrarian problem and the consequent ease with which the ancien régime was eliminated. Seen against the background of China and Russia, the cases of Iraq, Syria, and Egypt lead us to the conclusion that the bigger the predicament of the underprivileged classes before the revolution, the greater the odds that the break with past patterns will be almost total.

Quasi-Parliamentary Democracy:
Turkey and Lebanon

The Ottoman system has led, in a somewhat curious fashion, to the emergence of two democratic, parliamentary polities—Turkey and Lebanon. Lebanon is neither a true democracy nor a direct combination of the Ottoman polity; Turkey, on the other hand, is (at least partially) a parliamentary democracy. However, this statement may have been more valid before the events of the September 1980 army coup than it is today. There was much naïveté in the exuberance with which the Turkish transformation to democracy was hailed by well-wishers in the West. Briefly, the Turkish experience has shown repeatedly that the Turkish nation is ripe for democracy. For example, there was no large-scale following of extremist ideologies, nor were there major obstacles in the path of smooth-functioning, democratic institutions. The malaise of the Turkish political system has been either its inability to curb the violent activity of small extremist groups or the inability of political party leaders to cooperate in order to extricate the country from the parliamentary deadlocks characteristic of a multiparty system. These difficulties have led inevitably to a disastrous situation that reflects the structural problems beneath the surface; before democracy is securely anchored in Turkey, these issues will have to be resolved.

Turkey's democracy, therefore, is still far from perfect, and the substantial legacy of the despotic government of the Ottoman Empire cannot be easily eradicated. Fundamentally, however, it seems that Turkey may be viewed as a Western-style parliamentary democracy, which began in 1945 when President Ismet Inönü decreed the right to form political parties and free elections, and the opposition party then won a resounding victory at the polls in 1950. Inönü's measures seemed to create history ex nihilo. He was unhampered by historical obstacles such as sixty years of political despotism.

His act seemed to constitute a great triumph for the hero school of history and a great blow to social history. On closer inspection, however, it seems that the situation was more complex.

Some scholars have credited Western pressure on Turkey as the determining factor in the nation's sustained transition to parliamentary democracy; according to this view, democracy was a precondition for Turkey's acceptance as a member state by the United Nations. This explanation, however, is not valid. We need only recall other countries in the Middle East (Iraq or Egypt) that were under even greater pressure than Turkey to adopt Western-style democracy; their regimes collapsed at the first real challenge. If external pressure did, in fact, play a certain role in the advent of democracy in Turkey, this in itself would not have sustained the regime. For a political regime to function successfully, it must be consonant with the needs and proclivities of its society. Several trends characteristic of the Turkish polity since 1945 indicate that democracy rests on sound foundations.

One of the most interesting aspects of the functioning of democracy in Turkey has been the political behavior of the peasants, a pattern said to puzzle contemporary experts on Turkey. It has been observed by scholars that "interestingly, the RPP was challenged (from 1950 onwards) not so much in the regions where traditional notables were especially strong as in those areas where socio-economic developments were most permeating. . . . Due to the dyadic structure of notable politics in backward regions, the RPP and its principal contender, the Democrat Party (DP), split the votes almost evenly."[157]

This is a finding of considerable importance. On the whole "landlord politics" did not play an important role in Turkey. Rather, the individual peasant assessed his or her position and interests and lived according to them and not according to an order received from above. This would indicate that in Turkey parliamentary democracy was not premature, a conclusion also reached by W. F. Weiker on the state of modernization among the Turkish peasantry. Summarizing a wide variety of studies he said:

> Most of these [studies] found that, whatever the attitudes held by many villagers before the intense penetration of modernizing influences which took place after World War II, the typical Turkish peasant today is pragmatic, shrewd, cautious in dealing with outsiders. He is also aware of outside events to a very considerable degree, far from automatically averse to the acceptance of new things and new ways, increasingly mobile geographically, and has ambitions for himself and his children.[158]

Turkish democracy suffered at the same time from severe, fundamental structural problems, mainly remnants from the Ottoman past. Two of these problems were (and are) patrimonialism and patronage. Metin Heper saw the survival of patrimonialism as a hurdle to the smooth functioning of democracy in Turkey. Patrimonialism is defined as a political system where the relationship between superior and subordinate is strongly personal rather than rational and bureaucratic.[159] Although in a modern bureaucracy this relationship is limited to working hours, in a patrimonial system the subordination is total. The Ottoman political system was strongly permeated by patrimonialism; Heper's claim was that remnants of this system are still to be found in Turkish democracy today. He noted, for example, that Atatürk himself had no interest in the low echelons of the bureaucracy, with the result that the administration of the Turkish republic eventually reverted to late Ottoman norms of conduct.[160] Furthermore, public administration in Turkey today still wields enormous power vis-à-vis the civil society, far more than is compatible with a pluralistic democracy.

Another institutional remnant of the Ottoman period that mars the smooth functioning of parliamentary democracy is patronage. Of the many definitions of patronage, the only systematic and useful one I have found in the literature is given by Ernest Gellner. He stated that patronage is a political pattern that falls between kinship and full-fledged, Western-type bureaucratic domination.

> Power in a well-centralized and law-abiding bureaucracy is not a form of patronage. In as far as bureaucrats are selected for their posts by fair and public criteria, are constrained to observe impartial rules, are accountable for what they do, and can be removed from their positions without undue difficulty and in accordance with recognized procedures, they are not really patrons, even if they do exercise much power. It is only to the extent to which some or all of these features are lacking, that bureaucracies also become, as indeed they often do, a form of a patronage network.[161]

We can thus speak of a continuum between traditional domination based on kinship and bureaucratic-democratic domination, where patronage is in the middle. Democracy is transitional to the extent that patronage is widespread. Keeping this definition in mind, we may consider a study of patronage relations by Sabri Sayari. He emphasized the importance of patronage in Turkish politics, showing, for example, that one of the most active sections of the House of Parliament is the anterooms of the Members of Parliament. Indeed, he claimed that Turkish politics under the republic is the politics of patronage groups. "Following the transition to competitive politics, party strategies for peasant mobilization were based on the recruitment of notables into party ranks who were then entrusted with the task of providing "ready vote banks."[162] This thesis, however, is not wholly convincing. If it were, the crushing defeat of the ruling party in the 1950 elections would be totally incomprehensible. Indeed, Sayari himself showed that the continued activity of democratic parties has gradually eclipsed the pattern of patronage relations.[163]

In the final analysis the regime formed in Turkey in the wake of the 1950 elections may be considered a parliamentary democracy, albeit a defective version. Was it in fact created ex nihilo by Inönü? I strongly reject this notion. There were indications that democratic practice already existed in the Kemalist regime. The main chronology of events concerning this regime were as follows. In May 1919, Mustafa Kemal, a hero of World War I and a general in the now defunct Ottoman army, crossed from Istanbul into Anatolia and started to organize passive resistance to the occupation. In the second half of 1919, two congresses were held in Sivas and Erzurum, where the new movement crystallized. In 1920, free elections were held and a general assembly convened, which in effect was a constituent assembly in all but name. In 1920 and 1921, the main task of the new regime was to withstand an invading Greek army. With this mission successfully completed in 1922, the Kemalist regime was securely in the saddle, and the remnants of the old regime gradually were eliminated. First the sultanate was abolished, followed by the califate in 1924.

Concerning the nature of that regime from my viewpoint, it has been correctly observed that Atatürk himself was not head of a democratic state. But the basis of his strong Western orientation was a positive estimation of the liberal democratic model and a realization that authoritarianism was a necessary, but transitory evil.[164] In this context it behooves us to examine the views of Zia Gökalp, the most important ideologist of the Turkish national movement, who had a great influence on Atatürk. "The political regime which Gökalp desires to see established in Turkey is a national democracy. He regards democracy and nationalism, the dominant watchwords of the First World War, as two ideals closely linked with one another. Both are based on the same principle of equality among nations."[165]

Certain insights can be gained from a study of the formative years of the Kemalist revolution in Anatolia. In the formal ideology of Kemalism there is no trace of democracy as a principle, although populism may be viewed as approximating this concept. In the *Nutuk* Kemal stated that in December 1922 he announced his intention to establish the People's Party as a "democratic party," yet any democratic pointers in the incipient regime were to be found below the surface.[166]

In reading the *Nutuk,* one is impressed at the outset by the fact that many of the constitutional steps in Anatolia at the time were legislated independently of Kemal, sometimes even without his knowledge. A case in point was the ruling party. E. Özbudun has shown convincingly that this party was at least partially a popular movement that was established without a formal act.[167] Furthermore, although Atatürk himself was authoritarian, none of his major moves was carried out in a dictatorial manner. There were always elections, committees, and every decision was reached by democratic vote casting. The elections to the First Assembly were a case in point. Frey cites Halide

Edip, a distinguished eyewitness, as saying that "the elections took place in absolute freedom all over the country. I do not remember any election which had been so free, with the possible exception of the one in 1908."[168]

It would, however, be a grave error to conclude that democracy was achieved in Turkey purely as a result of ideological tendencies. Democracy developed from deep-rooted needs closely connected with the social structure and the material base of the society. If democracy in the West is the political expression of a society where the middle class predominates both quantitatively and politically, then clearly Turkey is not a middle class society in the Western sense of the word. Rather, in my view, parliamentary democracy here was an outcome of the lack of a dominant class of landlords and the creation, during the nineteenth-century reform process, of a ruling class possessing all the traits of a salaried middle class. Let us consider these two points in detail.

We saw in the last chapter that the emergent trend toward large-estate formation in all parts of the Middle East after 1858 was much less pronounced in Anatolia. As a result, the Turkish landholding regime is to this day still based on the small peasant and the independent peasant community. Consequently, large landlords enjoy much less influence on the national scene in Turkey than they did in old-regime Syria, Iraq, or Egypt. Frey analyzed in detail the professional structure of parliamentary delegates between 1920 and 1957.[169] The stage was entirely controlled by members with a bureaucratic background. Only 9 percent of the delegates were classified as agriculturists; some could not even be considered rural leaders but rather were agricultural officials and experts.[170] The peasantry itself seemed to have been completely inactive at the time of Kemal, who personally claimed that the peasant "carries very little weight."[171]

The total absence of class struggle in the Turkish revolution as well as the even division of various socioeconomic forces between government and opposition has led scholars to view the revolution as political rather than social.[172] Although there is much truth in this statement, it is my view that the development was not freely chosen by the nationalist leadership. It was rather a natural consequence of a social structure in which the main class cleavage of preindustrial society was lacking—namely, the cleavage between landlords and their subordinate peasantry. Özbudun toyed with the hypothetical possibility of the Kemalist elite choosing a more socialist line of development. I doubt whether objective conditions could have led the Kemalists in this direction. The peasants were not susceptible to large-scale mobilization because 87 percent of them were landowners.[173]

A comparison of Turkey and Russia reflects the partly imposed nature of the dominant ideology of the intellectual elite. I have shown how the first intellectuals who appeared in Russia in the nineteenth century embraced the cause of the peasants. This contrasts with the attitudes of the intellectuals in nineteenth-century Turkey. The predominant tone of the Young Ottomans was not a radical critique of the ruling regime. Most of them were low-level officials in the Ottoman bureaucracy, and thus, unlike the Russian intellectuals, they were in no way an alienated elite.[174] In Turkey the classical type of westernizer was not the uprooted intellectual lacking a well-defined position in the social structure of the old regime. Nor was he an aristocrat in an extremely ambiguous position. Here the classical figure of the westernizer was someone like Bihruz Bey, a literary hero in a novel by Recaizade Ekrem.[175] He was a high-ranking state bureaucrat, well to do and self-confident. That an important writer in Istanbul around 1870 chose to symbolize the problem of westernization in the Ottoman Empire in this hero was significant and probably indicated that at the time westernization was not associated with a major social cleavage threatening to undermine the entire structure of society.

The absence of a rural aristocracy or even landed upper class in Turkey was probably the most important factor facilitating the advent of democracy in Turkey. Although in Egypt, Iraq, and Syria a dominant class of large landlords required a strong repressive apparatus, this was not so in Turkey. In Turkey the transformation of the nineteenth-century Ottoman bureaucracy was an important element. Various aspects of its development lead us to view this bureaucracy at the end of the Ottoman period as a sort of "bureaucratic bourgeoisie"—that is, a relatively modern bureaucracy in the Weberian sense. Its members were salaried, professionally trained, and relatively cut off from the productive base of society, thus forming a distinct social group.

Contrary to what is often maintained, the fact that the bureaucracy that developed in the nineteenth century was a meritocracy was important. At least we may consider it a bureaucracy that was open to the admission of members of the lower classes, who could advance only on the basis of their inherent worth. Entry from below was in fact quite easy. The new professional schools that were established in the second half of the nineteenth century did not charge fees and qualified the graduate for a position in the administration. In fact, the principal politicians of the Ottoman Empire in the nineteenth century (Reshid, Ali, Fuad, Midhat) were all of dubious social origin, and none of their descendants ever rose to prominence. Similarly, all the illustrious *ulema* families of the past disappeared into oblivion in the nineteenth century.

An important social development of the Tanzimat period was that the Ottoman bureaucracy became a more closed social group. Although before 1839, 70 percent of those in high positions had antecedents without status, during the Tanzimat this figure dropped to 52 percent and under Abdülhamid to 49 percent. At the same time, a contrasting trend was underway. From the first to the last third of the nineteenth century the holders of "aristocratic," traditional titles (for example, *zade,* or son of) decreased by as much as one-third.[176] This meant that the Ottoman bureaucracy was now composed more of lower class recruits who were closing their ranks and showing some degree of esprit de corps.

An important related development was the special geographic pattern of recruitment. Available data showed that a huge proportion of recruits to high positions in the nineteenth-century Ottoman administration came from Istanbul (41 percent in the last quarter of the century). At the same time, 29 percent came from Anatolia and only 8 percent from Arab lands.[177] In terms of the present study (which compares developments in Turkey, Egypt, Syria, and Iraq), this means that Turkey was vastly favored over other areas in terms of bureaucratic development. This conclusion tallies perfectly with Dankwart Rustow's compilations, whereby "because of a long tradition of public service and because of systematic discrimination against Arabs in the late Ottoman period, the armistice also left this rump of the Ottoman Empire (which contained less than two-thirds of its population) with 93 per cent of its military officers and 85 per cent of its administrators."[178] In other words, it is evident that the development that transformed the Ottoman bureaucracy into a "bureaucratic bourgeoisie" favored Turkey over other countries in the defunct empire.

A comparison between Turkey and Egypt is in order here. We have seen that in the Ottoman Empire the role of Istanbul proper is a locus of recruitment was overwhelming. In nineteenth-century Egypt most of the Egyptians recruited to positions of importance "were drawn from families of provincial notables, the so-called *ayan* of the countryside."[179] The absence of a tangible landed upper class in Turkey gave the Istanbul urban middle class its opportunity to rise to positions of influence. However, in Egypt an alliance was forged between the central government and rural landed upper class, which was characteristic of most historical agrarian bureaucracies where the bourgeoisie remained the junior partner of the landed elite. Moreover, Donald Reid showed that late nineteenth-century Egypt experienced an impressive development of its professional middle class, which continued unabated through the first half of the twentieth century.[180] At the same time, these new organizations remained completely subservient to the ruling landed oligarchy. Many of this group came directly from landed families, and those that did not preferred to remain inconspicuous. Lawyers are in fact known to have become intimately associated with landlords in business and political matters.[181]

Robert Tignor wrote an extensive study on another aspect of the same phenomenon.[182] In the first half of the twentieth century Egypt witnessed a considerable growth in its business bourgeoisie. However, sociologically, most of those involved were not indigenous Egyptians; they were foreign nationals or members of the religious minorities (i.e., members of ethnic groups not originating in Egypt). They became strong enough to voice political demands for economic development but remained too feeble to challenge the power monopoly of the landed oligarchy, whose support they vitally needed.[183] Thus, the fact that Egypt's main bourgeois sector was not full-fledged Egyptian meant that the bourgeoisie was not in a position to challenge the landed elite. Naturally, nothing comparable to this took place in Turkey.

An important landmark in transforming traditional Ottoman bureaucracy into a bureaucratic bourgeoisie was the introduction into Turkey of Western-style elite education. The first institution was the Galatasaray Lycée in the 1860s, where French was the language of instruction. Lewis described the importance of this event. "The influence of the Galatasaray school on the rise of modern Turkey has been enormous. As the need for administrators, diplomats and others with a Western education and a capacity to handle Western administrative apparatus became more and more pressing, the graduates of Galatasaray came to play a preponderant role in the politics and administration of the Ottoman Empire, and after it, of the Turkish republic."[184]

These glowing words were criticized by A. M. Kazamias, who demonstrated that this school was not the main source of administrators.[185] He admitted, however, to the exceptionally important role of the school as the first high school and as a model for those that followed—that is, a high school staffed by French teachers, with French as the language of instruction, an almost entirely secular, modern curriculum, and where Muslims and non-Muslims were educated side by side.[186]

Another exceptionally prestigious school deserving mention here was the Mülkiye school for public administration, which in the early years of the republic was transformed into Ankara University's faculty of political science. This school became the most important reservoir for the recruitment of Ottoman administrators,[187] a trend that became even more pronounced under the Republic; it was claimed that a list of its graduates read like a "Who's Who in Turkey."[188]

There is little doubt that modern bureaucratic norms permeated late Ottoman bureaucracy to a much greater extent than they did at the beginning of the nineteenth century. I based this conclusion on a detailed study of the Ottoman administration of Jerusalem at the beginning of the twentieth century. These findings were confirmed for the whole empire by Carter Findley's study of bureaucratic reform in the Ottoman Empire. Summing up his findings the author said, inter alia:

> By the time of its collapse . . . the Ottoman Empire had acquired a unique position among the historic states of the Islamic world in a sense that went beyond the mere fact of its longevity. Now, it was unique as well in the extent to which it had acquired the legal and administrative apparatus of a

modern polity. The patent archaism of the overall imperial framework was obviously something that even the most extensive progress of this kind could not change. Yet, the Ottomans had made tremendous strides in creating a rationally regulated bureaucratic apparatus of a sort that could . . . provide the means for the kind of credible and effective administration to which they had by then aspired for a century and more.[189]

An important new norm that was evolving was that of service to the state. A major case in point was the career of Midhat Pasa, undoubtedly the greatest of the nineteenth-century reformers, whose devotion to the cause of reform was truly remarkable. I believe that his very appearance reflected a substantial change. Also notable in this respect was the case of Sati al-Husri, the foremost ideologue of Arab nationalism, who until the end of World War I was one of the most superior Arab bureaucrats in the central Ottoman administration, which he served faithfully, having grown up within the system.[190] In 1919, he went to Damascus and almost overnight became a major spokesman of Arabism. This sudden shift may appear somewhat puzzling. To my mind the explanation is to be sought in the process of bureaucratic education that inculcated in al-Husri and others a strong sense of devotion and duty to the state. His extraordinary intellectual contribution to the Ottoman bureaucracy is particularly relevant here. Only with the liquidation of that bureaucracy was he free to reveal his personal feelings—hence, the sudden shift.

In the final analysis, then, the group that rose to power in Turkey in the wake of World War I was a secular, modernized, westernized elite, possessing all the appropriate social traits to warrant the appellation "bureaucratic bourgeoisie."[191] The monopoly of power this elite held was total and unchallenged. Especially lacking was the kind of challenge present in most undemocratic regimes—that is, one that would originate in a strong landed upper class. I believe the advent of democracy is best understood in these terms.

Lebanon

Lebanon is the most unusual political phenomenon in the Middle East. In my opinion, it presents a major case study providing proof that there is a close connection between past social and agrarian structure and the modern political regime. It is possible to discern from the literature two interpretations of the nature of democracy in Lebanon, although these are rarely presented as dichotomous or mutually exclusive. The first is mainly functionalist. J. P. Entelis, for example, viewed the basis of democracy in Lebanon as the result of the need of several religious communities to share a common territory and build a common life. Confessionalism, in this view, was seen as a natural, rational choice. "Lebanon is a pluralistic confessional society; a society characterized by sharp cleavages between different sectarian groups. It is not a pluralistic society on the "democratic" model, however, where pluralism is conceived as a "dispersion of power between groups which are bound together by cross-cutting loyalties, and by common values."[192] Entelis further pointed out that when different religious communities live side by side, it is inevitable that one will be more preeminent than the others if an integrated polity is to be formed. In Lebanon this was not the case. The communities managed to live harmoniously, and a confessional form of government was a natural outcome of this equilibrium.

The need of the various communities in Lebanon to achieve a modus vivendi is one component of that regime, albeit not the only one. Several political systems in the world are based on religious communities predating the nation-state. Iraq, with its Sunnis, Shiites, and Kurds, is no less religiously fragmented than Lebanon, but in Iraq the question of confessional democracy never arose. Soviet Russia likewise comprises a great number of religious communities, with no discernible impact on the political regime. If in these countries one community is overwhelmingly dominant, this is less obvious in a country such as Yugoslavia and even less so in Albania, where the Muslim community never attempted to assert its dominance over the Christian community. Even in Lebanon these religious communities have lived together without the clearcut ascendancy of one community—for example, the princedom of Bashir II in the first half of the nineteenth century. This was a polity that combined the different communities in a manner considered more or less just by all of them. However, the rule was despotic and at times ruthless. It is therefore doubtful whether a democratic form of government is a natural derivation of the confessional structure of Lebanese society. I tend to see the rise of parliamentary democracy in Lebanon as interwoven with the historical development and socioeconomic institutions of that society. In this, I follow closely in the footsteps of Albert Hourani and Charles Issawi in this claim.[193]

Ecological factors played a major role in determining the modern structure of Lebanon. The region is one of the most mountainous in the Middle East and inaccessible from outside in terms of premodern technology. Consequently, direct control was problematic in the region. The Ottomans were therefore prepared to concede a wide measure of autonomy to local forces. Nevertheless, one should not underestimate the indirect contribution of the Ottomans to the creation of a democratic Lebanon. They were content to raise taxes centrally rather than to strive to introduce the *timar* system. What was true for Egypt was equally true for Lebanon—the centralized collection of taxes was the sine qua non of the *imara*, the princedom, which was the most important political institution in Ottoman Lebanon. Without this centralized control of taxation, it is reasonable to assume that the extreme fragmentation caused by geographical factors would not have made the rise of an institution like the princedom possible. The control of taxation gave a distinct advantage to the amir, the prince, over the feudalists, who were the local rulers, resembling feudal lords in medieval Europe. Hourani fully realized this when he said:

> The Ottoman government was able to intervene effectively when it wished. It did so several times when Fakhr al-Din [*amir* in the sixteenth century] grew too strong, and finally defeated and killed him. On the other hand, it was perhaps only because of Turkish approval that the princedom came into existence at all. It was convenient to have one tax-collector for the mountains, provided he did not become too strong and free; it was through Ottoman help that the Ma'nis had established their rule in the first instance.[194]

Hourani looked for the root of modern democracy in Lebanon in the tradition of rural independence and freedom from tyranny of the central Ottoman government. I have in fact shown that the villages and rural society during the Ottoman period enjoyed freedom to a much greater extent than was previously realized. But in Lebanon center-periphery relations (relations between the amir and the feudal chiefs) were based on a real division of power that was not present anywhere else in the empire.

Although nominally agricultural land in Lebanon was *miri* (as in other parts of the Ottoman Empire), there is a general consensus that this land was in fact private.[195] Most of it was under the ownership of feudal lords, who were political and social leaders of tiny mountainous regions. Within a ruling family the position was hereditary. This feudalistic agrarian regime disappeared in the first half of the nineteenth century, largely as a result of incessant conflict about the relative authority of the amir and the feudal chiefs. In the middle decades of the century all these powers were completely enmeshed in constant violent disturbances, petty wars, and sporadic massacres, which eventually weakened the Lebanese feudal institution. Small wonder that the final settlement of this period of chaos, the Lebanese Organic Law of 1861, promptly abolished feudalism once and for all.

In the second half of the nineteenth century there was a process of transfer of lands from former landlords to small peasants. Because feudal taxation in any form was abolished, these lands became less remunerative. It is quite probable that there were now new fields of potential investment, as evidenced by the phenomenal rise of Beirut and the coastal towns, due to the vastly expanding foreign trade between Syria and Europe. The old feudal elite was largely transformed into an urban business bourgeoisie. As a result, the land regime in Lebanon in the twentieth century became overwhelmingly one of small peasant proprietorship. This fact was reflected in several monographs written on Lebanese villages. I consider one of these an example—the mountainous village of Dahr, east of Tripoli. The villagers at the time of the study (the early 1940s) were a small homogeneous group, mainly proprietors.[196] In addition to the individually owned arable land of about 250 acres, the village community owned between 250 and 300 acres of grazing land. The author noted a great attachment to the land, "a mixture of profound love and reverential awe."[197] Strong adherence to traditional values also was apparent in the importance of the family and village as meaningful solidarity groups. "Family ties are, of course, the most important of all, but the feeling of community solidarity is also very strong. Villages tend to act as a unit in times of crisis, and bloody battles between villages are not uncommon."[198] Other village monographs from Lebanon reflected a similar pattern.

The village of Dahr raises an exceptionally interesting and elusive question. How do ancient modes of social organization and economic production manage to survive in the face of a purely capitalist formation? K. and P. Glavanis have dealt with this question extensively in the context of contemporary Egyptian agriculture. Their conclusion is applicable to Lebanon as well. Economic issues are not the sole consideration of any given production unit. There is also the question of security of future income and possibly a measure of clinging to traditional modes of social organization. However, it would appear that the predominance of small landlords in the Lebanese land regime was certainly an important factor in the development of a Western-style parliamentary democracy—as it was in France and the United States.

Due to the enormous economic boom of the coastal towns in Lebanon in the second half of the nineteenth century, the center of gravity of Lebanese society and polity shifted from the mountains to Beirut. Although Lebanese society has been based on the predominance of feudal leaders, it also has been a society based on an intricate network of patrons and clients, in which the wealthy businessman-leader is the inevitable cornerstone.[199] These leaders have not been feudal leaders as much as they have been feudalists-turned-capitalists. The pattern of relations between them and their followers has been far removed from the usual pattern found in typical Western democracies characterized by patron-client relations. In Lebanon every national leader "employs" a number of *kabadays* (strong men or bullies) whose task it is to ensure the electoral support of followers on election day. This support is mainly based on mutual interest. In exchange for their vote, the supporters expect the leader to help them by providing jobs, contracts, and other economic favors. Indeed, this description does not support the view of Lebanon as a Western-style parliamentary democracy. If I nevertheless claim that it has been such a democracy, it is because in Lebanon there is an absence of a landed upper class and the predominance of a class of small proprietors and the predominance of a commercial bourgeoisie centered mainly in Beirut, of which the political elite clearly has been an integral part. The confessional equilibrium is thus an indispensable component of the peculiar Lebanese democracy, as are its socioeconomic traits, which in themselves are decisive enough to create a bourgeois democracy.

CHAPTER EIGHT

Conclusion

In this book I have tried to trace the effect of the Ottoman socioagrarian regime on the sociopolitical structure of the modern Middle East. My starting point was the sixteenth century, during which the Ottoman land regime took its final shape. Its salient features were small landownership and independent village communities. The land regime was designed to help protect the Ottoman central government from a potential landed aristocracy, which, if permitted to emerge, would have threatened the supremacy of the Ottoman regime itself.

In subsequent centuries the land regime was subjected to great pressures; however, contrary to current scholarly opinion, it did not succumb to them. This point was illustrated by a detailed study of the archives of one limited region in western Anatolia in the seventeenth century. Archival materials indicated that, generally speaking, a land regime of smallholders was still predominant at the time, and the village community was as viable, strong, and independent as it had been in the previous century.

I further investigated the development of the land regime in the empire more generally from the sixteenth to the middle of the nineteenth century and specifically until 1858, when a new land law was enacted. In spite of clear tendencies toward land engrossment during this period, the old land regime remained substantially unchanged. I first examined and rejected a number of theories based on the assumption that this regime was eliminated after the sixteenth century; then I examined the various factors that worked for and against the preservation of the ancien régime. Chief among the former were those connected with the weakening of the central power in the seventeenth and eighteenth centuries, which led, among other things, to the strengthening of the nomadic fringe and a consequent cessation in the cultivation of large tracts of low-lying land. Insofar as plains were (and are) potentially more suitable than mountainous areas for large-estate formation, this served as an obstruction to such development.

The main factor at work in the opposite direction was also an outcome of the debilitation of the central government. There were several provinces outside the direct control of the central government, which were under the influence of rising provincial strongmen and notables (*ayan*) who ruled them politically and economically. But a perusal of the actual material relating to the records of these notables indicated quite clearly that they did not go so far as to bring about a change in the provincial land regime and did not establish for themselves landed estates in the full sense of the term. At most, they monopolized functions connected with taxation. The assumption that as far as they were concerned this amounted to actual estate ownership (the Weberian term "prebendal domain" is sometimes used in this context) is untenable. As actual landlords they could appropriate a further proportion of the produce as rent, an arrangement made possible by Islamic and Ottoman law; and due to the noninstitutionalization of their position vis-à-vis land and peasants, they were disinherited perfunctorily as a result of nineteenth-century reforms. Because it is unlikely that they were ignorant of these facts and possibilities, it is more feasible to draw the conclusion that the notables assessed their power as being insufficiently strong for carrying out a sociopolitical and legal revolution in the provinces. This could be considered proof that the power of the Ottoman central government in the seventeenth and eighteenth centuries did not decline as much as is generally supposed.

The key event for the beginning of the truly large-scale changes in the Ottoman socioagrarian regime was the enactment of the 1858 land law. This law was in effect a reenactment of the traditional Ottoman land law, with the introduction of relatively minor additions. The main addition was the enjoinment that each landowner register his or her land in the land registry. Linked to the simultaneous increase in public security and the salient growth in population, this law had a far-reaching effect. For the first time, it became possible to acquire land from the government "on paper," and for the first time there were sound economic reasons for doing so.

The aftereffects of the law were substantially different from those generally supposed. It is often assumed that it set the stage for a wholesale takeover of peasant tenures by city strongmen, but in fact the reality was more complicated. Such a takeover occurred in only a few places, such as lower Iraq, where the land law was utterly inappropriate for the basic social structure. The misdirected efforts of some local officials to enforce the law in Iraq against all odds had disastrous consequences and encouraged the rapid development of a repressive regime of large estates.

Egypt also underwent a rapid process of large-estate formation in the nineteenth century, mainly because of the large-scale economic boom, starting in the 1820s, that resulted from the introduction of cotton. But in other areas, such as the central mountainous region of Palestine and probably most of Anatolia, the 1858 land law was enforced with no unanticipated harmful results, such as land engrossment by unauthorized urbanites. I found in these regions large-scale estate formation in formerly uninhabited plains, from which the nomads were now being increasingly and permanently banished.

This development, which started in the last decades of the nineteenth century, gained momentum in the first half of the twentieth. In both Egypt and Iraq a process developed whereby smallholders were subjected to the control of large absentee landlords in a land regime quite reminiscent of a feudal regime. On the other hand, in most areas of Turkey small landowners continued to predominate; large landlordism remained confined mainly to eastern Anatolia or to uninhabited tracts elsewhere.

With this background we are now able to assess the effects of the land regime on the incipient sociopolitical regimes in the postindependence period. But before analyzing the purely political aspect, I must clarify the socioeconomic background. The traditional Ottoman socioagrarian structure has been accused of having constituted an obstacle to an industrial revolution. Barrington Moore saw the encouragement or discouragement of such a revolution as one of the most basic qualities of any agrarian system, but my comparative investigation has led in somewhat different directions. My fundamental conclusion is that the absence of an industrial revolution in the Ottoman Empire was not due to its agrarian structure. However, the usual strong association between the two obliged me to undertake a detailed analysis of the subject.

A detailed comparison of the Ottoman Empire and England led me to conclude that many of the factors usually proffered to explain the Industrial Revolution in England were by no means lacking in the Middle East. It will suffice here to mention such factors as the quality of individual entrepreneurship, crushing taxation, and the excessive greediness of governments. Some of these factors were exaggerated; others were false because their presence in similar cultures or at other periods in the history of the Middle East did not help bring about an industrial revolution.

All said and done, I arrived at the conclusion that the Industrial Revolution in England was an outcome of factors peculiar to English history and that other continental countries basically imitated the English. From a Middle Eastern perspective the fact that these European countries were able to imitate England was no small matter. No country in the Third World, with the exception of Japan, was sufficiently independent of Great Britain to do likewise.

A careful scrutiny of the economic history of England made clear that it is a mistake to seek the key to the Industrial Revolution in events or occurrences in mid–eighteenth-century England (the date usually given as the beginning of that revolution). Rather, its true origins are to be sought in the late Middle Ages or, more precisely, in the commencement of the large-scale demand for English wool on the part of European high-quality wool production centers, which led to an enormous rise in English wool exports.

No less important was the political situation that at that time characterized the English monarchy, especially the absolute political (and hence economic) weakness of the crown vis-à-vis other social factors in the realm. Kings Edward II and Edward III grasped at a solution. Because the monarch's main source of income was customs duties, prohibition of the export of raw wool would serve to augment the local output of finished woollen products, thus boosting the value added taxed at the ports. A strong textile industry thus became a crucial factor in English economic history in the subsequent centuries, with which, it would seem, most later developments were intimately connected. For example, this development may have helped England, centuries before the Industrial Revolution, to attain relatively high levels of income and capital accumulation, which in turn caused a lowering of interest rates—an acknowledged major factor in the events leading to the Industrial Revolution.

Agrarian developments in the Middle East that began in 1858, and continued with more urgent rapidity in the first half of the twentieth century, found clear expression in the political regimes. In Syria, Egypt, and Iraq the political regimes that came to power after World War I (and under the mandate) had the large landlord class as the main pillar of support. In Iraq and Syria in particular, an alliance came into being between large urban landlords and tribal chiefs cum large landlords. In contrast to these developments, Turkey followed a substantially different course of action, and the biographies of Turkish Members of Parliament during the years indicated that there was only a vestige of influence of large landlords on the national scene.

In regard to the realm of political regimes proper, the Ottoman agrarian regime exerted considerable influence in this field. Contrary to various other societies (such as France, Russia, China), the modern period in the Middle East did not begin with a great agrarian revolution, and no regime there was or is an outgrowth of such a revolution. A comparison of the Middle East with Russia and China indicated that the traditional Middle Eastern agrarian regime was much less repressive than that in either Russia or China and hence did not generate the necessary preconditions for revolution. Undoubtedly, the Middle Eastern peasantry had to part with a considerable proportion of its produce, but it was not a repressed peasantry with regard to legal title to the land. The historical facts showed that this was more important than is usually assumed, and in fact it does go a long way toward explaining why no major agrarian upheaval occurred in the Middle East.

Another major component in the modern Middle Eastern political formation is the dominance of army elites in some of the region's major countries. Army elites have become a popular research subject in recent years, but none of these studies offered adequate explanation for the predominance of army elites in the area. The usual argument for this predominance is that whereas in the West the armies developed into professional bodies, in the Middle East army elites were—and remained—the main pillar of society, and consequently there is nothing surprising about their predominance. On closer inspection the situation appeared to be less simple. The truth was that the separation between the military and civil authorities was no less far-reaching in the Middle East than in the major European countries. Likewise, the difference in levels of professionalization between Europe and the Middle East was not that great, for the Middle Eastern armies underwent a substantial measure of professionalization in the nineteenth century.

The real difference between the armies in the Middle East and Europe was one of class and socioagrarian structure. Whereas in South America and medieval Europe the traditional role of the army was to guard a social hierarchy, at the center of which stood a landed upper class, the Ottoman army had no such function, simply because no landed upper class worthy of the name existed. Middle Eastern armies therefore lacked the aristocratic aura that accompanied armies in Europe or South America. In the absence of such an aura, it was only natural that the army was recruited from among the lowest classes. Indeed, Ottoman sources indicated quite clearly that this was exactly the case. When a landlord elite came to power at the end of the Ottoman period, the army elite felt free of any bonds of solidarity toward it. The army then sided with its social class of origin, and when social unrest and resentment of the lower classes against the ruling elite mounted, the army revolted, thereby antedating a possible popular upheaval that might have erupted some years later.

It is interesting and important to underscore the fact that although traditionally Middle Eastern armies were characterized by recruitment from the lowest classes, the social origin most common to the twentieth-century officer corps has been the lower middle class. The reason for this, it seemed, was that the army was professionalized more intensely and earlier than other sectors, and it had come to require a certain modicum of prior education. As a major expression of the new national entity, the army's symbolic position has risen somewhat. As a result, the army has become a channel of promotion for those with both a drive for success and certain, if minimal, qualifications, which probably put them a notch above the lower social strata.

Incidentally, it is often suggested that the officer corps revolted exactly because their more modern education had alienated them from their traditional surroundings. Against this argument it must be pointed out that the armies of China and Russia were also more advanced technologically than other sectors of their societies, yet they both remained basically loyal to the traditional ruling system.

Another major aspect of the modern Middle Eastern political culture is the role of communism. In the 1950s, when the Middle East finally became free of colonial rule and could develop its own genuine political system, speculation was rife about the prospects of communism. From today's perspective it seems quite clear that communism has been distinctly unsuccessful in this area. I suggest that the true reason for its lack of success will emerge from a comparative analysis of the Middle East with some cases where communism prevailed and that the explanation will be in line with my suggestions concerning the absence of a peasant revolution. A prerequisite for a communist revolution, it seems, is a suitable prior socioagrarian background—that is, a long period of extremely repressive class structure. According to the record, the main drive behind the major communist revolutions was the destructive force of the peasantry, mainly directed at the landlords. Generally speaking, these masses were not striving for what proved to be the actual outcome of the revolution. What they wanted above all was a piece of land and a secure hold of it. In contrast, the traditional Middle Eastern social structure was not so repressive as to constitute a hotbed of resentment and sedition. In consequence, moderate social reform seemed to have been a much more common objective.

Democracy also has put in an appearance in the polities that are a direct outgrowth of the Ottoman Empire. This has happened mainly in Turkey and Lebanon, and this development also was not inexplicable. Turkey's political system can be characterized as partially democratic. The political vicissitudes that have pursued Turkey in recent years have not really changed this. I have tried to show that despite the obvious greatness of some of Turkey's modern leaders, the socioeconomic background for their activity is indispensable to an understanding of the path followed by that country. In nineteenth-century Turkey no class of large landlords emerged on a scale comparable to that of the main Arab countries where the landlords constituted the main obstacle to any form of democratic government; instead, small landowners remained numerically predominant. On the other hand, in the course of the nineteenth-century reforms there developed what can be described as a bureaucratic middle class. Not only did the Ottoman state become more bureaucratic in the nineteenth century, but also most of the new bureaucrats who had graduated from the new professional schools (and who were supposed to serve a large empire) remained after World War I at the disposal of the Turkish republic. Turkey thus possessed a bureaucratic middle class that was substantially larger than might have been expected under less abnormal conditions.

Lebanon presented an altogether different case. Here a truly feudal regime existed, stemming from the special ecology of Mount Lebanon. This regime collapsed in the mid-nineteenth century, mainly as an outcome of power conflicts between the feudal chiefs and the central ruler of the area. From an agrarian point of view the result of these developments was that the agrarian regime prevailing in the mountains from the middle of the nineteenth century was one of small landlords. At the same time Lebanon was ushered into its big economic boom as the entrepôt of Syrian external commerce, and Beirut became the scene of a burgeoning new middle class. One-time feudalists became big businessmen in a context devoid of a strong central government. This combination of beneficial factors seemed to be the main explanation for the rise of a democratic regime in Lebanon.

Notes

Chapter 1

1. L. Namier, "The Social Foundations," introductory chapter to *England in the Age of the American Revolution*, reproduced in D. A. Baugh (ed.), *Aristocratic Government and Society in Eighteenth-Century England* (New York, 1975), 218.

2. C. Brinton, *The Anatomy of Revolution* (London, 1938). Brinton was very much influenced by the American and English revolutions, where the main social relations were not between peasants and other groups.

3. M. R. Somers and W. L. Goldfrank, "The Limits of Agronomic Determinism: A Critique of Paige's *Agrarian Revolution*," in *Comparative Studies in Society and History* 21 (1979):443.

4. G. Baer, "Egyptian Attitudes Towards Land Reform, 1922–1955," in W. Z. Laqueur (ed.), *The Middle East in Transition* (London, 1958), 98–99.

5. B. Moore, *Social Origins of Dictatorship and Democracy: Lord and Peasant in the Making of the Modern World* (Boston, 1966).

6. L. Stone, *The Causes of the English Revolution* (London, 1972).

7. Moore, *Social Origins*, xvi.

8. T. Skocpol, "A Critical Review of Barrington Moore's Social Origins of Dictatorship and Democracy," in *Politics and Society* 1 (1973):1–34.

9. T. Skocpol, *States and Social Revolutions* (Cambridge, 1979); T. Skocpol, "France, Russia, China: A Structural Analysis of Social Revolutions," in *Comparative Studies in Society and History* 18 (1976):175–210.

10. Skocpol, "France, Russia, China," 178–179.

11. Ibid., 179.

Chapter 2

1. On center-periphery relations in the Ottoman Empire, see S. Mardin, "Center-Periphery Relations: A Key to Turkish Politics?" reproduced in E. D. Akarli and G. Ben-Dor (eds.), *Political Participation in Turkey* (Istanbul, 1975), 7–32. The best available introduction to the Ottoman political system is H. Inalcik, *The Ottoman Empire: The Classical Age, 1300–1600* (London, 1973).

2. Ö. L. Barkan, "Edirne Askeri Kassamina Ait Tereke Defterleri (1545–1659)" in *Belgeler* 3 (1966).

3. H. Gerber, *Economy and Society in an Ottoman City: Bursa 1600–1700* (Jerusalem, forthcoming).

4. See H. Gerber, "*Sharia, Kanun* and Custom in the Ottoman Law: The Court Records of 17th-Century Bursa," in *International Journal of Turkish Studies* 2 (1981):133–135.

5. H. Inalcik, *The Ottoman Empire,* 111ff.

6. A. K. S. Lambton, *Landlord and Peasant in Persia* (Oxford, 1953).

7. B. Lewis, *Notes and Documents from the Turkish Archives* (Jerusalem, 1952), 15–16.

8. H. Inalcik, "Osmanlilarda Raiyyet Rüsumu," in *Belleten* 23 (1959):575–610.

9. Khayr al-Din al-Ramli, *Al-Fatawi al Khayriyya* (Bulaq, A.H. 1300), 94ff.

10. There is also the question of the possible origin of the *miri* concept in pre-Ottoman Anatolian states. Osman Turcan, a Turkish historian, investigated the pre-Ottoman origins of this concept but did not come up with any conclusive proof of its origins. In any case, the concept had crystallized by the time of the Ottomans. See O. Turan, "Le droit terrien sous les Seldjoukides de Turquie," in *Revue des Etudes Islamiques* (1948):25–49.

11. The theory that the *timar* system existed because of the size of the tax can be augmented indirectly if we look at the case of Egypt. In places such as Anatolia the *timar* system was the most effective means the state had for disposing of the large quantities of grain accruing to it as tax revenue. But Egypt was one of the main granaries of wheat, supplying some of the important urban centers, especially Istanbul, and the holy cities of the Hijaz. Mecca and Medina apparently were fed almost entirely on Egyptian grain. Hence, the Ottomans had no need for the *timar* system in Egypt in order to dispense with this revenue in kind. See S. J. Shaw, *The Financial Organization and Development of Ottoman Egypt, 1517–1798* (Princeton, 1962), 30.

12. M. A. Cook, *Population Pressure in Rural Anatolia, 1450–1600* (London, 1972), 11.

13. This by no means detracts from my belief that class struggle is an analytic tool of major explanatory fruitfulness. On the Asian mode of production, see K. Marx, *Pre-Capitalist Economic Formations,* E. Hobsbawm (ed.) (London, 1964).

14. Barkan, "Edirne," 48–49.

15. See S. J. Shaw, *History of the Ottoman Empire and Modern Turkey,* vol. 1 (Cambridge, 1976), 185–186.

16. F. Braudel, *The Mediterranean and the Mediterranean World in the Age of Philip II* (London, 1972), 394ff.

17. Ibid., 403.

18. Ö. L. Barkan, "Essai sur les données statistiques des régistres des recensement dans l'empire Ottoman aux XVe et XVIe siècles," in *Journal of the Economic and Social History of the Orient* 1 (1958):9–36.

19. A. Cohen and B. Lewis, *Population and Revenue in the Towns of Palestine in the Sixteenth Century* (Princeton, 1978); B. Lewis, "Studies in the Ottoman Archives—I," in *Bulletin of the School of Oriental and African Studies* 16 (1954):469–501.

20. Braudel, *The Mediterranean,* 267ff.

21. Z. Klein, "Changes in the Level of the Dead Sea in the Last Nine Hundred Years," in *Teva ve Aretz* 23 (1981):212–218.

22. Issawi came up with very conflicting estimates, some of which were suggested by observers so vehemently anti-Ottoman (such as Eton) as to cast serious doubts on these estimates altogether. C. Issawi, "Population and Resources in the Ottoman Empire and Iran," in T. Naff and R. Owen (eds.), *Studies in Eighteenth Cen-*

tury Islamic History (Carbondale, 1977), 152–164.

23. See H. Gerber, "The Population of Syria and Palestine in the Nineteenth Century," in *Asian and African Studies* 13 (1979):76ff.

Chapter 3

1. The present study was based on the Sharia court records of Bursa, the central city of the region. The Bursa archive contained thousands of documents concerning peasants and agriculture and thus offered overwhelming proof that in this region peasants were so involved in urban life that village and city were almost inseparable. Bursa *kadi* records, the Archaeological Museum, Bursa. Documents are sorted into two series, A and B. I have also given the Muslim year of the document.

2. For examples of this last-mentioned phenomenon, see B118/332, 69a, 1027; B53/247, 3b, 1041; B50/244, 102b, 1039. On an en masse appearance in court of villagers from two disputing villages, see B116/330, 42a, 1082.

3. The phenomenon was observed in nineteenth-century Palestine. Villagers refrained from going to the *kadi* court and preferred a customary law called "Abraham's Law" (*Shariat al-Khalil*). See Mrs. Finn, "The Fellaheen of Palestine," *Palestine Exploration Fund, Quarterly Statement* (1879):38–39, 44–45.

4. For a general picture of the classical land regime of the Ottoman Empire, see H. A. R. Gibb and H. Bowen, *Islamic Society and the West*, vol. 1, part 1 (London, 1957), Chapter 5.

5. I summarize here in a few lines my article on "The Wakf Institution in 17th-Century Anatolian Bursa," in G. Baer (ed.), *Social and Economic Aspects of the Muslim Waqf* (Jerusalem, forthcoming).

6. Bashbakanlik Archive, Istanbul, M.D. 18560, date 1108–9.

7. B283/513, 3b, 1088.

8. B42/236, 191b, 1031.

9. B285/513, 15b–16a, 1088.

10. Gibb, *Islamic Society*, 253.

11. B36/230, 145a, 1026.

12. B53/247, 62b, 1042.

13. B94/300, 165a, 1108.

14. The wording is important. *Mukataa* here appeared to mean a specific *area* over which rights of collection were granted. With this meaning we know the term from eighteenth-century Palestine, eighteenth-century Izmir and its environs, and, of course, Mount Lebanon. In seventeenth-century Bursa the term was not encountered at all. Does this mean that adjacent regions were faster in this development than the Bursa region? Or was the development in the Bursa region totally different? These questions must await further research. On Palestine, see A. Cohen, *Palestine in the 18th Century* (Jerusalem, 1973), 121. On the region of Izmir, see G. Veinstein, "Ayan de la région d'Izmir et le commerce du Levant (deuxième moitié du XVIIIe siècle)," in *Revue de l'Occident Musulman et de la Méditerranée* 20 (1975):131–147.

15. A143/169, 46a, 995.

16. The *malikane* system was introduced only at the turn of the seventeenth

century. See, for example, Gibb, *Islamic Society,* 255–256.

17. Bashbakanlik Archive, Istanbul, M.D. 1617, date 1114, 108.

18. See footnotes 28–30 below.

19. B107/321, 42a ff, 1092.

20. Gibb, *Islamic Society,* 239; Ö. L. Barkan, "Türk Toprak Hukuku Tarihinde Tanzimat ve 1274 (1858) Tarihli Arazi Kanunnamesi," in *Tanzimat* (Istanbul, 1940), 325ff.

21. See the Introduction.

22. Ö. L. Barkan, *XV ve XVI inci Asirlarda Osmanli Imparatorluğunda Zirai Ekonominin Hukuki ve Mali Esasleri, I, Kanunlar* (Istanbul, 1943), 3 (art. 15), 7 (art. 7).

23. See Barkan, "Türk Toprak Hukuku," 344ff. It must, however, be emphasized that some *kanunnames* forbade transferring land to daughters.

24. B35/229, 26b, 1025.

25. D2 (Mudanya Sicilli), 4a, 1056.

26. P. Stirling, *Turkish Village* (London, 1965), 50–51.

27. B115/329, 44a, 1061.

28. B42/236, 78b, 1032.

29. B50/244, 110b, 1039; B255/249, 101a, 1040.

30. B140/355, 29a, 1088; B154/370, 44b, 1010; B154/370, 52a, 1010; B42/346, 97a, 1032; B36/230, 132a, 1026.

31. B59/253, 81b, 1044; B50/244, 95a, 1039; B42/236, 97a, 1032; B53/247, 6b, 1041.

32. B83/284, 49b, 1056; B53/247, 86b, 1042; B130/345, 17b, 1066; B42/236, 78b, 1032.

33. We know definitely that at least in some places this was not so. See, for example, K. Cuno, "The Origins of Private Ownership of Land in Ottoman Egypt, A Reappraisal," in *International Journal of Middle East Studies* 12 (1980):245–275.

34. Turkey, Ministry of Education, *Cenubi Marmara Havzasi: Bursa Vilayeti Jografyasi* (Istanbul, 1927), 204–205. In one single document this supposition could be verified. In this document a *chiftlik* was sold, which included 470 *kile* of sown grain (23.5 *mudd* or 12 tons). At the same time, the agricultural land appended to the *chiftlik* was sold, and the land was said to be 45 *muddluk tohum* (5 tons). These two figures tally only if we assume that about half the land was fallow. See B150/166, 31a, 1104.

35. For example, *on muddluk tohum istiab eden mezraa,* "a field [capable] of absorbing ten mudd of seed," see B53/247, 73a, 1042. Also see B150/366, 25b, 1104.

36. M. A. Cook, *Population Pressure in Rural Anatolia, 1450–1600* (London, 1972), 68.

37. B36/230, 17a, 1025.

38. Two types of plowing stock were found—water buffalo and oxen (the former was twice as costly as the latter).

39. B107/321, 42a, ff, 1092.

40. B152/368, 7a, 1105.

41. See, for example, B141/356, 119b, 1094; B55/249, 96a, 1040; B187/410, 94b, 1110.

42. B134/349, 69a, 1078.

43. B141/356, 84a, 1093.

44. B149/364, 56b, 1099. Also see B153/369, 99b, 1108; B187/410, 1110.

45. See, for example, A176/182, 32a, 982.

46. B142/357, 22a, 1092; B142/357, 14a, 1092; B204/428, 121b, 1090.

47. B139/354, 36a, 1088.

48. See, for example, B139/354, 36a, 1088.

49. I have come across a number of cases that implied that grown children had homesteads separate from those of their fathers'. In one example, a father and two sons died at short intervals, one after the other, and they were all from the village of Aksu near Bursa. The estates of the sons included the monetary value of their inheritances and the real estate they possessed individually. In one case this also included a house. See B134/349, 123b, 1079.

50. See B70/271, 23a, 1058; A156/207, 130a, 1012; B147/362, 67b, 1099; B118/332, 25a, 1027; A153/201, 23a, 1006; A153/201, 14a, 1006.

51. The problem of landlessness did exist in large parts of Latin America and even in parts of the Middle East, especially in the interwar period. See, for example, J. Weulersse, *Paysans de Syrie et du Proche Orient* (Paris, 1946), Chapter 3.

52. B53/247, 177b, 1042. For the other document, which was quite similar, see 850/244, 76b, 1039.

53. On this contract, see Ibrahim al-Halabi, *Multaka al-abhur* (Istanbul, A.H. 1309), 164–165.

54. Cook, *Population Pressure*, 11.

55. Ibid.

56. See, for example, the law of the province of Bursa in Barkan, *Kanunlar,* 3, art. 16.

57. See, for example, B17/197, 5b, 1010; A143/169, 72a, 995; A143/169, 12b, 993; A143/169, 10a, 993; B118/332, 35a, 1027.

58. B111/325, 25b, 1094.

59. See A143/169, 14a, 993; B90/295, 34b, 1081; B107/321, 7a, 1092; B140/355, 6b, 1088.

60. B17/197, 20a, 1010. For a similar example, see B71/272, 75b, 1059.

61. X. de Planhol, *De la Plaine Pamphylienne aux lacs pisidiens nomadisme et vie paysanne* (Paris, 1958), 222ff.

62. J. F. von Hammer, *Umblick auf einer Reise von Constantinopel nach Brussa* (Pest, 1818), 65–66 (footnote).

63. B17/197, 14a, 1010; also see B147/362, 67b, 1099; B50/244, 30a, 1038, where similar conflicts are reported in the same area.

64. B107/321, 85a, 1092. In the period studied here this herd no longer existed.

65. See, for example, B115/329, 86b, 1058.

66. B116/330, 32a, 1082.

67. The information presented here concerns two types of urbanites: (a) those who were engaged in agriculture as their main occupation, a fact that can be gauged from their estates; and (b) those who had some agricultural assets in their possession. Here I did not attend to cases of minor importance but gave much attention to

the important ones. References here are to the presence of *chiftliks* in the possession of people who were not professional agriculturalists. In the first part of this section I deal mainly with group (a).

68. See H. Gerber, *Economy and Society in an Ottoman City: Bursa 1600–1700* (Jerusalem, forthcoming), Chapter 2.

69. In my book on Bursa (ibid.) I dwelt at length on the *chiftliks* (Chapter 5). In the present section I devote more attention to other aspects.

70. See H. Inalcik, "Ciftlik," EI^2 (Leiden, 1965), 32–33.

71. See Cook, *Population Pressure,* 67.

72. M. Akdağ, *Türk Halkinin Dirlik ve Düzenlik Kavgasi* (Ankara, 1975), 67–68.

73. Bashbakanlik Archive, Kepeji 71, p. 279, 1017.

74. T. Stoianovich, "Land Tenure and Related Sectors of the Balkan Economy, 1600–1800," in *Journal of Economic History* 13 (1953):398–411.

75. Kepeji 71 (other details lost).

76. B53/247, 74b, 1042. On this man, Ebu Bekir Pasha, see Mehmed Sürreya, *Sicill-i Osmani,* vol. 1 (Istanbul, A.H. 1308), 173.

77. B55/249, 73a, 1040.

78. B46/240, 69a, 1085.

79. B149/364, 76a, 1100.

80. B55/249, 72b, 1040.

81. For a few examples, see B56/250, 12b, 1044; B46/240, 78b, 1039; A143/169, 59b, 995; B144/359, 73a, 1095.

82. B91/296, 6a, 1079. See Ismail Belig, *Güldeste-i Riyaz-i Irfan* (Bursa, A.H. 1302), 366.

83. B50/244, 79a, 1039.

84. B45/239, 34a, 1035.

85. B42/236, 40a, 1032; B144/359, 106b, 1096; B56/250, 132b, 1047; B56/250, 110a, 1047.

86. B91/296, 42b, 1080.

87. D2 (Mudanya Sicilli), 91a, 1095.

88. For examples of fragmentation of *chiftliks,* see B42/236, 49a, 1032 (an area of 2.5 *chift* was here divided into 16 fields); B42/236, 97a, 1032 (1 *chift* of land was here divided into 12 fields).

89. G. Baer, "The Dissolution of the Village Community," in his *Studies on the Social History of Modern Egypt* (Chicago, 1969), 17.

90. In one such document I found a conflict between the villages of Barak and Dere. One village demanded a tax contribution from the other. This document showed that the government fixed the number of *hane* units the village was to pay. The villagers themselves had to arrange a register in which they assessed the value of the property of each villager and evaluated the tax imposition due from each of them. The process struck me as being democratic in the extreme. See B75/276, 52b, 1090.

91. It is fitting to mention in this context that in one document the inhabitants of the village of Balbanjik came to court and complained to the *kadi* that they had encountered difficulties in the distribution of taxes among themselves and therefore wished to nominate a *kethüda* (head) over them. They also suggested a nominee.

Their wish was granted (see A143/169, 13b, end of the sixteenth century). This was further evidence that no official or de facto head existed in the villages of the area.

Chapter 4

1. See I. Wallerstein, *The Modern World System* (New York, 1974). For a shorter version, see I. Wallerstein, "Three Paths of National Development in Sixteenth-Century Europe," in *Studies in Comparative International Development* 7 (1972):95–101.
2. For the sake of the present summary, I have used the aforementioned shorter version.
3. Wallerstein, "Three Paths," 97.
4. H. Islamoğlu and C. Keyder, "Agenda for Ottoman History," in *Review* 1 (1977):31–55; I. Wallerstein, "The Ottoman Empire and the Capitalist World Economy: Some Questions for Research," *Review* 2 (1979):389–398.
5. See, for example, D. R. Sadat, "Rumeli Ayanlari: The Eighteenth Century," in *Journal of Modern History* 44 (1972):346–363; R. Busch-Zantner, *Agrarverfassung, Gesellschaft und Siedlung in Südosteuropa* (Leipzig, 1938); T. Stoianovich, "Land Tenure and Related Sectors of the Balkan Economy, 1600–1800," in *Journal of Economic History* 13 (1953):398–411.
6. B. McGowan, *Economic Life in Ottoman Europe* (Cambridge, 1979).
7. Ibid., 69ff.
8. K. M. Cuno, "The Origins of Private Ownership of Land in Egypt: A Reappraisal," in *International Journal of Middle East Studies* 12 (1980):249.
9. McGowan, *Economic Life*, 46.
10. Ibid., 171–172 (italics added).
11. Ibid., 72.
12. Ibid., 163.
13. H. Gerber, *Economy and Society in an Ottoman City: Bursa, 1600–1700* (Jerusalem, forthcoming), Chapter 6.
14. M. A. Cook, *Population Pressure in Rural Anatolia 1450–1600* (London, 1972), 1–2.
15. A. Raymond, *Artisans et commerçants au Caire au XVIIIᵉ siècle*, vol. 1 (Damascus, 1973), 193ff.
16. Ibid., table.
17. By large-estate formation I mean large estates in the physical structural sense, as against large ownership units, which did make an appearance, apparently due more to political rather than to strictly economic factors, as I show later in this chapter.
18. See H. Inalcik, *The Ottoman Empire, The Classical Age, 1300–1600* (London, 1973); R. Jennings, "Loans and Credit in Early 17th-Century Ottoman Judicial Records," in *Journal of the Economic and Social History of the Levant* 16 (1973):168–216.
19. W. Turner, *Journal of a Tour in the Levant*, vol. 3 (London, 1820), 151, 179–180.

20. L. Erder, "The Making of Industrial Bursa: Economic Activity and Population in a Turkish City, 1835–1975" (Ph.D. diss., Princeton University, 1976).

21. Ibid., 96.

22. H. Gerber, "Jews and Moneylending in the Ottoman Empire," in *Jewish Quarterly Review* 72 (1982):100–118.

23. See H. Gerber, "Jews and Moneylending: Edirne Jewry in the Sixteenth and Seventeenth Centuries," in *Sefunot,* n.s., 3 (1983):35–52.

24. Ö. L. Barkan, "Edirne Askeri Kassamina Ait Tereke Defterleri (1545–1659)," in *Belgeler* 3 (1966): no. 78.

25. D. Chevallier, "Western Development and Eastern Crisis in the Mid-Nineteenth Century: Syria Confronted with the European Economy," in W. R. Polk and R. L. Chambers (eds.), *Beginnings of Modernization in the Middle East* (Chicago, 1968), 205–206.

26. H. Gerber, "Modernization in Nineteenth-Century Palestine: The Role of Foreign Trade," in *Middle Eastern Studies* 18 (1982):250–264.

27. E. Weakley, *Report upon the Conditions and Prospects of British Trade in Syria* (London, 1911), 25.

28. For more details, see Gerber, "Modernization in Nineteenth-Century Palestine."

29. O. Kurmuş, "Some Aspects of Handicraft and Industrial Production in Ottoman Anatolia, 1800–1915," in *Asian and African Studies* 15 (1981):85–102.

30. Ibid., p. 87.

31. Ibid., p. 89.

32. Ibid., pp. 89–90.

33. For the express purpose of the present chapter I have made extensive use of a source that remains to date almost entirely untapped for the socioeconomic history of the Ottoman Empire: the *fetva* collections. The collections consulted were the following: Ali al-Murtaza (ed.), *Ilaveli Mejmua-i Jedida* (Istanbul, A.H. 1326) (a compilation of *fetva*s); Abdallah Efendi Yenishehiri, *Behjetül-Fetavi* (Istanbul, A.H. 1266); Ali Efendi Chataljali, *Fetava* (Istanbul, n.d.); Abd al-Rahim Efendi Menteshizade, *Fetava* (Istanbul, n.d.); Feyzüllah Efendi, *Fetava-i Feyziyye* (Istanbul, A.H. 1266); Cheshmi-zade Mehmed Halis Efendi (ed.), *Hulasat el-Ejviba* (Istanbul, A.H. 1289) (compilation); Muhammad Khalili, *Kitab Fatawi al-Khalili* (Cairo, A.H. 1289); Khayr ad-Din al-Ramli, *Al-Fatawi al-Khayriyya* (Bulaq, A.H. 1300).

34. U. Heyd, *Studies in Old Ottoman Criminal Law* (Oxford, 1973), 152ff.

35. Ali al-Murtaza, 649.

36. Ali Efendi, 543; Cheshmi-zade Mehmed, 248 (Abd al-Rahim, no. 182).

37. Abd al-Rahim, 31; Ali al-Murtaza, 646, 661, 663.

38. Abd al-Rahim, 37; Ali Efendi, 16, 18, 19, 176, 262; Abdallah Efendi, 32, 35.

39. Ali Efendi, 133 (three cases).

40. For example, Ali Efendi, 733.

41. Examples: Ali Efendi, 735; Cheshmi-zade Mehmed, 194 (Abd al-Rahim, no. 194).

42. I. Abbas, "Hair ad-Din ar-Ramli's Fatawa: A New Light on Life in Palestine in the Eleventh/Seventeenth Century," in U. Haarmann and P. Bachmann (eds.), *Die Islamische Welt zwischen Mittelalter und Neuzeit (Festschrift Hans Robert Roemer)* (Beirut, 1979), 1–19.

43. Khayr al-Din al-Ramli, vol. 2, 184.

44. Ibid., p. 165.

45. Ibid., vol. 1, 177, 247; vol. 2, 126.

46. The Ottoman agrarian system of the sixteenth century took over in its entirety the former Mamluk land revenue administration. This was called *qasm* or *muqasama*, and by it taxes were assessed as a proportion of the produce, usually one-fifth, one-quarter, or one-third of the produce in question. The difference, in this respect, between Palestine and Anatolia was a major proof that the sixteenth century Ottoman agrarian regime was basically a continuation of the pre-Ottoman situation. On the *qasm* system, see B. Lewis, *Notes and Documents from the Turkish Archives* (Jerusalem, 1952), 15–16; A. N. Poliak, *Feudalism in Egypt, Syria, Palestine and the Lebanon, 1250–1900* (London, 1939), 65–67.

47. Khayr al-Din al-Ramli, vol. 1, 95.

48. For examples, see ibid., vol. 1, 96–97.

49. Ibid., vol. 1, 98–99; vol. 2, 184.

50. H. A. R. Gibb and H. Bowen, *Islamic Society and the West*, vol. 1, part 1 (London, 1950), 255.

51. H. Ongan, *Ankara'nin Iki Numarali Şeriye Sicili* (Ankara, 1974), documents 1508, 1528, 1679, 1685, 1754.

52. Ihsan al-Nimr, *Tarikh Jabal Nablus wal'Balqa*, vol. 2 (Nablus, 1962), 233.

53. Ibid., 261–263.

54. A. Cohen, *Palestine in the Eighteenth Century* (Jerusalem, 1973), 179ff.

55. A. Rafeq, "Economic Relations Between Damascus and the Dependent Countryside, 1743–71," in A. L. Udovitch (ed.), *The Islamic Middle East, 700–1900* (Princeton, 1981), 653–685.

56. Ibid., 656.

57. Cohen, *Palestine,* 184ff. This was also the background to the Azms' rise to prominence in Damascus. See Rafeq, "Economic Relations," 655.

58. Chavush-zade Mehmed Aziz, *Durr al-Sukuk,* vol. 2 (Istanbul, A.H. 1288), 17.

59. Ibid., 18–19.

60. Examples: Ali Efendi, 173; Abd al-Rahim, 53, 54–55; Abdallah Efendi, 193; Ali al-Murtaza, 188–189.

61. Examples: Ali Efendi, 172, 173, 174, 315; Feyzüllah Efendi, 166.

62. Ali Efendi, 163; Abd al-Rahim, 50, 55, 56; Feyzüllah Efendi, 165; Abdallah Efendi, 192–193.

63. Abd al-Rahim, 55.

64. For example, Ali Efendi, 172, 173, 174.

65. For examples, see Abd al-Rahim, 55; Feyzüllah Efendi, 168; Ali Efendi, 173.

66. See. S. J. Shaw, *Between Old and New* (Cambridge, Mass., 1971), 211–217 and *passim.*

67. A. Bryer, "The Last Laz Risings and the Downfall of the Pontic Derebeys, 1812–1840," in *Bedi Kartlisa* 26 (1969):192.

68. G. Veinstein, "Ayan de la région d'Izmir et le commerce du Levant (deuxième moitié du XVIIIe siècle)," in *Revue de l'Occident Musulman et de la Méditerranée* 20 (1975):131–147.

69. Ibid., 136.

70. Ibid., 137.

71. Ibid., 137 (note 22).

72. M. L. Meriwether, "The Notable Families of Aleppo, 1770–1830: Networks and Social Structure" (Ph.D. diss., University of Pennsylvania, 1981), 179–182, 185ff.

73. M. M. Aktepe, "Kara Osman Oğlu Mehmed Ağa bn. Haci Omer Ağa," in *Vakiflar Dergisi* 11 (1976):57–66.

74. H. Gerber, "The Wakf Institution in Seventeenth-Century Anatolian Bursa," in G. Baer (ed.), *Social and Economic Aspects of the Muslim Waqf* (in press).

75. G. G. Güzelbey, *Gaziantep Şeri Mahkeme Sicilleri*, Fasikül 2 (Gaziantep, 1966).

76. B. Yediyildiz, "Türk Vakif Kurucularinin Sosyal Tabakalaşmadaki Yeri, 1700–1800," in *Osmanli Araştirmalari* 3 (1982):143–164.

77. Mustafa Nuri, *Netaij el-Vukuat*, vol. 1 (Istanbul, A.H. 1274), 124.

78. Feridun Bey, *Munshaat al-Salatin*, vol. 2 (Istanbul, A.H. 1274), 368–369.

79. N. W. Werry, "Rural Syria in 1845," in *Middle East Journal* 16 (1962):508–514.

80. Y. Firestone, "Crop-Sharing Economics in Mandatory Palestine," in *Middle Eastern Studies* 11 (1975):3–23, 175–194.

81. Khayr al-Din al-Ramli, vol. 2, 164, 168–171.

82. L. Bianco, *Origins of the Chinese Revolution, 1915–1949* (Stanford, 1971), 101.

83. Ibid., 92.

84. Muhammad Khalili, vol. 1, 233.

85. Ali Efendi, 575, 576.

86. Ali Efendi, 730.

87. Feyzüllah Efendi, 570.

88. Ali Efendi, 731.

89. Ibid.

90. Feyzüllah Efendi, 570.

91. Ali Efendi, 730.

92. Ibid., 731.

93. Ali al-Murtaza, 490, 492, 493.

94. Ibid., 675.

95. Ibid., 652.

96. Y. Nagata, *Some Documents on the Big Farms (Ciftliks) of the Notables in Western Anatolia* (Tokyo, 1976).

97. Ibid., 5. Negata erred in assuming that all the documents pertained to estates of deceased. Such documents would have been edited by the *kadi*; the documents relating to the first five cases were not. Inheritance documents also included the monetary value of all the items contained in them without which it would have been impossible to divide these items among the heirs. The estates of these five people appeared to have been confiscated by the government, which may have been the reason why they were drawn up in the first place. Only the later documents were for estates of deceased, and not surprisingly, the documents included monetary values affixed to arable lands. See ibid., 37ff.

98. Ibid., 16–17.

99. Ibid., 37ff.

100. Ali al-Murtaza, 646, 647, 648, 650, 666, and many more.

101. Chavush-zade Mehmed Aziz, vol. 2, 107–108, 180–181, 196–197.
102. Cuno, "The Origin of Private Ownership," 246.
103. Ibid., 247.
104. Ibid., 251.
105. S. J. Shaw, *The Financial Organization and Development of Ottoman Egypt, 1517–1798* (Princeton, 1962), 22.
106. Cuno, "The Origin of Private Ownership," 251–252.
107. Khayr al-Din al-Ramli, vol. 2, 96.
108. Cuno, "The Origin of Private Ownership," 249.
109. C. Issawi, *The Economic History of Turkey, 1800–1914* (Chicago, 1980), 203.
110. Ibid.
111. Ibid.

Chapter 5

1. See *Düstur* (Ottoman Statute Book), vol. 1, 165–229, with translations into several languages. I made use mainly of Tute's translation. R. C. Tute, *The Ottoman Land Laws with a Commentary on the Ottoman Land Code of 7th Ramadan 1274* (Jerusalem, date of preface 1927). French translation by M. Belin, "Etude sur la propriété foncière en pays Musulmans, et spécialement en Turquie," in *Journal Asiatique* (April-May 1862):291–358.
2. Detailed explanations of these terms are given in Articles 1–5 of the land law.
3. D. Warriner, "Land Tenure in the Fertile Crescent," in C. Issawi (ed.), *The Economic History of the Middle East* (Chicago, 1966), 73.
4. Ibid.
5. G. Baer, "The Development of Private Ownership of Land," in his *Studies in the Social History of Modern Egypt* (Chicago, 1969), 67–68. It must be emphasized, however, that Baer's main objective in his study was to show that although the Egyptian land law was explicitly intended to enlarge landowners' rights to their land, the Ottoman land law meant nothing of the sort. In this he was entirely correct because, as I show in this chapter, the intention of the law was neither to augment nor to curtail rights but merely to reflect an existing situation.
6. Ibid., 66.
7. Tute, *Ottoman Land Laws,* 2 (note 1).
8. Baer, *Studies,* 70.
9. Ideally we should expect to find explicit discussion of these terms in the classical collection of provincial agrarian *kanuns*—Ö. L. Barkan, *XV ve XVI inc Asirlarda Osmanli Imparatorluğunda Zirai Ekonominin Hukuki ve Mali Esaslari, Kanunlar* (Istanbul, 1943). However, none of the numerous references to the terms *mulk* and *miri* gave a definition, which was obviously taken for granted. Apparently, the only theoretical differentiation was to be found in the writings of Sheyhulislam Ebu Suud Efendi. See, for example, *Budin Kanunnamesi,* Sadik Albayrak (ed.) (Istanbul, date of preface 1973), 112. It was noteworthy that I nowhere encountered the

term *meturke* (communal land) in the classical Ottoman sources, but there was no doubt that substantially the term existed.

10. Ebu Suud, *Budin,* 127.

11. *Düstur,* vol. 1, 172–173 (art. 68).

12. Ibid., 178 (art. 54).

13. Barkan, *Kanunlar,* 4 (art. 19).

14. See Tute, *Ottoman Land Laws,* 119; Belin, *Etude,* 356; M. Dukhan, *Dinei Qarqa'ot be Eretz Yisrael* (Jerusalem, 1925), 214. The erroneous translation has for *kanunen* "in law" instead of "according to the *kanun*" as I suggest (in the text of Article 131 of the land law, as reproduced here). The mistake was made evident by the fact that no known law had any reason to define *chiftlik* as a certain measure of land, for when it said anything substantial on the term, the law invariably spoke of an estate in the full sense of the word. In contrast, the classical *kanun* gave for *chiftlik* the exact definition given in the first sentence of Article 131 of the land law.

15. Land Law, Art. 130, Tute, *Ottoman Land Laws,* 119.

16. Land Law, Art. 99, ibid., 94.

17. Article 3 of the 1858 land law, and several others.

18. See, for example, P. J. Klat, "The Origins of Landownership in Syria," in *Middle East Economic Papers* (London, 1958), 60–61.

19. J. Weulersse, *Paysans de Syrie et du Proche Orient* (Paris, 1946), 113ff., particularly 119; J. Weulersse, *Le Pays des Alouites* (Tours, 1940), 220ff., 362–363.

20. For Iraq in general, I have relied on the following studies: S. Haider, "Land Problems of Iraq," in C. Issawi (ed.), *The Economic History of the Middle East* (Chicago, 1966), 164–178; A. Jwaideh, "Midhat Pasha and the Land System of Lower Iraq," in *St. Anthony's Papers,* no. 16 (1964):106–136; J. Batatu, *The Old Social Classes and the Revolutionary Movements of Iraq* (Princeton, 1979), Chapter 5.

21. Haider, "Land Problems," 164.

22. Ibid., 165.

23. Batatu, *The Old Social Classes,* 55.

24. Haider, "Land Problems," 164.

25. Jwaideh, "Midhat Pasha."

26. Haider, "Land Problems," 166.

27. Jwaideh, "Midhat Pasha," 130–131.

28. See A. Jwaideh, "The *Sanniya* Lands of Sultan Abdul Hamid in Iraq," in G. Makdisi (ed.), *Arabic and Islamic Studies in Honor of Hamilton A. R. Gibb* (Leiden, 1965), 326–336. On reviewing all the evidence it appeared that Abdülhamid pursued a systematic policy of purchasing vacant or disputed lands throughout the empire and not just in Iraq. For Anatolia, see for example, X. de Planhol *De la plaine pamphylienne aux lacs pisidiens, nomadisme et vie paysanne* (Paris, 1958), 140–141.

29. Batatu, *The Old Social Classes,* 56.

30. H. Gerber, "The Population of Syria and Palestine in the Nineteenth Century," in *Asian and African Studies* 13 (1979):58–80.

31. See, for example, W. Hütteroth, "The Pattern of Settlement in Palestine in the Sixteenth Century," in M. Maoz (ed.), *Studies on Palestine During the Ottoman Period* (Jerusalem, 1975), 3–9.

32. A. Granott, *The Land System of Palestine* (London, 1952).

33. H. Gerber, *Ottoman Rule in Jerusalem, 1890–1914* (Berlin, 1985), Chapter 9.

34. The documents that have survived actually covered only three years at the beginning of the twentieth century.

35. R. Kark and H. Gerber, "Land Registry Maps in Palestine During the Ottoman Period," in *The Cartographic Journal* 21 (1984):30–32.

36. Land Law, Art. 8.

37. De Planhol, *De la Plaine Pamphylienne*, 336 (footnote).

38. S. Bergheim, "Land Tenure in Palestine," *Palestine Exploration Fund, Quarterly Statement* (1894), 195.

39. L. Oliphant, *Haifa or Life in Modern Palestine* (Edinburgh and London, 1887), 59.

40. A. Cohen, *Arab Border Villages in Israel* (Manchester, 1965), 10.

41. On Sursoq, see Oliphant, *Haifa*, 60; and L. Oliphant, *The Land of Gilead* (New York, 1881), 277ff.

42. This point should not, however, be pushed too far; after all, although in the case of Sursoq this reasoning was apparently borne out, to my knowledge this pattern of entrepreneurship generally had very meager results. Obviously, much more energetic encouragement was needed to achieve such results.

43. The original document is reportedly lost. I am, therefore, forced to cite from a book of dubious scientific validity—A. L. Avneri, *The Jewish Land Settlement and the Arab Claim of Dispossession* (in Hebrew) (Tel Aviv, 1980), 252–253.

44. K. W. Stein, "Legal Protection and Circumvention of Rights of Cultivators in Mandatory Palestine," in J. S. Migdal (ed.), *Palestinian Society and Politics* (Princeton, 1980), 233–260.

45. See, for example, Z. Vilnay, "Emeq Izrael (Plain of Esdraelon)," in *Ariel, A Geographical Encyclopaedia*, vol. 6 (Tel Aviv, 1978), 5895–5915, where a map showing such villages is reproduced. But it is quite clear that in other instances the villagers were relatively new settlers, and hence the big landlords' legal claims were sound. Thus, Firestone described the sharecroppers of the Abd al-Hadi family in the Plain of Esdraelon as "largely immigrants from the hill country and perhaps sedentarizing semi-nomads." See Y. Firestone, "Crop-Sharing Economics in Mandatory Palestine," in *Middle Eastern Studies* 11 (1975):9.

46. Oliphant, *Gilead*.

47. Central Zionist Archives, Jerusalem, S/25, file 7433.

48. See M. Maoz, *Ottoman Reform in Syria and Palestine* (Oxford, 1968), 188ff.

49. Personal information supplied by Adil Manna, who is working on the court records of Jerusalem at the beginning of the nineteenth century.

50. See, for example, Weulersse, *Paysans de Syrie*; and Weulersse, *Le Pays des Alouites*.

51. On the career of the Abd al-Hadis, see, for example, Firestone, "Crop-Sharing Economics," 3–23, 175–194 (the article was based on records of that family); M. Abir, "Local Leadership and Early Reforms in Palestine, 1800–1834," in Maoz, *Studies*, 184–310.

52. Unfortunately, Firestone did not say what proportion of Arabeh's land was

actually owned by the Abd al-Hadis, but the study contained several hints that there were many smallholders. See, for example, "Crop-Sharing Economics," 183.

53. G. Post, "Essays on the Sects and Nationalities of Syria," *Palestine Exploration Fund Quarterly Statement* (1891), 104–105, essay 2.

54. G. L. Bell, *Syria: The Desert and the Sown* (New York, 1973), 223–227.

55. Ibid., 207.

56. Ibid., 235.

57. M. Refiq and M. Behjet, *Beirut Vilayeti*, vol. 2 (Beirut, A.H. 1336), 442.

58. Ibid., 520–521.

59. Ibid., 556–557.

60. Ibid., 494.

61. Ibid., 332–333.

62. "Law Relating to Broadening the Right of Succession," *Düstur*, vol. 1, 223–224. The law introduced the new principle whereby other relatives could succeed the deceased without paying the *tapu*.

63. *Ilaveli mejmua-i Jedida*, Ali al-Murtaza (ed.) (Istanbul, A.H. 1326), 653.

64. For examples of relatives succeeding through "simple succession" according to the new law, see ibid., 656, 658, 664, 672, and many more. In fact, most of the *fetvas* in this collection that related to the post-1858 period concerned problems connected with this law. This may be due to the fact that it was new and of an unfamiliar nature; but whatever the reason, it further enhanced my impression that these *fetvas* related to real life situations.

65. See, for example, ibid., 663.

66. Ibid., 656, 667, 670, 672, 673.

67. Ibid., 649, 665, 666.

68. P. Benedict, *Ula, An Anatolian Town* (Leiden, 1974), 58.

69. Ibid.

70. De Planhol, *De la Plaine Pamphylienne*, 122–130.

71. J. S. Szyliowicz, *Political Change in Rural Turkey: Erdemli* (Paris, 1966), 22–30.

72. M. B. Kiray, "Social Change in Çukurova; A Comparison of Four Villages," in P. Benedict, E. Tümertekin, and F. Mansur (eds)., *Turkey: Geographic and Social Perspectives* (Leiden, 1974), 179. Similarly, Eberhard wrote: "Local tradition says that Cukurova was quite unhealthy until the early twentieth century. It was strongly malarial and largely uninhabited. The few existing settlements were along the main caravan route connecting Asia Minor with Iraq on one side, Syria and Palestine on the other." See W. Eberhard, *Settlement and Social Change in Asia*, vol. 1 (Hong Kong, 1967), 283.

73. Eberhard, *Settlement and Social Change*, 291.

74. E. F. Nikoley, "Agriculture," in E. G. Mears (ed.), *Modern Turkey* (New York, 1924), 294.

75. Cited by C. Issawi, *The Economic History of Turkey, 1800–1914* (Chicago, 1980), 246.

76. Ibid., 244.

77. D. Quataert, "Agricultural Trends and Government Policy in Ottoman Anatolia, 1800–1914," in *Asian and African Studies* 15 (1981):75–76.

78. Great Britain, *A Handbook of Asia Minor*, vol. 1 (London, 1919), 230.

79. Benedict, *Ula*, 58–60.
80. *Ottoman Land Laws*, Art. 68.
81. B. Moore, *Social Origins of Dictatorship and Democracy: Lord and Peasant in the Making of the Modern World* (Boston, 1966), 218–219, 353ff.
82. D. Quataert, "The Commercialization of Agriculture in Ottoman Turkey," in *International Journal of Turkish Studies* 1 (1980):71.
83. Ibid., 42–43.
84. Quataert, "Agricultural Trends," 73–74.
85. Ibid., 77.
86. Ibid., 75.

Chapter 6

1. J. Batatu, *The Old Social Classes and the Revolutionary Movements of Iraq* (Princeton, 1979), 75.
2. Ibid., 86ff.
3. Ibid., 94ff.
4. Ibid., 94.
5. Ibid., 95.
6. Cited in ibid., 96–97.
7. Ibid., 98–99.
8. Ibid., 83–85.
9. Ibid., 75.
10. Ibid., 83–84.
11. Ibid., 110.
12. Cited in ibid., 114.
13. D. Pool, "From Elite to Class: The Transformation of the Iraqi Leadership, 1920–1939," in *International Journal of Middle East Studies* 12 (1980):347.
14. Batatu, *The Old Social Classes*, 133.
15. Ibid., 146.
16. Ibid., 148.
17. R. A. Fernea, "Land Reform and Ecology in Postrevolutionary Iraq," in *Economic Development and Cultural Change* 17 (1968–69):356–381.
18. That these problems have not yet been solved is attested by a recent study of R. Theobald and S. Jawad, "Problems of Rural Development in an Oil-Rich Economy," in T. Niblock (ed.), *Iraq: The Contemporary State* (London, 1982), 191–218.
19. Batatu, *The Old Social Classes*, 1115.
20. D. Warriner, *Land Reform and Development in the Middle East* (Oxford, 1962), 157.
21. J. Weulersse, *Paysans de Syrie et du Proche Orient* (Paris, 1946), 113–114 (translation by Haim Gerber).
22. Ibid., 120 (translation by Haim Gerber).
23. P. S. Khoury, "The Tribal Shaykh, French Tribal Policy, and the Nationalist Movement in Syria Between Two World Wars," in *Middle Eastern Studies* 18 (1982):187.

24. J. Weulersse, *Le Pays des Alouites* (Tours, 1940), 362–363.

25. Ibid., 364.

26. An example is found in ibid., 362, note 2.

27. Ibid., 363.

28. Ibid., 366–368.

29. G. Baer, *Introduction to the History of Agrarian Relations in the Middle East* (in Hebrew) (Tel Aviv, 1971), 97.

30. L. E. Sweet, *Tell Toqaan: A Syrian Village* (Ann Arbor, 1960), 59ff.

31. Ibid., 39.

32. R. A. Hinnebusch, "Local Politics in Syria: Organization and Mobilization in Four Village Cases," in *Middle East Journal* 23 (1976):1–24.

33. R. A. Hinnebusch, *Party and Peasant in Syria* (Cairo, 1979), 66.

34. Hinnebusch, "Local Politics," 8.

35. Ibid., 19.

36. Hinnebusch, *Party and Peasant*, 72.

37. Ibid., 77.

38. Ibid., 86.

39. Hinnebusch, "Local Politics," 11.

40. Ibid., 16.

41. Hinnebusch, *Party and Peasant*, 89–90.

42. R. T. Antoun, *Arab Village* (Bloomington, 1972), 15–26.

43. Ibid., 19.

44. G. Baer, "Land Tenure in the Hashemite Kingdom," in *Land Economics* 33 (1957):194.

45. G. E. Walpole, "Land Problems in Transjordan," in *Journal of the Royal Central Asian Society* 35 (1948):63.

46. Antoun, *Arab Village*, 25.

47. R. B. Winder, "Syrian Deputies and Cabinet Ministers," in *Middle East Journal* 16 (1962):38f.

48. A. Hourani, *Syria and Lebanon* (London, 1946), 91–92.

49. G. Baer, *A History of Landownership in Modern Egypt, 1800–1950* (London, 1962); L. Binder, *In a Moment of Enthusiasm* (Chicago, 1978); R. Owen, *The Middle East in the World Economy* (London, 1981).

50. Owen, ibid., 146.

51. Ibid.

52. Ibid., 228.

53. Ibid., 230.

54. A. Richards, "The Political Economy of *Gutswirtschaft*: A Comparative Analysis of East Elbian Germany, Egypt and Chile," in *Comparative Studies in Society and History* 21 (1979):488–489.

55. Owen, *The Middle East*, 148.

56. A. Güriz, "Land Ownership in Rural Settlements," in P. Benedict, E. Tümertekin, and F. Mansur (eds.), *Turkey: Geographic and Social Perspectives* (Leiden, 1974), 71.

57. C. Keyder, "Paths to Rural Transformation in Turkey," in *Journal of Peasant Studies* 11 (1983):43–49; C. Keyder, "Small Peasant Ownership in Turkey," *Review* 7 (1983):53–107.

58. B. Denker, "Die Siedlungs—und Wirtschaftsgeographie der Bursa-Ebene" (Ph.D. diss., University of Freiburg, 1963), 92–95.

59. O. Ozankaya, *Toplumsal Yapi ve Siyasal Kultur* (Ankara, 1971), 33ff.

60. Ibid., 35.

61. I. Yasa, *Sindel Köyü'nün Toplumsal ve Ekonomik Yapisi* (Ankara, 1960).

62. Ibid, 43.

63. Ibid, 44–45.

64. Ibid., 4.

65. Ibid., 46.

66. P. Stirling, *Turkish Village* (London, 1965).

67. Ibid., 54–56.

68. Ibid., 48–50.

69. I. Yasa, *Hasanoğlan, Socio-Economic Structure of a Turkish Village* (Ankara, 1957), vi.

70. Ibid., 66.

71. J. D. Szyliowicz, *Political Change in Rural Turkey: Erdemli* (The Hague, 1966), 70.

72. J. E. Pierce, *Life in a Turkish Village* (New York, 1964), 66.

73. Ibid., 68.

74. W. C. Brice, "The Anatolian Village," in *Geography* 40 (1955):161–168.

75. Ibid., 162.

76. Ibid., 163–164.

77. R. B. Scott, *The Village Headman in Turkey* (Ankara, 1968), 30–33.

78. J. Kolars, *Tradition, Season and Change in a Turkish Village* (Chicago, 1963), 32.

79. N. Berkes, *Bazi Ankara Köyleri Uzerinde Bir Araştirma* (Ankara, 1942).

80. Ibid., 48.

81. Ibid., 43.

82. Ibid., 46–47.

83. N. Helburn, "A Stereotype of Agriculture in Semiarid Turkey," in *The Geographical Review* 45 (1955):375–384.

84. Ibid., 380.

85. Ibid., 381.

86. Ibid., 383–384.

87. D. Kandiyoti, "Social Change and Social Stratification in a Turkish Village," in *Journal of Peasant Studies* 2 (1975):206–219.

88. Ibid., 207.

89. Ibid.

90. Ibid.

91. Ibid., 208. This situation also was implied in other sources. Robinson, who conducted field work in Turkey in the early 1950s, had this to say:

Substantial evidence exists that Turkey is running out of uncultivated arable land in many sections and that pressure on the land has been felt for several years. Within a ten-day period in May 1951, intervillage fights over land use were reported from four areas. In one battle, two persons were killed, four wounded; in a second, one was killed and two wounded; in a

third, four persons were seriously wounded and ten suffered minor in-
juries; in the fourth, a watchman on a farm attacked and wounded a trespas-
sing shepherd. . . . These fights over the use of land have become so important and frequent that the national press has begun to take notice. In 1954,
newspapers reported a general increase in the number of such battles,
both between villages and between farmers and herdsmen. In one central
Turkish *kaza* (county), the number of disputes over land totalled 93 during 1950 and 89 during 1951. . . . This increase in disputes over land arises
out of growing land pressure and the importance of affixing the ownership
of remaining arable land lying between villages. In past years, relatively
few villages lacked land on which to expand. Hence, the establishment of
exclusive ownership of land adjoining that of another village was seldom
of concern. Now, however, the ownership of that buffer land has become
important. Other evidence that pressure on the land is building up rapidly
is the settlement of nomadic groups, in part occasioned by the difficulty in
moving from place to place across privately-owned land.

From R. D. Robinson, "Turkey's Agrarian Revolution and the Problem of Urbaniza-
tion," in *Public Opinion Quarterly* 22 (1958):398 (note).

    92. L. Bianco, *Origins of the Chinese Revolution* (Stanford, 1971), 90–91.

    93. Kandiyoti, "Social Change," 214.

    94. For example, in Tell Toqan (northern Syria). See Sweet, *Tell Toqaan*, 39.

    95. W. Eberhard, *Settlement and Social Change in Asia*, vol. 1 (Hong Kong,
1967), pp. 317–318.

    96. Ozankaya, *Toplumsal Yapi*, 69.

    97. Stirling, *Turkish Village*, 228.

    98. Ibid., 53 (note).

    99. Ibid., 145–146.

    100. Ibid.

    101. Kolars, *Tradition, Season and Change*, 86.

    102. Scott, *The Village Headman*, 21ff.

    103. P. Benedict, *Ula, An Anatolian Town* (Leiden, 1974), Chapter 3.

    104. Ibid., 94–95.

    105. M. E. Meeker, "The Great Family Aghas of Turkey: A Study of a Changing
Political Culture," in R. Antoun and I. Harik (eds.), *Rural Politics and Social Change
in the Middle East* (Bloomington and London, 1972), 237–266.

    106. Ibid., 165 (note 5).

    107. Keyder, "Small Peasant Ownership," 53–107.

    108. Ibid., 60, 68.

    109. D. Chirot, *Social Change in a Peripheral Society: The Creation of a Balkan
Colony* (New York, 1976).

    110. Ibid., 161–162.

    111. O. Kurmuş, *Emperyalizmin Türkiye'ye Girişi* (Istanbul, 1974), 99ff.

Chapter 7

1. See, for example, T. S. Ashton, *The Industrial Revolution, 1760–1830* (Oxford, 1970); R. M. Hartwell (ed.), *The Causes of the Industrial Revolution in England* (London, 1967); C. Hill, *Reformation to Industrial Revolution* (London, 1969); J. Hicks, *A Theory of Economic History* (Oxford, 1969).

2. On the 1838 commercial convention, see C. Issawi, *The Economic History of the Middle East* (Chicago, 1966), 38ff.

3. Hill, *Reformation,* Chapter 3.

4. Ibid., 154.

5. See E. L. Jones and S. J. Woolf (eds.), *Agrarian Change and Economic Development* (London, 1969), 1–2. Jones and Woolf admit the fallacy of this argument by pointing out, for example, that in pre-modern China substantial increments were made in the peasants' net incomes, but this led only to population growth.

6. E. E. Power, *The Wool Trade in English Medieval History* (Oxford, 1941), 12–13. See also M. M. Postan, *The Medieval Economy and Society* (Harmondsworth, 1975), 213–214.

7. E. Lipson, *The Economic History of England,* vol. 1 (London, 1937), 391ff.

8. B. Braude, "International Competition and Domestic Cloth in the Ottoman Empire, 1500–1650: A Study in Undevelopment," *Review* 2 (1979):437–451.

9. Hill, *Reformation,* 65.

10. Ibid., 72.

11. R. Brenner, "Agrarian Class Structure and Economic Development in Pre-Industrial Europe," in *Past and Present,* no. 70 (1976):30–75, at page 66.

12. L. Stone, *The Causes of the English Revolution, 1529–1642* (London, 1972), 71.

13. F. F. Mendels, "Proto-industrialization: The First Phase of the Industrialization Process," in *Journal of Economic History* 32 (1972):241–261.

14. E. R. J. Owen, *Cotton and the Egyptian Economy, 1820–1914* (Oxford, 1969).

15. See, for example, A. Richards, "Growth and Technical Change: 'Internal' and 'External' Sources of Egyptian Underdevelopment," in *Asian and African Studies* 15 (1981):45–68.

16. Ibid., 48.

17. Ibid., 49 (table).

18. See, for example, C. Issawi, "The Economic Development of Egypt, 1800–1960," in his (ed.), *The Economic History of the Middle East* (Chicago, 1966), 361ff.

19. Hill, *Reformation,* 30–33 (italics added).

20. Brenner, "Agrarian Class Structure."

21. Ibid., 51.

22. Ibid.

23. Hill, *Reformation,* 66.

24. C. N. Cipolla, *European Culture and Overseas Expansion* (Harmondsworth, 1970), 28.

25. Ibid., 73–78.

26. Ibid., 82–89.

27. Cited by Cipolla, *European Culture,* 160.

28. Ibid., 26.

29. D. Landes, "The Creation of Knowledge and Technique: Today's Task and Yesterday's Experience," in *Daedalus* 109 (1980):111–120.

30. Ibid., 115.

31. Ibid., 116.

32. Ibid.

33. Ibid., 117.

34. Hicks, *Theory of Economic History,* 141ff.

35. Mendels, "Proto-industrialization."

36. C. Tilly and R. Tilly, "Agenda for European Economic History in the 1970s," in *Journal of Economic History* 31 (1971):187.

37. Ibid., 189.

38. G. Baer, "Fellah Rebellion in Egypt and the Fertile Crescent," in his *Fellah and Townsman in the Middle East* (London, 1982), 253–323.

39. Ibid., 253ff.

40. See, for example, C. Uluçay, *18. ve 19. Yüzyillrarda Saruhan'da Eşkiyalik ve Halk Hareketleri* (Istanbul, 1955).

41. M. A. Cook, *Population Pressure in Rural Anatolia, 1450–1600* (London, 1970), 41 (note 1).

42. E. R. Wolf, *Peasant Wars of the Twentieth Century* (London, 1969), 52.

43. Baer, "Fellah Rebellion," 311.

44. D. Djordjevic and S. Fischer-Galati, *The Balkan Revolutionary Tradition* (New York, 1981).

45. E. J. Hobsbawm, *Bandits* (New York, 1981), 70ff.

46. Ibid., 71.

47. Ibid., 73.

48. T. Skocpol, "France, Russia, China: A Structural Analysis of Social Revolutions," in *Comparative Studies in Society and History* 18 (1976): 179.

49. Moore, *Social Origins of Dictatorship and Democracy: Lord and Peasant in the Making of the Modern World* (Boston, 1966), 459.

50. Ibid., 967.

51. Y. Porath, "The Peasant Revolt of 1858–61 in Kisrawan," in *Asian and African Studies* 2 (1966):77–157; Baer, "Fellah Rebellion."

52. Baer, "Fellah Rebellion," 300–301, 309, 312.

53. Ibid., 309.

54. Cited by T. Skocpol, *States and Social Revolution* (Cambridge, 1979), 134.

55. Aside from Moore's chapter on China, I have relied mainly on L. Bianco, *Origins of the Chinese Revolution, 1915–1949* (Stanford, 1971).

56. Bianco, *Origins,* 101.

57. Ibid., 92.

58. Ibid., 90.

59. I have relied mainly on the following sources: L. Kochan and R. Abraham, *The Making of Modern Russia* (Harmondsworth, 1983); E. N. Williams, *The Ancien Regime in Europe* (Harmondsworth, 1979), Chapters 9–12; A. Gerschenkron, *Europe in the Russian Mirror* (Cambridge, 1970); Skocpol, *States and Social Revolutions.*

60. Gerschenkron, *Europe in the Russian Mirror*, 72.
61. Ibid., 74.
62. Ibid., 75.
63. Wolf, *Peasant Wars*, 52–53.
64. Gerschenkron, *Europe in the Russian Mirror*, 92.
65. Ibid., 93.
66. Wolf, *Peasant Wars*, 55–56.
67. I. Berlin, *Russian Thinkers* (New York, 1978), 211.
68. Skocpol, *States and Social Revolutions*, 132.
69. "The *mir* was more than a form of social organization. Its role as a kind of collective superego imparted to it a truly religious aura. The term *mir* signifies both commune and universe, comparable to the Greek word *kosmos*. . . . It would not be inappropriate to translate *mir* as 'congregation.'" (Wolf, *Peasant Wars*, 62.)
70. Cited in Skocpol, *States and Social Revolutions*, 135.
71. Cited in A. Richards, "The Political Economy of *Gutswirtschaft*: A Comparative Analysis of East Elbian Germany, Egypt and Chile," in *Comparative Studies in Society and History* 21 (1979):499.
72. R. Fernea, *Shaykh and Efendi* (Cambridge, Mass., 1972), 151.
73. J. Batatu, *The Old Social Classes and the Revolutionary Movements of Iraq* (Princeton, 1979), 611–613.
74. Ibid., p. 664.
75. Ibid., 467–468.
76. Ibid., 865–889.
77. Ibid., 886.
78. G. Baer, "The Dissolution of the Village Community," in his *Studies in the Social History of Modern Egypt* (Chicago, 1969), Chapter 2.
79. G. Baer, "A Note on the Controversy over 'The Dissolution of the Egyptian Village Community,'" in *International Journal of Middle East Studies* 6 (1975–76):241–244.
80. H. H. Ayrout, *The Egyptian Peasant* (Boston, 1968), 111.
81. A. Tannous, "The Arab Village Community of the Middle East," in *Annual Report of the Smithsonian Institution* (Washington, D.C., 1943), 523–543.
82. Ibid., 542.
83. A. M. Lutfiyya, *Baytin, A Jordanian Village* (The Hague, 1966), 175.
84. J. Gulick, *Social Structure and Culture Change in a Lebanese Village* (New York, 1955), 162–163.
85. L. E. Sweet, *Tel Toqaan: A Syrian Village* (Ann Arbor, 1960), 189–190.
86. J. F. Kolars, *Tradition, Season and Change in a Turkish Village* (Chicago, 1963), 83–85.
87. P. J. Magnarella, *The Peasant Venture* (Boston, 1979), 91.
88. N. Berkes, *Bazi Anakara Köyleri Uzerzinde Bir Araştirma* (Ankara, 1942), 114–117.
89. R. B. Scott, *The Village Headman in Turkey* (Ankara, 1968).
90. P. Stirling, *Turkish Village* (London, 1965).
91. Ibid., 264.
92. F. W. Frey and L. L. Roos, "Social Structure and Community Development in Rural Turkey: Village and Elite Leadership Relations," Rural Development Re-

search Project, Report no. 10, Center for International Studies, MIT (Cambridge, Mass., 1967), 25, 41–42.

93. S. Bergheim, "Land Tenure in Palestine," in *Palestine Exploration Fund, Quarterly Statement* (1894), 191–199.

94. J. L. Burckhardt, *Travels in Syria and the Arab Land* (London, 1822), 300.

95. H. Gerber, *Ottoman Rule in Jerusalem* (Berlin, 1985), Chapter 9.

96. J. Weulersse, *Paysans de Syrie et du Proche Orient* (Paris, 1946), 104.

97. E. Be'eri, *Army Officers in Arab Politics and Society* (Jerusalem, 1969); S. N. Fischer (ed.), *The Military in the Middle East* (Columbus, Ohio, 1963).

98. See S. E. Finer, *The Man on Horseback: The Role of the Military in Politics* (London, 1962), Chapter 4.

99. Be'eri, *Army Officers.*

100. Ibid., 296.

101. P. J. Vatikiotis, *The Modern History of Egypt* (London, 1969).

102. D. Farhi, "Nizam-i Cedid—Military Reform in Egypt under Mehmed Ali," in *Asian and African Studies* 8 (1972).

103. H. A. R. Gibb and H. Bowen, *Islamic Society and the West,* vol. 1, part 1 (London, 1957), 182.

104. Ibid., 60 (note 1).

105. S. J. Shaw, *Between Old and New* (Cambridge, Mass., 1973), 112ff.

106. Ibid., 120.

107. H. L. Bodman, *Political Factions in Aleppo, 1760–1826* (Chapel Hill, 1963). This pattern of political relations no doubt existed at that time in several places in the Ottoman Empire. Cf. M. Maoz, *Ottoman Reform in Syria and Palestine* (Oxford, 1968), 6–7. I chose to concentrate on Aleppo because it is the best known and best researched example. To all appearances it also must have been the most far-reaching case of urban autonomy at that time.

108. A. Cohen, *Palestine in the Eighteenth Century* (Jerusalem, 1973).

109. M. E. Yapp, "The Modernization of Middle Eastern Armies in the Nineteenth Century," in V. J. Parry and M. E. Yapp (eds.), *War, Technology and Society in the Middle East* (London, 1975), 330–366, an article that demonstrated lucidly that, mutatis mutandis, the nineteenth-century Ottoman army underwent a technical reform along the lines of the European armies. For a detailed case study, see G. E. Swanson, "War Technology and Society in the Ottoman Empire from the Reign of Abdulhamid II to 1913: Mahmud Şevket and the German Military Mission," in Parry, *War, Technology and Society,* 367–385. The article showed how hard Ottoman officers had to work and learn (among other things from Prussian experts and from translated European literature) in order to reach the top. Although this generalization may not have been always true, it does hold, and superbly so, for the case study at hand.

110. Gibb, *Islamic Society,* part 1, 56ff.

111. Shaw, *Between Old and New,* 127.

112. Ibid., 130.

113. A. Rafeq, "The Local Forces in Syria in the Seventeenth and Eighteenth Centuries," in Parry, *War, Technology and Society,* 277–307.

114. Ibid., 277–307.

115. Be'eri, *Army Officers,* 302.

116. Ibid.

117. Ibid.

118. Ibid., 331.

119. Ibid., 317–321.

120. J. Batatu, "Some Observations on the Social Roots of Syria's Ruling Military Group and the Causes for Its Dominance," in *Middle East Journal* 35 (1981):342.

121. M. Janowitz, "Some Observations on the Comparative Analysis of Middle Eastern Military Institutions," in Parry, *War, Technology and Society*, 412–439.

122. For a somewhat different view, see M. Howard, *War in European History* (Oxford, 1976), 106ff.

123. Ibid., 107.

124. J. J. Johnson, "The Latin American Military as a Political Competing Group in Transitional Society," in his (ed.), *The Role of the Military in Underdeveloped Countries* (Princeton, 1962), 94–95.

125. Ibid., 99.

126. J. Nun, "The Middle-Class Coup," in C. Veliz (ed.), *The Politics of Conformity in Latin America* (Oxford, 1970), 66–118.

127. P. Kemp, "Mosuli Sketches of Ottoman History," in *Middle Eastern Studies* 17 (1981):310–333.

128. D. Lerner, *The Passing of Traditional Society* (New York, 1966), 280–283.

129. P. Seale, *The Struggle for Syria* (London, 1965), Chapter 11.

130. It must be emphasized that this explanation was probably true only in general terms. Finer criticized the universal applicability of the class explanation of the army-in-politics phenomenon by citing specific coups where it is not feasible (Finer, *Man on Horseback*, 40). This was no doubt true. The class explanation seems to be applicable only to the general phenomenon of army politics during an extended period of time and to the general social orientation pursued by the officer corps.

131. P. J. Vatikiotis, *Politics and the Military in Jordan* (London, 1967). Also see M. Heller, "Politics and the Military in Iraq and Jordan, 1920–1958," in *Armed Forces and Society* 4 (1977–8):75–99.

132. Vatikiotis, *Politics and the Military*, 1–2.

133. Heller, "Politics and the Military," 94.

134. This discussion, originally published in *Comparative Studies in Society and History*, was reproduced in A. Perlmutter, *Political Roles and Military Rulers* (London, 1982), 41–129.

135. M. Halpern, *The Politics of Social Change in the Middle East and North Africa* (Princeton, 1962), Chapter 4.

136. G. Ben-Dor, "Civilianization of Military Regimes in the Arab World," in *Armed Forces and Society* 1 (1974-5):320ff; A. Baram, "Saddam Hussein: A Political Profile," in *The Jerusalem Quarterly*, no. 17 (1980):119ff.

137. E. Be'eri, "The Waning of the Military Coup in the Middle East," in *Middle Eastern Studies* 18 (1982):69–81.

138. Ibid., 75.

139. C. Issawi, "Economic Trends in the Middle East and Future Prospects," in *The Political Economy of the Middle East* (Washington, D.C., 1980), 7–19.

140. See G. Germani and K. Silvert, "Politics, Social Structure and Military Intervention in Latin America," in *Archives Européennes de Sociologie* 2 (1961):77; R. D.

Putnam, "Toward Explaining Military Intervention in Latin American Politics," in *World Politics* 20 (1967):83–110.

141. M. Rodinson, *Marxism and the Muslim World* (New York, 1981), Chapter 10; A. Abd al-Malek, *Egypt, Military Society* (New York, 1968), Introduction.

142. Rodinson, ibid., 288 (italics added).

143. B. Lewis, "Communism and Islam," in *International Affairs* 3 (1954):1–12.

144. Halpern, *The Politics of Social Change,* Chapter 9.

145. T. Y. Ismael, *Government and Politics of the Contemporary Middle East* (Homewood, Ill., 1970), 89.

146. J. Batatu, *The Old Social Classes and the Revolutionary Movements of Iraq* (Princeton, 1979), 462, 465.

147. Ibid., 465.

148. Ibid., 894.

149. Ibid., 896.

150. Ibid., 897.

151. Ibid., 903–904.

152. Ibid., 1084.

153. P. Mansfield, "Saddam Hussein's Political Thinking: The Comparison with Nasser," in T. Niblock (ed.), *Iraq: The Contemporary State* (London, 1982), 71.

154. Ibid.

155. R. A. Hinnebusch, "Local Politics in Syria: Organization and Mobilization in Four Village Cases," in *Middle East Journal* 30 (1976):10–11.

156. R. A. Hinnebusch, *Party and Peasant in Syria* (Cairo, 1979), 63.

157. See E. D. Akarli, "The State as a Socio-Cultural Phenomenon and Political Participation in Turkey," in E. D. Akarli and G. Ben-Dor (eds.), *Political Participation in Turkey* (Istanbul, 1975), 146.

158. W. F. Weiker, *The Modernization of Turkey* (New York, 1981), 4.

159. M. Heper, "Patrimonialism in the Ottoman Turkish Public Bureaucracy," *Asian and African Studies* 13 (1979):4.

160. Ibid., 14.

161. E. Gellner, "Patrons and Clients," in E. Gellner and J. Waterbury (eds.), *Patrons and Clients in Mediterranean Societies* (London, 1977), 1.

162. S. Sayari, "Political Patronage in Turkey," in Gellner, ibid., 107.

163. Ibid., 107ff.

164. R. Frye, *The Turkish Political Elite* (Cambridge, Mass., 1965), 335–336.

165. U. Heyd, *Foundations of Turkish Nationalism* (London, 1950), 133.

166. Mustafa Kemal, *Speach* (Leipzig, 1929), 598.

167. E. Özbudun, "The Nature of the Kemalist Political Regime," in A. Kazancigil and E. Özbudun (eds.), *Atatürk, Founder of a Modern State* (London, 1981), 82.

168. Frye, *The Turkish Political Elite,* 425.

169. Ibid., Chapter 4.

170. Ibid., 80, 124–125. I found a certain confirmation for this whole thesis in the case of Costa Rica and Uruguay (the two relatively more democratic polities in Latin America). Germani and Silvert ("Politics, Social Structure," p. 79) had this to say on this question:

Costa Rica was unattractive to early Spanish colonizers, for it had a small indigenous population and no readily available minerals. As a result the Costa Rican central valley was an area of slow and secondary settlement, peopled by persons who had to work the land themselves. This emergence of a landed peasantry permitted the development of a type of bourgeoisie (in the figurative sense of the word) which, as in the case of Uruguay, has had long experience in the organization and application of its power to the detriment of armed pretenders.

171. But there was a divergence of opinion concerning the interpretation of this evidence. I have come across only one study that set out to investigate the relations between Kemalism, the peasantry, and landowners at the time of the Kemalist revolution. This study, by Feroz Ahmed, arrived at conclusions that were the very opposite of those I reached. Ahmed suggested that the peasants were passive and powerless politically because the peasantry was "fragmented . . . by ethnic and religious loyalties and totally dependent for its very survival on local forces." The fact is that no tangible, empirical evidence of this statement was put forward. See F. Ahmed, "The Political Economy of Kemalism," in Kazancigil, *Atatürk,* 145–163 (citation at 156).

172. Özbudun, "The Kemalist Political Regime," 83.

173. Ibid., 87.

174. S. Mardin, *The Genesis of Young Ottoman Thought* (Princeton, 1962), 202–204, Chapter 4.

175. I relied here on a study by S. Mardin, "Super Westernization in Urban Life in the Ottoman Empire in the Last Quarter of the Nineteenth Century," in P. Benedict, E. Tümertekin and F. Mansur (eds.), *Turkey, Geographic and Social Perspectives* (Leiden, 1974), 403–446, who, it seemed to me, erred in presenting the cultural problem connected with Westernization as less serious in Russia than in Turkey (409).

176. J. S. Szyliowicz, "Changes in the Recruitment Patterns and Career-Lines of Ottoman Provincial Administrators During the Nineteenth Century," in M. Maoz (ed.), *Studies on Palestine During the Ottoman Period* (Jerusalem, 1975), 265–266.

177. Ibid., 262, table 3.

178. D. A. Rustow, "Political Ends and Military Means in the Late Ottoman and Post-Ottoman Middle East," in Parry, *War, Technology and Society,* 394.

179. F. R. Hunter, "Egypt's High Officials in Transition from a Turkish to a Modern Administrative Elite, 1849–1879," in *Middle Eastern Studies* 19 (1983):283.

180. D. M. Reid, "The Rise of Professions and Professional Organizations in Modern Egypt," in *Comparative Studies in Society and History* 16 (1974):24–57.

181. Ibid., 56.

182. R. Tignor, "The Economic Activities of Foreigners in Egypt, 1920–1950: From Millet to Haute Bourgeoisie," in *Comparative Studies in Society and History* 22 (1980):416–449.

183. Ibid., 440.

184. B. Lewis, *The Emergence of Modern Turkey* (London, 1966), 120.

185. A. M. Kazamias, *Education and the Quest of Modernity in Turkey* (London, 1961), 103ff.

186. Ibid., 64ff.

187. Szyliowicz, "Changes in Recruitment Patterns," 271.

188. L. L. Roos and N. P. Roos, *Managers of Modernization* (Cambridge, Mass., 1971), 22.

189. C. V. Findley, *Bureaucratic Reform in the Ottoman Empire* (Princeton, 1980), 347.

190. W. L. Cleveland, *The Making of an Arab Nationalist* (Princeton, 1971), Chapter 1.

191. For a study that used this term, see J. Sarnoff, "The Bureaucracy and the Bourgeoisie: Decentralization and Class Structure in Tanzania," in *Comparative Studies in Society and History* 21 (1979):30–62.

192. J. P. Entelis, *Pluralism and Party Transformation in Lebanon* (Leiden, 1974), 1.

193. A. Hourani, *The Emergence of the Modern Middle East* (London, 1981); C. Issawi, "Economic and Social Foundations of Democracy in the Middle East," in A. M. Lutfiyya and L. W. Churchill (eds.), *Readings in Arab Middle Eastern Societies and Cultures* (The Hague, 1970), 259–277.

194. Hourani, ibid., 129.

195. W. R. Polk, *The Opening of South Lebanon, 1788–1840* (Cambridge, Mass., 1963), 82.

196. R. E. Crist, "The Mountain Village of Dahr, Lebanon," in *Annual Report of the Smithsonian Institution* (Washington, D.C., 1953), 408ff.

197. Ibid., 408.

198. Ibid., 419.

199. S. K. Farsoun, "Family Structure and Society in Modern Lebanon," in L. E. Sweet (ed.), *Peoples and Cultures of the Middle East*, vol. 2 (New York, 1970), 281; M. Johnson, "Political Bosses and Their Gangs: Zuama and Qabadayat in the Sunni Muslim Quarters of Beirut," in Gellner, *Patrons and Clients,* 207–224.

Selected Bibliography

I. Abbas. "Hair ad-Din ar-Ramli's Fatawa: A New Light on Life in Palestine in the Eleventh/Seventeenth Century." In U. Haarmann and P. Bachmann, eds. *Die Islamische Welt zwischen Mittelalter und Neuzeit (Festschrift Hans Robert Roemer)*. Beirut, 1979, 1–19.

E. D. Akarli and G. Ben-Dor (eds.). *Political Participation in Turkey*. Istanbul, 1975.

R. T. Antoun. *Arab Village*. Bloomington, 1972.

H. H. Ayrout. *The Egyptian Peasant*. Boston, 1968.

G. Baer. "Egyptian Attitudes Towards Land Reform, 1922–1955." In W. Z. Laqueur, ed. *The Middle East in Transition*. London, 1958, 80–99.

————. *Studies in the Social History of Modern Egypt*. Chicago, 1969.

Ö. L. Barkan. "Türk Toprak Hukuku Tarihinde Tanzimat ve 1274 (1858) Tarihli Arazi Kanunnamesi." In *Tanzimat*. Istanbul, 1940, 321–421.

J. Batatu. *The Old Social Classes and the Revolutionary Movements of Iraq*. Princeton, 1979.

E. Be'eri. *Army Officers in Arab Politics and Society*. Jerusalem, 1969.

P. Benedict. *Ula, An Anatolian Town*. Leiden, 1974.

N. Berkes. *Bazi Ankara Köyleri Uzerinde Bir Araştirma*. Ankara, 1942.

L. Bianco. *Origins of the Chinese Revolution 1915–1945*. Stanford, 1971.

B. Braude. "International Competition and Domestic Cloth in the Ottoman Empire, 1500–1650: A Study in Undevelopment." In *Review* 2 (1979):437–451.

F. Braudel. *The Mediterranean and the Mediterranean World in the Age of Philip II*. London, 1972.

R. Brenner. "Agrarian Class Structure and Economic Development in Pre-Industrial Europe." In *Past and Present*, no. 70 (1976), 30–75.

C. N. Cipolla. *European Culture and Overseas Expansion*. Harmondsworth, 1970.

Abner Cohen. *Arab Border Villages in Israel*. Manchester, 1965.

Amnon Cohen. *Palestine in the Eighteenth Century*. Jerusalem, 1973.

A. Cohen and B. Lewis. *Population and Revenue in the Towns of Palestine in the Sixteenth Century*. Princeton, 1978.

M. A. Cook. *Population Pressure in Rural Anatolia, 1450–1600*. London, 1972.

K. Cuno. "The Origins of Private Ownership of Land in Ottoman Egypt, A Reappraisal." In *International Journal of Middle East Studies* 12 (1980):245–275.

R. Fernea. *Shaykh and Efendi*. Cambridge, Mass., 1972.

————. "Land Reform and Ecology in Postrevolutionary Iraq." In *Economic Development and Cultural Change* 17 (1968–69):356–381.

C. V. Findley. *Bureaucratic Reform in the Ottoman Empire*. Princeton, 1980.

Y. Firestone. "Crop-Sharing Economics in Mandatory Palestine." In *Middle Eastern Studies* 11 (1975):3–23, 175–194.

R. Frye. *The Turkish Political Elite*. Cambridge, Mass., 1965.

E. Gellner and J. Waterbury (eds.). *Patrons and Clients in Mediterranean Societies*.

London, 1977.

H. Gerber. "*Sharia, Kanun* and Custom in the Ottoman Law: The Court Records of 17th-Century Bursa." In *International Journal of Turkish Studies* 2 (1981):131–147.

———. *Ottoman Rule in Jerusalem.* Berlin, 1985.

A. Gerschenkron. *Europe in the Russian Mirror.* Cambridge, 1970.

A. Granott. *The Land System of Palestine.* London, 1952.

J. Gulick. *Social Structure and Culture Change in a Lebanese Village.* New York, 1955.

A. Güriz. "Land Ownership in Rural Settlements." In P. Benedict, E. Tümertekin, and F. Mansur, eds. *Turkey: Geographic and Social Perspectives.* Leiden, 1974.

N. Helburn. "A Stereotype of Agriculture in Semiarid Turkey." In *The Geographical Review* 45 (1955):375–384.

M. Heller. "Politics and the Military in Iraq and Jordan, 1920–1958." In *Armed Forces and Society* 4 (1977–8):75–99.

U. Heyd. *Studies in Old Ottoman Criminal Law.* Oxford, 1973.

R. A. Hinnebusch. "Local Politics in Syria: Organization and Mobilization in Four Village Cases." In *Middle East Journal* 23 (1976):1–24.

———. *Party and Peasant in Syria.* Cairo, 1979.

E. J. Hobsbawn. *Bandits.* New York, 1981.

F. R. Hunter. "Egypt's High Officials in Transition from a Turkish to a Modern Administrative Elite, 1849–1879." In *Middle Eastern Studies* 19 (1983):277–300.

H. Inalcik. *The Ottoman Empire: The Classical Age, 1300–1600.* London, 1973.

A. Jwaideh. "Midhat Pasha and the Land System of Lower Iraq." *St. Anthony's Papers,* no. 16 (1964):106–136.

D. Kandiyoti. "Social Change and Social Stratification in a Turkish Village." In *Journal of Peasant Studies* 2 (1975):206–219.

A. Kazancigil and E. Özbudun, eds. *Atatürk, Founder of a Modern State.* London, 1981.

C. Keyder. "Paths to Rural Transformation in Turkey." In *Journal of Peasant Studies* 11 (1983):43–49.

———. "Small Peasant Ownership in Turkey." In *Review* 7 (1983):53–107.

P. S. Khoury. "The Tribal Shaykh, French Tribal Policy, and the Nationalist Movement in Syria Between Two World Wars." In *Middle Eastern Studies* 18 (1982):180–193.

M. B. Kiray. "Social Change in Çukurova; A Comparison of Four Villages." In P. Benedict, E. Tümertekin, and F. Mansur, eds. *Turkey, Geographic and Social Perspectives.* Leiden, 1974, 179–203.

J. Kolars. *Tradition, Season and Change in a Turkish Village.* Chicago, 1963.

D. Lerner. *The Passing of Traditional Society.* New York, 1966.

B. Lewis. *Notes and Documents from the Turkish Archives.* Jerusalem, 1952.

A. M. Lutfiyya. *Baytin, A Jordanian Village.* The Hague, 1966.

M. Maoz. *Ottoman Reform in Syria and Palestine.* Oxford, 1968.

B. McGowan. *Economic Life in Ottoman Europe.* Cambridge, 1979.

B. Moore. *Social Origins of Dictatorship and Democracy: Lord and Peasant in the Making of the Modern World.* Boston, 1966.

Y. Nagata. *Some Documents on the Big Farms (Çiftliks) of the Notables in Western Anatolia.* Tokyo, 1976.

Ihsan al-Nimr, *Tarikh Jabal Nablus wal'Balqa,* vol. 2. Nablus, 1962.

H. Ongan. *Ankara'nin Iki Numarali Şeriye Sicili.* Ankara, 1974.

R. Owen. *The Middle East in the World Economy.* London, 1981.

D. Pool. "From Elite to Class: The Transformation of the Iraqi Leadership, 1920–1939." In *International Journal of Middle East Studies* 12 (1980):331–350.

Y. Porath. "The Peasant Revolt of 1858–61 in Kisrawan." In *Asian and African Studies* 2 (1966):77–157.

Khayr al-Din al-Ramli. *Al-Fatawi al Khayriyya.* Bulaq, A.H. 1300.

D. M. Reid. "The Rise of Professions and Professional Organizations in Modern Egypt." In *Comparative Studies in Society and History* 16 (1974):24–57.

A. Richards. "Growth and Technical Change: 'Internal' and 'External' Sources of Egyptian Underdevelopment." In *Asian and African Studies* 15 (1981):45–68.

L. L. Roos and N. P. Roos. *Managers of Modernization.* Cambridge, Mass., 1971.

R. B. Scott. *The Village Headman in Turkey.* Ankara, 1968.

P. Seale. *The Struggle for Syria.* London, 1965.

S. J. Shaw. *The Financial Organization and Development of Ottoman Egypt, 1517–1798.* Princeton, 1962.

———. *History of the Ottoman Empire and Modern Turkey,* vol. 1. Cambridge, 1976.

T. Skocpol. "A Critical Review of Barrington Moore's Social Origins of Dictatorship and Democracy." In *Politics and Society* 1 (1973):1–34.

———. "France, Russia, China: A Structural Analysis of Social Revolutions." In *Comparative Studies in Society and History* 18 (1976):175–210.

———. *States and Social Revolutions.* Cambridge, 1979.

P. Stirling. *Turkish Village.* London, 1965.

L. Stone. *The Causes of the English Revolution.* London, 1972.

L. E. Sweet. *Tell Toqaan: A Syrian Village.* Ann Arbor, 1960.

J. S. Szyliowicz. *Political Change in Rural Turkey: Erdemli.* The Hague, 1966.

A. Tannous. "The Arab Village Community of the Middle East." In *Annual Report of the Smithsonian Institution.* Washington, D.C., 1943, 523–543.

P. J. Vatikiotis. *Politics and the Military in Jordan.* London, 1967.

G. Veinstein. "Ayan de la région d'Izmir et le commerce du Levant (deuxième moitié du XVIIIe siècle)." In *Revue de l'Occident Musulman et de la Méditerranée* 20 (1975):131–147.

I. Wallerstein. *The Modern World System.* New York, 1974.

———. "The Ottoman Empire and the Capitalist World Economy: Some Questions for Research." In *Review* 2 (1979):389–398.

D. Warriner. *Land Reform and Development in the Middle East.* Oxford, 1962.

J. Weulersse. *Paysans de Syrie et du Proche Orient.* Paris, 1946.

E. R. Wolf. *Peasant Wars of the Twentieth Century.* London, 1969.

I. Yasa. *Hasanoğlan, Socio-Economic Structure of a Turkish Village.* Ankara, 1957.

Index

217

About the Book and Author

Dr. Gerber traces the effects of the Ottoman socioagrarian structure on political formation and revolution in the modern Middle East (ca. 1500 to the present). The sixteenth century Ottoman regime was characterized by small and independent village communities and the absence of a landed aristocracy. This configuration lasted until the mid-nineteenth century, despite strong pressures toward the formation of large estates. Finally, however, the effects of the 1858 Ottoman Land Law, together with a substantial increase in public security throughout the Middle East, made it both possible and profitable in some areas to establish large estates on a massive scale, at the expense of the peasantry.

Elaborating on Barrington Moore's theory of the agrarian origins of civilization and on Theda Skocpol's work on social-agrarian revolution, Dr. Gerber attributes to these developments the absence of massive peasant revolutions in the Middle East. In contrast to their plight in Russia and China, peasants in the Middle East did not experience centuries of subjugation and exploitation by a landed upper class. The historical absence of a landed aristocracy also made possible strong military regimes, which, because of the lack of extreme unrest among the peasant class, typically did not enforce immoderate social policies.

Once a landed upper class did develop, the consequent unrest came to a head in the army revolutions of the 1950s. Dr. Gerber explains this unusual military role and explores the two cases—Lebanon and Turkey—where there was no major assumption of power over the last century by a repressive landed class and where, therefore, regimes have developed at least in the direction of democracy.

Haim Gerber is senior lecturer in the Department of Islam, the Hebrew University of Jerusalem.